Quintessence...
Realizing the Archaic Future

ALSO BY
Mary Daly

THE CHURCH AND THE SECOND SEX

BEYOND GOD THE FATHER:
TOWARD A PHILOSOPHY OF WOMEN'S LIBERATION

GYN/ECOLOGY: THE METAETHICS OF RADICAL FEMINISM

PURE LUST: ELEMENTAL FEMINIST PHILOSOPHY

WEBSTERS' FIRST NEW INTERGALACTIC
WICKEDARY OF THE ENGLISH LANGUAGE

OUTERCOURSE: THE BE-DAZZLING VOYAGE

2048 BE (BIOPHILIC ERA) EDITION

....

*Containing Cosmic Comments
and Conversations with the Author*

Quintessence...
Realizing the Archaic Future
A RADICAL ELEMENTAL FEMINIST MANIFESTO

Mary Daly

ILLUSTRATIONS BY
SUDIE RAKUSIN

ORIGINALLY PUBLISHED IN 1998 AD

BEACON PRESS

BOSTON

PUBLISHED ON LOST AND FOUND CONTINENT
BY ANONYMA NETWºRD (AN INTERGALACTIC
ENTERPRISE OF ANONYMA NETWORK)

IN CELEBRATION OF THE
50TH ANNIVERSARY OF THE WORK

BEACON PRESS
25 Beacon Street
Boston, Massachusetts 02108-2892
www.beacon.org

BEACON PRESS BOOKS
are published under the auspices of
the Unitarian Universalist Association of Congregations.

03 02 01 00 99 98 8 7 6 5 4 3 2 1

This book is printed on recycled acid-free paper that contains at least
20 percent postconsumer waste and meets the uncoated paper
ANSI/NISO specifications for permanence as revised in 1992.

Text design by Anne Chalmers
Composition by Wilsted & Taylor Publishing Services

Library of Congress Cataloging-in-Publication Data

Daly, Mary, 1928–
Quintessence . . . realizing the archaic future : a radical
elemental feminist manifesto / Mary Daly.
        p.   cm.
Includes bibliographical references and index.
ISBN 0-8070-6790-3 (hardcover)
1. Feminist theory.   2. Ecofeminism.   3. Patriarchy.
    I. Title.   HQ1190.D35   1998
       305.42′01—dc21   98-15286

To

E M I L Y   E R W I N   C U L P E P P E R,

Gorgon-identified fighter, visionary, dreamer, and schemer;

Be-Lasting, Be-Laughing, Be-Loving Friend

who is "in it for the long haul"

To my Wondrous Feline Familiar, Á I L L E   Ó G

(which means in Irish "Young Beauty"), who has followed

in the paw-steps of my Fore-Familiar, W I L D   C A T,

guiding this book to completion

And,

as always,

to my parents,

A N N A   A N D   F R A N K,

whose Presence intensifies in the course of Time

Contents

Preface to the 2048 BE (Biophilic Era)
Edition of *Quintessence* . . . . · xi

Author's Introduction to the Original 1998 Edition · 1

CHAPTER ONE · 27
The Fifth Spiral Galaxy: Expanding Here
*Cosmic Comments and Conversations
in 2048 BE Concerning Chapter One*

57

CHAPTER TWO · 81
Nemesis and the Courage to Create
*Cosmic Comments and Conversations
in 2048 BE Concerning Chapter Two*

109

CHAPTER THREE · 123
Re-awakening the X-Factor/Faculty
and Creating the Archaic Future
*Cosmic Comments and Conversations
in 2048 BE Concerning Chapter Three*

151

CONTENTS

CHAPTER FOUR · 167

The Fifth Element and the Fifth Direction
*Cosmic Comments and Conversations
in 2048 BE Concerning Chapter Four*

190

CHAPTER FIVE · 204

Breaking into the Fifth Dimension:
Dis-covering the Light of Quintessence
*Cosmic Comments and Conversations
in 2048 BE Concerning Chapter Five*

233

Notes
Acknowledgments
Index

PREFACE TO THE
2O48 BE (BIOPHILIC ERA) EDITION of
QUINTESSENCE

by Anonyma

I AM HAPPY *to have the opportunity to write this Preface to my Fore-sister/Firesister Daly's seventh Radical Feminist book. I know that she also is pleased that this work is being reissued in 2048 BE* (Biophilic Era). *She recognizes the significance of the victory symbolized by this singular Re-Vision of Time and of, well, everything.**

This work was originally published in 1998. Writing such a book as Quintessence *near the end of the twentieth century was no small feat for Daly, who must sometimes have felt that she was a voice screaming into the void in that terrible time. When standing onstage before her audiences she had frequently yelled out her battle cry: "Even if I were the only one, I would still be a Radical Feminist!" Although this hypothetical fate—becoming a cognitive minority of one—did not seem a foregone conclusion at that time, Daly glimpsed the misogynist "handwriting on the wall." Her project was to erase that "handwriting" which was intended to erase women. Her method was to keep on creating—from a Background perspective—blasting away the negativity with flashes of light.*

Our Archives contain much evidence of the fragmentation of women in the late twentieth century—by extreme oppression, poverty, burnout, isola-

----

*A few points may need explanation. First, I call myself "Anonyma" in order to honor and signify my bonding with the countless women of the patriarchal era who could not publish under their own names. As scholars living in that era, such as Virginia Woolf, have noted, "Anonymous" was often a woman. They could not have foreseen that we would reverse the patriarchal reversals and form a Network Named "Anonyma." A second point is that I write of Daly in the present tense because, of course, she is Present, together with Sappho, Sojourner, Woolf, and our countless other Foresisters who survived patriarchy.

tion, discouragement on many levels. Many had been assimilated into the role of tokens/gatekeepers, blocking women from access to knowledge and power. How did Daly and other Journeyers keep going?

In Quintessence she explains the process by which she and her "Cronies," as she fondly Names them, managed to Leap onward into "The Fifth Spiral Galaxy," which is the Realm of Expanding Here/Presence. They soared away . . . and Out, saving all they could save, and arriving Here.

Recently I tried an experiment. I had been reading Daly's work in our Archives and came to realize how frequently she Conjured her Foresisters— when she was writing, lecturing, teaching, or just simply Spinning ideas. So when I went home I decided to Invoke her in order to have a conversation about her work and what it was like to live in those times. Of course, I expected that I, in turn, would tell her about my own experiences. Well! As soon as I had clearly formed the thought, she just popped up in front of me. "Mary Daly!" I exclaimed. "Is that you?"

Perhaps I jumped in surprise, because Daly was laughing at me. "So, what did you expect?" she asked. "By the way, please just call me Mary. Who are you?"

"My name is Annie," I said. We were both a bit shocked. I announced in amazement that I could actually see and hear her. We both laughed. "So, Here we are!" we exclaimed in unison.

We were actually in my study. My visitor blinked and looked around curiously. She stared at her hands and feet to make sure she was really all Here. Impulsively she walked across the room and stuck her head out the window, sniffing the air inquisitively and studying my garden, which was in full bloom.

While this was going on with Mary I decided to heat a kettle of water, stalling for time to give us both a chance to adjust. After a few minutes I invited my stunned guest to sit down and have a cup of tea.

When we were seated, we savored the wonder of this Transtemporal experience. I remarked that the year was 2048 BE (Biophilic Era). "Big Brother has been soundly defeated," I proclaimed. "He finally shriveled up and died ignominiously of his own inherent rottenness."

We both burst into laughter and congratulated ourselves and all our Foresisters on this victory.

"What a relief!" said Mary. "I look forward to hearing more about it."

I promised to fill her in on the cosmic events of the twenty-first century. I suggested that meanwhile I should tell her something about myself, and she agreed to this. Since I am an ardent student of twentieth century Feminist philosophy, I naturally had the advantage of having read Daly's work and knew something about her life, while she knew nothing about me. I began by relating a bit of my own history, which I summarized as follows:

"I was born in 2018 BE, which was the very first year in which BE became widely accepted as a replacement for the obsolete AD and CE. BE (Biophilic Era) signifies the end of the necrophilic era, that is, patriarchy. My mother and grandmother, together with many of their Cronies in the Anonyma Network, worked to bring about this Tremendous Transition. They didn't bother to renumber years, partly because this would involve tedious complexity, but especially because they wished to signify their bonding and continuity with all the Foresisters who lived in the age of Big Brother. Moreover, those Foreseeing Foresisters were already participating in the Biophilic Era. They were, to use a rather common expression, 'ahead of their time.'

"As a member of the Network, I choose to write under the noble name Anonyma, but my friends just call me Annie. My mother, whose name is Kate, was born in 1980, so she was a young woman during the terrible millennial times. From her earliest years she imbibed understanding of the Women's Movement from her mother, Johanna. My grandmother, Johanna, who was born in 1942, participated wholeheartedly in the Movement. She was twenty-six in 1968 and fought exuberantly through the cresting of Feminism's so-called 'second wave.' Johanna survived the hideous backlash against women in the 1980s and 1990s and lived far into Cronehood. From the time I was a small child she regaled me with stories of A-mazing Amazonian adventures and battles.

"I was enthralled with my grandmother's tales and with the twentieth century books by and about women which she first read to me and later gave me to read by myself. My collection of these books is like a treasure trove. When

I walk into the room where they are proudly displayed on the shelves I feel their auras and sense their powerful vibrations.

"And—on top of this—my grandma's Memory went far back into her own childhood, when she imbibed great stories from her mother, Honora, who was born in 1904. My great-grandmother had related wondrous tales to Johanna about the suffragists. So for me there are auras upon auras of orally (aurally) transmitted memories of strong and courageous women."

When I finished my almost breathless recounting I saw that Mary was in such a high state of ecstasy that she was practically flying around the room. "WOW!" she exclaimed. "This is Quintessential!"

Before she could come down from the ceiling I told her of my desire to write a Preface to the 2048 BE Edition of Quintessence *. . . with her permission. With mounting excitement I added: "We could get it out just in time for the 50th anniversary of* Quintessence—*and for the 200th anniversary of the first Woman's Rights Convention at Seneca Falls, New York, in 1848. Besides that, '48 reverses '84 in the title of Orwell's famous novel 1984."*

Daly listened intently, nodding her head vigorously in agreement. Then she exclaimed, "There should be more by you *in this edition than just a Preface, Annie."*

"Agreed!" I said happily. I told her that I would be excited to contribute more extensively to the 2048 BE edition of Quintessence, *adding that I already had some ideas in mind.*

So we began to discuss what my contribution would be. I pointed out that a number of my contemporaries are intrigued by Quintessence, *which is viewed by some as very much in harmony with our understanding of the transformations that have already happened and that continue to occur. I told Mary that members of the Anonyma Network are eager to know about her own experiences in the 1990s of the realities she describes in this book.*

"For example," I said, "we are curious to learn more about the conditions of the diaspora of Wild Women in that dreadful era and how you and your Cronies worked toward overcoming this scattered state. We would like to know how women experienced Magnetic Magic then. (Of course, such Magic brought about our meeting each other Here and Now!) Perhaps more than

anything, we want to discuss our mutual quest to Realize the Archaic Future.* I understand that at the end of the twentieth century women were forced to confront the horror of necrotechnocracy's attempt to control evolution—and hence the future—by manipulating the genes of plants, animals, and humans."

At this point I was interrupted by my guest. "Hold on, Annie!" she commanded. "I have an idea. Why don't you write your own comments after each chapter?"

I agreed with this general plan. We decided to have further visits and sort of "play it by ear." Mary gave me a big grin. "Just call me up anytime, and I'll be Here."

So that was the origin of my Cosmic Comments and Conversations *which follow each chapter of the 2048 BE Edition of Quintessence.*

----

*Daly has written that the Archaic Future *is the real future, which transcends the stagnation/timelessness of archetypal deadtime. It is the direction of the movements of Original Creative Time (Archaic Time), beyond the stifling grasp of archetypal molds and measures. It is reality created through successions of Original Acts/Actions. See* New Archaic Afterwords, *in her book* The Church and the Second Sex, *pp. xviii, xxvii, xxviii. See also* Wickedary, *p. 62.*

Author's Introduction

THE WRITING of this book is a Desperate Act performed in a time of ultimate battles between principalities and powers. More than ever all sensate and spiritual life on this planet and anywhere within reach is threatened with extinction. The Boundary-violating necrotechnologists of the "millennial time" are executing the "divine plan" that has been laid out for them in hideous self-fulfilling prophecies/myths. The words of Dr. Richard Seed which were broadcast in January 1998 say it precisely—more accurately than the fanciful mutterings of his more successful and sophisticated colleagues: "God made man in his own image. . . . We are going to become one with God. . . . Cloning and the reprogramming of DNA is the first serious step in becoming one with God. Very simple philosophy."

Ecologist Jerry Mander succinctly summarizes the societal context in which such statements can be made and taken seriously:

> Our society is characterized by an inability to leave anything in nature alone. Every piece of land, every creature, every mineral in the oceans, every growing plant, every mountain, every inch of desert is examined for its potential contribution to commercial development and exploitation, and to the expansion of technological society.[*][1]

---

*Mander continues this line of thought, stating that "the last two frontiers of this expansionist process, the last two relatively underdeveloped wildernesses [are] space and the genetic structure of life." See Jerry Mander, *In the Absence of the Sacred* (San Francisco: Sierra Club Books, 1991), p. 161.

Whenever we encounter such lists of "every's" that are described by ecologists as exploited by "our society," the Wild Women who Roam and Howl our ways through the pages of *Quintessence* Declare there are Glaring omissions, namely, ourSelves. We, of course, are unrecognized and not named. Glaring, Gorgonish Women, happy in our knowledge that we are *not* made in the image of the malegod, experience no need or desire to become one with this fictitious entity (nonentity). We point to the fact that we are Prime Targets of his animosity and ghoulish intent, which is faithfully executed by his followers.

Dreadful/Dreadless Women willfully join with the whole crowd of "every's"—the mountains, the minerals, the atoms, the protons, the critters of all kinds—Naming ourSelves not simply as targets but especially as choosing to win the war that is waged against all life by necrophiliacs/nothing-lovers. We *will* succeed in our Quest for Quintessence.

THE TITLE OF THIS BOOK

This brings me to the title of this book, *Quintessence . . . Realizing the Archaic Future.* This may seem to be rather an intimidating title. Moreover, its connection with the subtitle, *A Radical Elemental Feminist Manifesto,* may not be immediately evident to the reader. It all comes together for Canny Women, however, when we begin to understand the extremity of the conditions under which we struggle to survive and thrive. At the end of the twentieth century—the turn of the millennium—we are faced with the reality of hideous manipulation and the probability of ultimate extinction, not only of our own bodies/minds (ourSelves), but of all nature.

Even as I write these words in 1998, dull voices of denial drone around me . . . "Nah! You're getting carried away. Don't be so extreme!" Then I glance at the front page of the newspaper, any newspaper, or turn on the TV, struggling to decode the disinformation, and feel suffocated by the smog of distractions and lies.

The voices of denial are getting weaker, though, as all the evidence comes pouring in. Yes, they are invading and destroying the genetic wilderness and the space wilderness. Molecular engineering (nanotechnology) threatens to reduce anything and everything to a heap of molecular dust. And this technology is controlled by—well, yes, mad and evil scientists. It would seem that nothing can stop them. They rush ahead blindly, faster and faster.

Life is being irreversibly destroyed. Forests are dead or dying. The oceans are dying. More species of plants and animals are becoming extinct every few minutes. The whales and dolphins have their own reasons for beaching themselves. Everything is being turned inside out and upside down. When an unexpected tornado hurls a Dodge through the wall of a house and it lands on someone's bed in central Florida, the weakening deniers' voices continue to croak: "Well there's nothing new about tornadoes, and El Niño has been around before."

It all keeps happening faster and faster. The space-rapists say they intend to strip-mine the moon. They say that by the year 2003 they will "blacken the skies with spacecraft." The moon! The sky! My heart breaks. The hearts of all Other-Wise Women are breaking.

In February 1998 a little girl asks a superscientist on the nightly news if there will be hotels and restaurants on other planets when she grows up. He tells her yes. He calls the process terraforming. Meanwhile his buddies are busy harpooning a comet, just to see what's inside.

The hearts of Truth-Saying Women are broken again and again. The remains of mindbindings are slipping off our brains. We are ripping off the mummy wrappings from our souls. Grief and Desperation propel us. Be-Longing for transcendence and harmony, for the splendor and beauty of life draws us on, opens our eyes to the sky—and, as always, to the Earth, Beloved Earth.

Ignoring phony promises of a "better future," Wayward Women *will* to find and create a Real Future. We Time-Space travel beyond archetypal deadtime and reach deep into our Memories, our Deep Past, to Dis-cover the roots of an Archaic Future, beyond the limits of patriarchal linear time.

That is why this book is called *Quintessence . . . Realizing the Archaic Future.* Because seeing into the manmade pit of horror can force us to break through the brain-killing casings that are crushing our skulls, stifling our souls. Facing the ultimate horror that is all around us can free Fiery Women into Fearlessness, so that we can Spring ahead, ready, finally, for the greatest adventure of our lives. It really is a case of Now or Never.

Quintessence is a Name for what Wild Women have always been seeking. It has a Misty quality about it. It was not as visible to me at the beginning of the Voyage of this book as it later became. It is that which has drawn me on in my writing and searching. The Quest for Quintessence is the most Desperate response I know to the Call of the Wild. It means throwing one's life as far as it will go. The explosion of information about nectech horror in the 1990s brought the absolute necessity of this Quest into Focus.

The Quest for Quintessence is all that matters. It means Realizing our own inherent integrity and participating in Integrity beyond that integrity—the ever moving Dance of the Universe, the Harmony of the Spheres.

Quintessence is not a noun but a Verb. It attracts us magnetically into its Vast and Luminous context. And it is perfectly Natural that we should move and thrive in its Wondrous Realms. What is unnatural is the soul-shrinking, stinking manmade mess that they have made of "the globe" and everything else within reach. When Wild Women are awakened to Quintessence, we are multidimensionally Present. We move into further dimensions and yet are more than ever determined to fight for life on Earth.

ABOUT REALIZING THE ARCHAIC FUTURE:
WHAT DOES THIS MEAN NOW?

Throughout patriarchal history women have experienced surges of Memories of an Archaic Past. Patriarchal men have done everything they could to stop women from this Re-membering. They are doing this today—by deadening and killing off Women's Studies, by erasing Feminist books, i.e., making them inaccessible, putting them out of print, keeping them out of libraries, forcing women's bookstores out of business. They try to kill our Deep Memories by tokenizing/taming women faculty members and other professionals. (What if Madeleine Albright had found it within her capacity to turn down her appointment as Secretary of State and had chosen instead to devote her life's work to her Sisters? A few cases like that would cause the world to crack open.)

In the early 1970s Elizabeth Gould Davis and Monique Wittig were outstanding examples of Memory Bearers of an Archaic Past. That period was marked by Volcanic Eruptions of Memories which were recognized by and assumed into the consciousness of many women. In the late nineteenth century Matilda Joslyn Gage was such a Memory Bearer. And there were many before that.

Those Memories are still alive. The Volcanic Eruptions that occur from Time to Time spew forth Lava that enriches the soil for the flowering of Elemental Feminist Genius. When the predictable backlash from the patriarchy occurs after each Eruption women become exhausted and feel betrayed. It appears that the Volcanic soil is also exhausted. We often have described this experience as "having to reinvent the wheel over and over."

It is Time Now to put the picture together and See through the pattern. Because the patriarchs have interrupted our tradition—also because they have continued to kill us in countless ways—we have not had a chance to finish putting all the pieces of the puzzle together completely. Now Wild Women must recognize that the Waves of Feminism are Volcanic Waves. The accumulated Lava has enriched our Powers sufficiently for yet another Eruption. It has nourished our capacity for continuing progress into the Future that is rooted in Archaic Memory.

The patriarchal machine grinds on, working to cover over (overcome) our Past. As we come into the twenty-first century we Know more. We have had practice. We know that what have appeared to be our "new" insights are really explosions of knowledge from the Deep Past. We can count on our Archaic Knowledge to pull us through.

Now is very possibly our Ultimate Chance. The demonic forces of technomadness are armed not merely to kill off but also to *hideously and irreversibly mutate and mutilate all Elemental Life.* The obscene experiments of the necrotechnologists are like nothing we have ever seen before. Their plans and activities continue and expand the "tradition" of Nazi eugenics and other atrocities. The manufacture of "new species" of animals and plants is already here. And "new humans" are on the way.

We Know that a massive evil effort is under way, that a demonic necrophilic campaign is in operation to block the possibility of Survival and Bonding of Wild Women with all of Nature. *Realizing the Archaic Future* does not mean simply waking up and Seeing. It means working to open the Way for Transtemporal/Trans-spatial and Interspecies Bonding.

This battle of principalities and powers Now is Extreme. Memory-Bearing Women are Here and Now charged with the responsibility of blasting open the walls that have been installed in our minds/souls and opening the way to participation in the Biophilic Elemental Integrity of the Universe, which is Quintessence. This means Seeing in its Light, Moving in its Rhythm. We can have Faith that the Volcanic Flow which we have inherited from our Foresisters—Past, Present, and Future— will guide and guard us. It will help us find our Way into Realizing the Archaic Future. But we have to Work our Way Here. And, Metaphorically Speaking, that is, Deeply Be-Speaking, Goddess is on our side. This enCouraging assurance brings me to the project of defining the subtitle of this work.

THE SUBTITLE OF THIS BOOK:
A RADICAL ELEMENTAL FEMINIST MANIFESTO

In this work I am re-claiming and expanding the Original insight that Radical Feminism is a Spirit-filled, Enspiriting Revolution.* I am ex-

---

*Elsewhere I have defined *Radical Feminism* as "be-ing *for* women and all Elemental Life, which implies going to the roots of the oppression of all Others." This definition is followed by a list of criteria for Radical Feminism. These are "(a) an Awesome and Ecstatic sense of Otherness from patriarchal norms and values (b) conscious awareness of

panding the expression *Radical Feminism,* however, to emphasize even more explicitly the inherent connections between women, especially Wild Women, and all Elemental/Natural Reality, and the necessity of Realizing this connectedness more and more.

All of my books have made these connections explicit. *Gyn/Ecology,* for example, is a title which contains the word *Ecology. Pure Lust* has as its subtitle *Elemental Feminist Philosophy.* The word *ecofeminism* has never seemed to me to be strong enough. So . . . This is A *Radical Elemental Feminist Manifesto.*

The word *manifesto,* according to *Webster's Third New International Dictionary,* means "a public declaration of intentions, motives, or views." I am Now declaring that the intentions, motives, and views of Radical Elemental Feminists are focused on one central cause: the expansion of *Biophilia,* which means "the Original Lust for Life that is at the core of all Elemental E-motion; Pure Lust, which is the Nemesis of patriarchy, the necrophilic state." In simpler words, *Biophilia* means love of life. (See *Gyn/Ecology, Pure Lust, Wickedary, Outercourse,* and *Quintessence.*)

Over twenty years ago when I was writing *Gyn/Ecology* I looked for the word *Biophilia* in various dictionaries and was alarmed to find that it wasn't there. However, all of these dictionaries did offer the word *necrophilia.* Well, I thought, these are all patriarchal dictionaries. So I made up the word, housed it in books, and have promoted it ever since.

The absence of the word *Biophilia* from the dictionary is significant. It is related to the absence of love of life from the patriarchal world.*

---

the sadosociety's sanctions against Radical Feminists (c) moral outrage on behalf of women *as women:* WOMAN-IDENTIFICATION (d) commitment to the cause of women that persists, even against the current, when feminism is no longer 'popular': CONSTANCY." See *Pure Lust,* pp. 397–98, and *Wickedary,* p. 75. In these times both the Name and the Reality of Radical Feminism are under attack. The writing of this book is an affirmation that they will not and cannot be obliterated.

*Several years after the publication of *Gyn/Ecology* the word *Biophilia* was used as a book title by Edward O. Wilson to promote his views on the new/old field of sociobiology. I don't know where he found it or what it really means to him.

I am now declaring also that the motives of RadicalElemental Feminists focus on one central emergency: the hideous expansion and intensification of rapism on this planet. By *rapism* I mean:

the fundamental ideology and practice of patriarchy, characterized by invasion, violation, degradation, objectification, and destruction of women and nature; the fundamental paradigm of sexism, racism, classism, speciesism, and all other oppressive -isms. (See *Beyond God the Father* and all my other books. See *Wickedary*, p. 91.)

Countless Wild Women have described the behavior of the ruling necrophiliacs/rapists toward women. Jane Caputi has written:

Throughout male supremacist societies, all women (even the most tokenized, privileged, and/or numb among us), by virtue of our femaleness, are variously beaten, brainwashed, disrespected, objectified, incested, harassed, mutilated, battered, raped, tongue-tied, defamed, enslaved, or systematically murdered by men.[2]

Disgusted Women, including Andrée Collard, Joyce Contrucci, Suzanne Bellamy, Susan Griffin, Batya Bauman, and Carol Adams, have analyzed atrocities against animals and nature. And many other Wolfish and Catty Women present supporting evidence . . .

At this point I seem to hear a few readers muttering, "Just *who* are these hordes of Wild Women who parade through this Introduction and through the book?" One woman, who looks quite Wild herSelf, asks: "Who calls herself a 'Radical Elemental Feminist,' anyway?"

"Good question," I respond. "*I* do. This Manifesto is issued for mySelf and any woman who Hears the Call of the Wild and follows it. Wild Women recognize ourSelves. It doesn't matter to me whether we all use the same words. Words generate their own energy. They move around a lot, especially in subconscious realms. If I Be-Speak certain words, they're in the air, as it were. They're free and available. They have influence, and they follow their own Spiraling paths."

"But throughout the book you have these raving bands of women, it seems, who 'howl' and make pronouncements. They seem to be something like a Greek chorus . . . "

"Well, that's an interesting point," I reply. "I happen to enjoy Raving Bands of Wild Women. I wouldn't say they function exactly as a Greek chorus, though. They're too Rowdy for that role. Of course some of them may well be Wild Greek Women . . . "

By now my questioner's eyes show gleams of interest. "Well, *I* don't see or hear them," she says. "Maybe I'd like to, though."

"I *do* See and Hear them," I say. "But I can understand your problem. You seem to be stuck in the diaspora that's been plaguing Wild Women during the dulled-out 1990s. You need to open your Third Eye and your Inner Ear and try some Transtemporal/Trans-spatial travel."

"Do you give lessons?" asks the same woman, whose face is visibly brightening.

"Not exactly, but you could start with reading *Quintessence* and sharing it with Other Women, and then find some other books as well. There's no need to become braindead."

"Well, O.K., I'll try. But what's this 'Anonyma Network' stuff? That's just *so* far out."

"Yes, it is," I respond. I feel myself drifting off into another dimension. "Speak with you again sometime," I say.

ABOUT THE "ANONYMA NETWORK" STUFF

There are a few points that may require explanation to the general reader:

Due to a peculiar "wrinkle in Time"[3] that happened in the course of writing this book I had the unexpected privilege of meeting a group of Fantastic Women who live (will live?) in a place they call Lost and Found Continent in the year 2048 BE. They said that "BE" stands for Biophilic Era.

You see, one of them, a woman who calls herSelf "Anonyma" ("Annie" for short) actually Invoked me and I found mySelf there/

then—on Lost and Found Continent in 2048 BE. This woman and her friends, who obviously live in the Future, told me they had read *Quintessence* and found it thought provoking. I was thrilled to hear that they liked it. Needless to say I am fascinated by their ideas and experiences.

When Annie told me that Anonyma Netword (an Intergalactic Publishing Enterprise of Anonyma Network) wanted to publish a 50th Anniversary Edition of *Quintessence* on Lost and Found Continent I was excited at this prospect. They suggested that I propose to my twentieth-century publisher in Boston the idea of "simultaneous publication" (Transtemporally speaking). When I returned from that visit to Lost and Found Continent I did in fact bring their proposal to my publishing house, where it was welcomed with respect and enthusiasm. I think it is a very good omen for the Future that a highly respected publisher has been willing to take the risk of cooperating in this unusual undertaking.

I know this Transtemporal/Trans-spatial travel and communication sounds mind-boggling but I'm really glad it has begun to happen. I was deeply Disgusted by the condition of "the world" in the late 1990s and delighted to get out of that time/space for my visits to Lost and Found. Those women from 2048 BE generate such Hope! They have inspired me to complete my writing of the 1998 edition of this book in Time for them to bring out their 50th Anniversary Anonyma Edition—simultaneously, as it were. And, as Annie wrote in her *Preface*, it's all happening on the 200th anniversary (from a 2048 BE perspective) of the Woman's Rights Convention at Seneca Falls, New York, in 1848.*

As I am writing this I look forward to seeing the 2048 BE edition of *Quintessence ... Realizing the Archaic Future*, which will contain the Original 1998 edition, actually in print. I suspect that contemporary readers will be intellectually stimulated by Annie's *Preface* and her *Cosmic Comments and Conversations with the Author*.

These Comments and Conversations seemed to come from Else-

---

*I have just heard from Annie that the Anonyma Book Club will be adopting this book—as well as a number of other twentieth-century Radical Feminist books—for its workshops across Lost and Found and on a few of the other continents.

where/Elsewhen. Don't get me wrong, please. I am not a "channeler." I take full responsibility for these (ad)ventures. After all, since I have been Conjuring Foresisters, Past, Present, and Future in the course of public lectures for years, it shouldn't be too surprising that a Future Foresister began to Conjure me. It just takes getting used to the idea.

Annie and her friends continue to inspire me to expand my horizons to include Transtemporal, Trans-spatial and Interspecies Bonding in Elemental Sisterhood. I hope that these Glimpses and Intuitions of the Future will be enCouraging for readers, as they have been for me. This brings me to some introductory musings on the subject of Quintessence and Courage.

QUINTESSENCE AND COURAGE

In Pythagorean mysticism, *Quintessence* is Spirit that fills the universe and gives it life and vitality. In ancient and medieval philosophy, *Quintessence* Names the fifth and last or highest essence, above fire, air, water, and earth, that permeates all nature. When I use this Word— *Quintessence*— it Names the unifying Living Presence that is at the core of the Integrity and Elemental connectedness of the Universe and that is the Source of our power to Realize a true Future—an Archaic Future.

Radical Elemental Women participate in and expand Quintessence by Re-Calling Outrageous Contagious Courage. In these times there is a tremendous need for women to Re-member such Courage. A terrible war is being waged against women and all of nature, especially against our souls. For this death battle the patriarchs are bringing out their big guns—their media, their religions, their technologies, their education, et cetera. As always. But in the late 1990s the battle is more blatant than ever, more insidious than ever. My analysis of the strategies currently being employed by the sadosociety to destroy our bodies, minds, and souls and to annihilate all Elemental Reality is woven throughout the chapters of this book. It is impossible for Radical Elemental Feminists to go "too far" in our fight for our lives, for all Life. . . .

For this struggle it is empowering to Re-Call the words of Foresister Elizabeth Cady Stanton, who proclaimed in 1851:

The manner in which all courage and self-reliance is educated out of the girl, her path portrayed with dangers and difficulties that never exist, is melancholy indeed. Better, far, suffer occasional insults or die outright, than live the life of a coward, or never move without a protector. The best protector any woman can have, one that will serve her at all times and in all places, is courage; this she must get by her own experience, and experience comes by exposure.[4]

In 1870 Susan B. Anthony pondered the problem of compelling women to see "the abject degradation of their present position."

The fact is, women are in chains, and their servitude is all the more debasing because they do not realize it. O, to compel them to see and feel, and to give them the courage and conscience to speak and act for their own freedom, though they face the scorn and contempt of all the world for doing it![5]

"The abject degradation of our present position" continues, and Radical Elemental Feminists continue to face the scorn and contempt of all the world for Be-Speaking and Acting.

RE-CLAIMING THE WONDERLUST OF WOMEN

Quintessence is a Wild work of Radical Elemental Feminist philosophy. The word *Radical* (which suggests going to one's roots) implies *Elemental*. As a woman becomes more Radical she Dis-covers Elemental reality. Her reason is rooted in instinct, intuition, passion. Breaking out of tame/tracked modes of thinking and feeling, she returns to the experiences and questions of her childhood and listens to the promptings of ancestral Memory.

The very word *philosophy* terrifies many women. In *Quintessence* I strive to exorcise this patriarchally embedded fear that undermines our intelligence and passion. We were all philosophers when we were five years old. Re-Calling our connections with nature at that age, many women can Re-member our sense of wonder and our urgent need to *know.* We were always asking "Why?" This state of mind can be called *Wonderlust*—meaning a strong and unconquerable longing for Elemental adventure and knowledge.

So what happened to our Wonderlust? Our visions, dreams, and far-out questions have been stunted by phallocratic society and its institutions. When we come into contact with our own deep and passionate intellectuality, we become intolerably threatening to the patriarchy. This is why there is an overwhelming taboo against women becoming philosophers, that is, seekers of wisdom on our own terms/turf.

Philosophy—of our own kind, for our own kind—is a source of wholeness and power that rightfully belongs to women. Breaking the patriarchal taboo against it—against us—we break out of the state of deception. Moreover, we open gateway after gateway into our own Otherworld, our Homeland. From this perspective we can See, Name, and Act to end the atrocities perpetrated against ourSelves and all Biophilic beings.

HOW *QUINTESSENCE IS CONNECTED* WITH MY OTHER BOOKS

Quintessence Bio-logically and Crone-logically follows all my other books.* It flows from them on a Course that can be compared to that of

---

*Bibliographic information on earlier books:

The Church and the Second Sex (1968; reissued with Autobiographical Preface to the 1975 Edition and Feminist Postchristian Introduction, 1975; reissued with New Archaic Afterwords, Boston: Beacon Press, 1985).

Beyond God the Father: Toward a Philosophy of Women's Liberation (1973; reissued with Original Reintroduction by the Author, Boston: Beacon Press, 1985).

Gyn/Ecology: The Metaethics of Radical Feminism (1978; reissued with New Intergalactic Introduction by the Author, Boston: Beacon Press, 1990).

Pure Lust: Elemental Feminist Philosophy (1984; 1992; London: The Women's Press, 1984; distributed in the U.S. by Trafalgar Square Publishing).

a deep river.[6] As an Explorer on that river I have never known exactly what will come next. I have been greeted by astonishing events at every turn. *Quintessence* has come as a Startling Surprise—which is, of Course, a familiar experience.

My first Feminist book, *The Church and the Second Sex* (1968), might on the surface seem incompatible with everything I have written since.* In fact, in my Feminist Postchristian Introduction to the 1975 edition of that work I referred to the author of the original edition as "the early Daly," and as a "quaint foresister." Yet, despite serious disagreements, I remained respectful of her, recognizing that "it hardly seems appropriate for me to pass judgments upon an author who was not an astronaut before it was possible to become one," and that "if it were not for Daly's early work, I myself probably would never have tried on a feminist space suit."

In fact, in the original edition of *The Church and the Second Sex* she/I was "constructing a launching pad for a future space trip which she could not have foreseen clearly." Had she/I fully understood the implications of this project, "she would have been rocketed into the postchristian era."

Instead of immediately rocketing into the Postchristian era, in that early book I produced a thoroughly Searched historical record and critique of the misogynism of the catholic church. My effort was based on

---

Websters' First New Intergalactic Wickedary of the English Language, Conjured in Cahoots with Jane Caputi (1987; 1993; London: The Women's Press, 1988; distributed in the U.S. by Trafalgar Square Publishing). Hereafter cited as *Wickedary.*

Outercourse: The Be-Dazzling Voyage (1992; London: The Women's Press, 1993; distributed in the U.S. by Trafalgar Square Publishing).

*This surface impression is one example of the effects of time warps. *The Church and the Second Sex* might seem "liberal" rather than "Radical" to someone who cannot see it in historical context. As I view it, the adjective *Radical* describes the Original impulse of a work, not only its material content. *The Church and the Second Sex* was Radical enough to launch me on an A-mazing Voyage.

the premise that by clear reasoning and presentation of evidence of the church's androcentrism I could *change* that institution. That book's history and its infamous consequences served to illustrate the absurdity of this presupposition.* Thus without realizing what I was doing, I actually wrote mySelf Out of the catholic church and, by logical extension, Out of christianity in general and Out of all patriarchal religion. So by my construction of this initial Launching Pad I freed mySelf to rocket in the direction of *Beyond God the Father: Toward a Philosophy of Women's Liberation* . . . and beyond. My Course was set. It was and is toward liberation from the tyranny of patriarchy and into fullness of Be-ing.

At its core, the driving impulse of *Quintessence* is in line, that is, in Spiral, with the direction of *Beyond God the Father* (1973; 1985), whose organic, unifying theme is that the movement for women's liberation is an *ontological* movement propelled and fired by existential Courage. Such profound Courage to Be is the key to the revelatory power of the Feminist revolution.

In a special way *Quintessence* follows both *Gyn/Ecology: The Metaethics of Radical Feminism* (1978; 1990) and *Pure Lust: Elemental Feminist Philosophy* (1984; 1992). I wrote these books with the idea that they could be the first two volumes of a trilogy describing the Metapatriarchal Journey of Exorcism and Ecstasy.

Gyn/Ecology conveys the spirit of the Journey and the identities of many of the Journeyers, e.g., the Hags, Harpies, Crones, Furies, Spinsters, Witches, A-mazing Amazons, and Others who roam through

---

*These consequences included my being fired from my teaching job at jesuit-run Boston College in the spring of 1969; four months of widely publicized student protests; a petition on my behalf signed by 2,500 persons; a seven-hour teach-in; the decoration of the central B.C. administration building (Gasson Hall) at night with brilliant red graffiti. The university backed down when caught by the media in its own indecent act of self-exposure, and it attempted to save face by granting my overdue promotion and tenure in June 1969. But it was too late. The whole affair had functioned as a microcosm, revealing the entrenched conservatism of the stubborn old men who control the church and its educational institutions and who are terrified of the intellectual power of women.

three Passages. It establishes the direction of the Voyage, charting its Passages, Naming the demons who try to block our way. These demons are personifications of eight Deadly Sins of the Fathers. Namely:

Processions	(deception)
Professions	(pride)
Possession	(avarice)
Aggression	(anger)
Obsession	(lust)
Assimilation	(gluttony)
Elimination	(envy)
Fragmentation	(sloth)

Gyn/Ecology takes on all of the demonic Deadly Sins, but focuses especially on the first three: *Processions, Professions,* and *Possession*. In this process it breaks patriarchal myths and symbols and exposes phallocratic atrocities, analyzing their interconnectedness. It frees Journeyers to Leap into Ecstatic Spooking, Sparking, and Spinning.

Pure Lust carries on by confronting *Aggression* and *Obsession*. As the Voyage continues, Wonderlusting women who are the Furious Fighters of these infernal molesters increase in numbers and in Spirit-force. Fired by Elemental E-motion, we Move onward, upward, downward, outward, traversing New Realms of Spheres. We first A-maze our way through *Archespheres*, the Realm of Origins. Then we Charge into and through *Pyrospheres*, the Purifying Realm of Fire. Finally we soar through *Metamorphospheres*, the Be-Witching Realm of graceless/ Graceful transformations.

In a specific way *Pure Lust* is a direct predecessor of *Quintessence* for it focuses upon Elements in clusters of four.* *Quintessence* breaks through to the Dis-covering of yet an Other Element.

Elements traditionally have been defined as "1: the spoken letters of the alphabet; the primal Race of Words—their cosmic sounds, meanings, rhythms, and connections 2: fire, air, earth, water, constituting the deep Realms of Reality with which all sentient beings are naturally and Wildly connected 3: the larger cosmos including the sun, moon, planets, and stars; the vast context within which the Primal Powers of Witches and all

This, my seventh Radical Feminist book, is the third volume of the Original trilogy, comprising *Gyn/Ecology*, *Pure Lust*, and *Quintessence*. In this book the traveler on the Otherworld Journey of Exorcism and Ecstasy, first described in *Gyn/Ecology*, encounters the final three Deadly Sins of the Fathers: *Assimilation* (Gluttony), *Elimination* (Envy), and *Fragmentation* (Sloth).

Strangely enough, this book did not appear immediately after *Pure Lust*. Instead, I found that I was compelled to create two more books before I could write *Quintessence*. These works are *Websters' First New Intergalactic Wickedary of the English Language*, Conjured in Cahoots with Jane Caputi (1987; 1994) and *Outercourse: The Be-Dazzling Voyage*—Containing Recollections from My *Logbook of a Radical Feminist Philosopher* (Be-ing an Account of My Time/Space Travels—Then, Again, Now, and How) (1992).

If these books are viewed in a superficial manner, they might appear to have been "detours." However, this would not be an adequate or accurate estimation of their respective places in the Course of the Voyage. Both *Wickedary* and *Outercourse* have been necessary prerequisites for the emergence of *Quintessence*, for these provide a Field of Force that is strong enough to allow this book to Spring forth.[7] Both of these earlier books, which "intervened" between *Pure Lust* and *Quintessence*, are summations (but not consummations) as well as Leaps. Specifically, the *Wickedary* gathers together Tribes of New Words, while *Outercourse* is a Philosophical Autobiography, in which I Re-member Momentous Moments of my own Voyage.

The *Wickedary* is a Source Book of New Words. The Original Sources for most of these New Words are my more Archaic Tomes: *The Church and the Second Sex*, *Beyond God the Father*, *Gyn/Ecology*, and *Pure Lust*. However, a significant number of Words made their first appearance in the *Wickedary*. The *Wickedary* embellishes upon all of these, providing precise, colorful, and often multiple definitions, as well

---

Wild beings must be understood 4: Elemental Spirits/Angels/Demons." See *Pure Lust*, pp. 178–79, and *Wickedary*, pp. 73–74.

as meta-etymologies, examples, Canny Comments, and cockaludicrous comments.

In addition to offering its proliferation of New Words, which are contained in three Word-Webs, the *Wickedary* takes off from the format of dick-tionaries, which commonly contain (in addition to words and their definitions) a number of tedious essays. Avoiding tedium at all cost, the *Wickedary* Presents nine A-mazing essays, five of which are Named Preliminary Webs, while four are Called Appendicular Webs.

All of these Words, Embellishments, and Wicked Webs have continued to act as Sources and Aids, offering their services to the writer and readers of both *Outercourse* and *Quintessence*. Moreover, the Magnetic Auras of these Wicked Words and Webs have attracted even more New Words and ideas, which spontaneously have "popped up" in my subsequent books.

In *Outercourse* I have described Four Spiral Galaxies of my Voyage. I Re-member my Acts in the course of this Voyage primarily as feats of a Radical Feminist Pirate.

The Courageous Acts of Radical Feminist Pirates who sail the Subliminal Sea (the vast realm of unconscious memories of women's history) include Plundering—that is, Righteously Ripping Off—treasures that have been stolen from Wild Women by the patriarchal thieves, and Smuggling these back to our Sisters.

As I have explained in *Outercourse*, using my Pirate's Craft—which is also my WitchCraft—I have Sailed through Myriad Moments of Meta-patriarchal Time Travel, adventurously Leaping into Other dimensions. In The Fourth Spiral Galaxy I have experienced Be-Dazzling Moments of Momentous Re-membering. Indeed my arrival in this Galaxy coincides with my entry into an *Expanding Now*—a Now which encompasses the Past, thereby enriching the Present and Touching a New Future.

THE SPIRALING OF QUINTESSENCE

My Voyage into The Fourth Spiral Galaxy of *Outercourse* brought me to the point of Dis-covering yet an Other Galaxy. As a consequence of my arrival in an Expanding Now/Present, the Way Opened for me to Leap into an Expanding Here/Presence. Moving more deeply into the Background Realms, I was ready to begin Spiraling into The Fifth Spiral Galaxy.

The idea of *Quintessence* began brewing in 1992, when a woman in an audience, after my reading from the manuscript of *Outercourse*, asked me: "Is there a Fifth Spiral Galaxy?" Time and Again this question Re-turned, Nagging my Craft onward. Before I could ask Why—in the Blink of an Eye—I found mySelf Here—in the Expanding Here which also implies Expanding Now.

The chapters of this book continue the Otherworld Journey of Exorcism and Ecstasy that was begun in *Gyn/Ecology*. Each chapter reflects the sense of urgency that marks the millennial time. Each, like the Labrys—the ancient Cretan Double-Ax—is double-edged, both Naming/confronting the escalating atrocities of the late twentieth century against women and nature and summoning Courage and Hope to transcend the atrocities. Finally, each chapter is intended to invite the Voyagers of this book into deeper communication with our Elemental Sisters of all kinds as we pursue the Quest for Quintessence.

Chapter One, "The Fifth Spiral Galaxy: Expanding Here," Names and confronts specific contemporary manifestations of the escalating state of atrocity that is phallocracy, in which abominations are normalized, ritualized, repeated, legitimized, sacralized. The focus initially is on the genocidal/gynocidal rape of Muslim women by the Serbs in Bosnia-Hercegovina in the early 1990s and the use of pornography by the Serbian rapists, especially in their rape/death camps, as stimulus for rape. This chapter emphasizes the escalating worldwide state of terror which intensifies the prevailing condition of dividedness/diaspora among women everywhere.

The challenge is to overcome diaspora by Expanding the Presence of Wild Women to ourSelves and each other and to all Elemental creatures—trees, for example. This involves recognizing and cultivating such realities as Magnetic Magic, Elemental Feminist Genius, our deep Rootedness in nature, our profound connection with all Elemental Reality. The project of Wild Women in diaspora is to transform this condition—which is marked by exile, scattering, and enforced migration—into Positive Diaspora. This project requires recognizing our condition as replete with Outlandish opportunities for inventing New modes of Exile, Scattering, and Migration into Quintessential Freedom.

Chapter Two, "Nemesis and the Courage to Create," confronts the worldwide surge of religious fundamentalism in the 1990s and its suppression of women. I examine this woman-destroying plague as it has spread in the Middle East and in the U.S., where it is exemplified in the rise of "Promise Keepers." My analysis sets the scene for moving beyond mere re-acting against injustice to Concreation of Nemesis, a process that requires Magnetic Courage and Courage to Create, which evolves into Creative Courage.

The chapter next takes on technological pseudocreativity, as this displays itself in the "creation" of mutant species and clones. Biotechnology is exposed as necrotechnology ("nectech"). After examining the phenomenon of male motherhood as this manifests itself in the late twentieth century I move on to countering this pseudocreativity with the Wildness of Creative Courage. Next follows a Spin-off from powerful words of Elizabeth Oakes Smith, who calls for "subversion and dissolution of the entire patriarchal order."[8] In order to describe the project of Radical Elemental Feminism I Call for *Meta-subversion* and *Meta-dissolution* of the entire patriarchal order. This involves putting that "order" into the past, getting behind it into the Background, changing and transforming everything.

This project is less daunting than it might appear, because that "order" is killing itself and rapidly succumbing to its own inherent and incurable decrepitude. Since patriarchy is hell-bent on dragging all Biophilic Reality down with it, Voyagers of this chapter are invited to find a Way Out. For Wanderlusting, Wonderlusting Women this involves Discovering the "X-Factor/Faculty," which is the unpredictable, unpossessable nature of Wild Elemental Genius.

Chapter Three, "Re-awakening the X-Factor/Faculty and Creating the Archaic Future," confronts the dis-spiriting state of con-fusion. In this state tricksters/mind-twisters blend words and images which have opposite meanings, producing mixed-up meaninglessness. Ultimate con-fusion is manifested in such nectech phenomena as splicing and mapping genes, mixing species, and penetrating celestial bodies. Refusing to be trapped in this arena of atrocities, Defiant Women seek to Re-member beyond it.

This leads to a discussion of Moments of Unforgetting. The extremity of our Be-Longing is sometimes so strong that Elemental Women break into our hidden Heritage of Memories of the Future—Re-Calling Momentous Acts of our Foresisters. These provide inspiration for Focused Acts of Desperation. My analysis of Desperation leads to reflections upon the resurging of Elemental Feminist Genius that began to occur in the early 1970s.

The chapter next forges ahead to an analysis of the taming of Feminist Genius by the tricks of academia/academentia. These include the intrusive and con-fusing use of "gender" jargon to inhibit all Radical Feminist thought. They also include preoccupation with postmodern theory and specifically the oxymoronic entity known as "postmodern feminist theory." Students are sometimes taught that the word "women" is "essentialist" and should be replaced by such phrases as "persons gendered as feminine." I examine the invasion of Women's Studies by such theory and re-turn to the writings of Virginia Woolf for guidance and passionate insight.

The seven-point Sado-Ritual Syndrome, which I Dis-covered and used in *Gyn/Ecology* in my analysis of worldwide atrocities against women here serves as a method for exposing "postmodern feminist theory" as a cause of mindbinding and inability to Name and Act against oppression.

This chapter concludes with Metamorphic Leaping into an Archaic Future, which is a Real Future, rooted in the Archaic Past. We reach it by transforming foreground diaspora into Transtemporal Diaspora. This we accomplish by Unforgetting our Deep Past and by performing actions and generating works that can affect/effect the Future. These actions and works can be Re-membered and Realized in the minds and actions of those who come after us. Transmuting the condition of diaspora into a heretofore unimaginable manifestation of an "Outsiders' Society" (Virginia Woolf's expression) is a consequence of Desperately Hopeful Foreknowledge, and it is rooted in understanding of our history, our Past.

Chapter Four, "The Fifth Element and the Fifth Direction," begins with unveiling reversals that are omnipresent in patriarchal "spirituality." It warns women who are disgusted by the blatant misogynism of christianity against seduction by less obvious but equally woman-erasing messages and practices that are pervasive in eastern religions. After a discussion of bamboozlement of women by the institution of "gurudom," the chapter moves on to an analysis of mythic foreshadowings of cloning, east and west. These foreshadowings are manifested in apparently diverse phenomena such as the Tibetan tulku system, the Greek myth of Dionysus, and the christian myth of the "Virgin Birth of Christ."

In the section on the Fifth Element, traditionally known as Ether, this chapter Spins off from John Milton's tirade against the killing (by men) of books authored by men, which he says "strikes at that ethereal and fifth essence, the breath of reason itself [and] slays an immortality rather than a life." Noting that there can be no comparison between the piddling offenses of males against each other and the unspeakable erasure of Female Creativity under patriarchy, I Name the current massacre/bookburning of Wild Women's books and bookstores in the context of patriarchy's slaying of *our* immortality, that is, our Heritage. I note the bland erasure of such erasure in phallic philosophy. Our recognition of such massacre/erasure gives rise to the Passion of Grief. The Grief of Wild Women combines with Rage. Our Wailing *is* our Railing, and it moves us to Be-Speaking.

The Fifth Direction is identified as our Core/Center by Voyaging

Women who are Centering/Balancing/Focusing, reaffirming our Original Integrity. This consideration leads to a decoding and reinterpretation of the Greco-Egyptian Sphinx, which is an embodiment of ancient energy forms that are reclaimable by Wise Women. In this Radical Elemental Feminist analysis, the Sphinx signifies the unified integrity of all Five Elements. The Fifth Element, Ether, represented by the head and bust of a woman, is a unifying principle. The Sphinx is a symbolic message to Wild Women, summoning us to participation in the Transtemporal/Trans-spatial Integrity and Harmony of all creation, which is Quintessence.

Chapter Five, "Breaking into the Fifth Dimension: Dis-covering the Light of Quintessence," begins with a description of typical Fifth Dimensional experiences, notably seeming "coincidences," which are recognized by Canny Crones as not merely coincidental. In reality, they are deeply purposeful synchronicities, also known by Shrewd Women as Syn-Crone-icities.

As Eccentric Women Voyage ever further Out we become more threatening to the demonic daddies of the deadzone, who try to block our Ways. These fathers of a fake future, working to make everything unnaturally disconnected from everything else, are revoking inherent knowledge of life cycles from the genes of seeds, animals, and women.

This chapter exposes current incarnations of patriarchal myths and symbols which have served as paradigms for hell on earth and in space in the twenty-first century. Symbols include the triune god that would keep us trapped in a three-dimensional world and that provides a paradigm for cloning and other productions of the monoculture. The scenario is one of infinite immutability, ineffable sameness, and supreme narcissism. The section on "demonic dissociation" shows how necro/biotechnology and the technology of nuclearism concur in promoting the destruction of nature, while generating indifference to the suffering they create.

This leads into Naming of the rampant boundary violation manifested in such phenomena as xenotransplantation, the patenting of life forms, the new reproductive technologies, and the "creations" of the human genome project. These are manifestations of the deadly sin of assimilation, that is, gynocidal, biocidal gluttony which expresses itself in vampirism/cannibalism, feeding upon the *living* flesh, blood, and spirit of its victims.

The Call of the Wild summons us to Movement beyond this brain-dead, deadly state into the Fifth Dimension. This is a State of Natural Grace in which Journeying Women Dis-cover our Elemental Harmony with the Universe. In Touch with the joy of Quintessence, we find that we cannot conveniently block out our knowledge of evil. Our intensified E-motional and intellectual powers enable us to understand atrocities and their interconnections on deep levels. We come to Realize all our Biophilic Acts as significant, because we are participating in Quintessential Creation.

Quintessence...
Realizing the Archaic Future

Chapter One

The Fifth Spiral Galaxy: Expanding Here

ILD WOMEN are Present to each other across Space and Time. For example, when we choose to hold an Intergalactic Congress on the other side of the moon, Hags of the millennia are Here Now.

On a more mundane plane, we do this all the time. Especially when we deeply hear each other's words, we magnetize/summon our Foresisters as well as our Present and Future Selves. This great Summoning Summons the "sum total" of our energy/Gynergy,* which ultimately amounts to participation in Be-ing. The sum of our powers manifests itself in a Wild Call echoing across the Etheric Realms, as each woman awakens to the words "I Am!"

Wanderlusting Women are always on the move. Our Voyages of Exorcism and Ecstasy comprise Moments of participation in Be-ing which carry Journeyers beyond imprisonment in fatherland. These Moments are Acts of Courage. Each Moment leads/leaps to another because it has consequences in the world which impel us to move onward.

The paths formed by our Moments/Movements constitute Spiral Galaxies, which, like the galaxies of the universe, are in perpetual whirling motion. At certain points in this Spinning progression the accumulated Gynergy of New Moments enables Voyagers to take extreme Qualitative

---

*The word *Gynergy*, which was invented by Emily Culpepper, is defined as "the female energy which both comprehends and creates who we are; that impulse in ourselves that has never been possessed by the patriarchy." See *Wickedary*, p. 77.

Leaps and thus begin New Galaxies. Adventurously hurling ourselves into Galaxy after Galaxy, we Realize Other dimensions.*

In The Fifth Spiral Galaxy—the Realm of *Expanding Here/Presence*—we encounter the Fifth Cause, the Fifth Element, the Fifth Direction, and the Fifth Dimension. In this Galaxy we Dis-cover *Quintessence*, the Metamorphic Manifestation of Cosmic Integrity, Harmony, and Luminous Splendor in the Unfolding Universe.[1] And we are arriving Here just in Time. For we must dispel the demonic destruction that is being inflicted upon women and nature by the frauds and fiends who rule fatherland.

THE STATE OF ATROCITY: THE STATE OF TERROR

As the patriarchal death marchers relentlessly strut into their "millennial time," they work to undermine the Expanding Presence of Elemental Women. Wild Women witness and experience ubiquitous terrorism, striving to thrive through and beyond the increasing horrors of the state of atrocity, in which abominations are normalized, ritualized, repeated, legitimized, sacralized.

The state of atrocity is characterized by *rapism*, the fundamental ideology and practice of patriarchy.[2] The primary analogate for the wider concept of rapism is, of course, rape. In her classic work *Against Our Will: Men, Women, and Rape*, Susan Brownmiller speculates that one of the earliest forms of male bonding must have been the gang rape of one woman by a band of marauding men. She continues:

This accomplished, rape became not only a male prerogative, but man's basic weapon of force against woman, the principal agent of his will and her fear. His forcible entry into her body, despite her physical

---

*Elsewhere I have described my own experience of arrival in The Fourth Spiral Galaxy, where Voyagers experience Moments of Momentous Re-membering, retracing our earlier Moments as with a Pen of Light. This coincides with entry into *Expanding Now*. Our arrival in *Expanding Now/Present* opens the way for the Great Leap into *Expanding Here/Presence*. See my philosophical autobiography, *Outercourse: The Be-Dazzling Voyage*, esp. pp. 1–21 and 335–415.

protestations and struggle, became the vehicle of his victorious conquest over her being, the ultimate test of his superior strength, the triumph of his manhood. . . . From prehistoric times to the present, I believe, rape has played a critical function. It is nothing less than a conscious process of intimidation by which *all* men keep *all* women in a state of fear.[3]

Throughout patriarchal history, in times of "peace" as well as periods of war, rape has been an omnipresent threat and reality. Worldwatch Institute estimated in 1996 that in the United States between one in five and one in seven women will be the victim of a completed rape in her lifetime.[4] Mass rapes of women occur especially in war-torn countries. The intentional strategy often is to punish and terrorize large parts of civilian populations. Women are prime targets of sexual violence especially in areas where such violations are seen as attacks against their families' (read: men's) honor.

Escalation of such atrocities was manifested in the last decade of the twentieth century. Naomi Neft and Ann D. Levine, in their international report on the status of women, published in 1997–1998, state:

In recent years mass rapes and other sexual assaults have been reported in Bangladesh, Burundi, Cambodia, Liberia, Peru, Rwanda, Somalia, and Uganda. Perhaps the most shocking reports of large-scale organized rape in recent years have come from the countries that made up the former Yugoslavia,* where 20,000 or more women and

---

*I suggest that one reason why "the most shocking reports" appear to have come from the former Yugoslavia is that hardly anyone is talking about the other cases. Concerning Rwanda, Jan Goodwin reports: "Despite the enormous numbers of women raped . . . and the thousands of infants fathered by their attackers, there has not yet been a single rape indictment handed down by the U.N. International Criminal Tribunal for Rwanda. Nor is there likely to be, say international observers." Goodwin cites human rights lawyer Binaifer Nowrojee, who stated that there is a view at the U.N. that rape is not a crime of genocide, that rape is not really an international crime. See Jan Goodwin, "Rwanda: Justice Denied," *On the Issues: The Progressive Woman's Quarterly*, Fall 1997, pp. 26–33. See also Nowrojee's Human Rights Watch report *Shattered Lives: Sexual Violence During the Rwandan Genocide and Its Aftermath.* In contrast to the silence about

girls were raped during the first few months of the war that followed the country's dissolution in 1992. Although all three parties to the conflict—Muslims, Croats, and Bosnian Serbs—were guilty of committing sexual assaults, the main abusers were the Bosnian Serbs, who were ordered to rape Muslim women as part of a brutal ethnic cleansing campaign as well as a deliberate attempt to terrorize civilians and drive them from their homes.[5]

An estimated 200,000 people, perhaps 80 percent Muslim, were killed in Bosnia by the Serbian military. On January 4, 1993 *Newsweek* reported that Serb forces had raped an estimated 30,000 to 50,000 women, most of them Muslim.[6] Catharine A. MacKinnon pointed out that the mass rape of Muslim and Croatian women and girls by Serbs was not simply a practice of misogyny, but also a tactic for "ethnic cleansing," that is, genocide.[7] Serb military policy *mandated* the systematic gang rape of Muslim and Croatian women and girls, many of whom were taken from their homes and raped in the streets, or in schools, factories, motels, or concentration camps. There were an estimated ninety Serb-controlled camps, in which victims were chosen at random to be raped as part of torture preceding death. In addition there were more than twenty infamous rape/death camps, where women were subjected to ongoing rape unto death. Acts of torture included mutilation, especially amputation of breasts. Serb soldiers also raped some women as part of a program of forced impregnation to produce "Serbian children."* These atrocities against women were acts both of genocide *and gynocide.*†

Of crucial importance was the fact that the Serbs used advanced,

---

Rwanda, there have been some condemnations and actions against the Bosnian Serb killers and rapists.

*The offspring of the raped women are considered Serbs by the Serbs, whose ignorance of biology makes it possible for them to see enforced pregnancy as a method of genocide. The mothers are seen simply as vessels, contributing nothing to the identity of their offspring.

†I have defined the word *gynocide* as "the fundamental intent of global patriarchy: planned, institutionalized spiritual and bodily destruction of women; the use of deliber-

sophisticated moving-picture technology to make violent pornography, which was distributed widely in the former Yugoslavia to whet the appetites of soldiers to obtain sexual pleasure from raping, torturing, and killing women. According to MacKinnon, this "paved the way for the use on television of footage of actual rapes, with the ethnicity of the victims and perpetrators switched, to inflame Serbs against Muslims and Croatians."[8] The Serbs made pornography of their crimes and disseminated it, adding further dimensions to the atrocities. The same author also states: "In the conscious and open use of pornography, in making pornography of atrocities, in the sophisticated use of pornography as war propaganda, this is perhaps the first truly modern war."[9]

Andrea Dworkin described this situation in 1993 in her inimitable way as follows:

In this war, pornography is everywhere: plastered on tanks; incorporated into the gang rapes in the prostitution-prison brothels. Soldiers have camcorders to do the military version of "Beaver Hunt"— women tortured for the camera, raped for the camera, knifed and beaten for the camera; and of course, for the man behind it, the rapist-soldier turned—in Amerikan parlance—into an expresser. Of what? Oh, ideas.[10]

Dworkin has pointed out that such true-to-life/death pornography can be disseminated elsewhere in the world, stimulating other men to copy the acts and take more pictures.[*11] It does not require an un-

---

ate systematic measures (such as killing, bodily or mental injury, unlivable conditions, prevention of births), which are calculated to bring about the destruction of women as a political and cultural force, the eradication of Female/Bio-logical religion and language, and ultimately the extermination of the Race of Women and all Elemental being; the master model of genocide; paradigm for the systematic destruction of any racial, political, or cultural group." See *Gyn/Ecology*, throughout, and *Wickedary*, p. 77.

*The nazis set a precedent for this by taking pictures in death camps of naked women running to their deaths and other horrors. However, they did not have the sophisticated technologies that became available in the nineties.

realistic leap of the imagination to consider the possibility that porno-graphic propaganda produced by the Serbs has in fact spread to other countries.[12]

Women who look to male-controlled organizations for help against gynocide can expect disappointment. It has been reported that some United Nations troops participated in raping Muslim and Croatian women taken from Serb-run rape/death camps.[13] Moreover, the patri-archal political powers of the world, including the U.S. government, did not intervene to stop the Serb atrocities against women. As MacKinnon wrote in 1994:

> Whether or not these practices [rape, prostitution, pornography, and sexual murder] are formally illegal . . . they are widely permitted un-der both domestic and international law. . . . They are legally rational-ized, officially winked at, and in some instances formally condoned.[14]

It has also been demonstrated that we would be unwise to count on patriarchal religious leaders to acknowledge any of this reality. In fact, Wickedly Wise Women can see a further extension of the genocidal, gynocidal rape in the former Yugoslavia in the advice of pope John Paul II to atrocity victims in Croatia, described tamely as "ill-treated women" (*misshandelten Frauen*) to "transform the act of violence into an act of love" and "to accept the enemy inside them." He told the women not to abort.[15]

It would appear that there has been some progress on the interna-tional level. Neft and Levine report:

> In 1996 an International Criminal Tribunal, in an unprecedented ac-tion, indicted several Bosnian Serb military, paramilitary, and police officers for raping Muslim women. This was the first time in history that organized rape and other sexual assaults had been recognized as war crimes in international law.[16]

It is understandable that many women remain skeptical concerning the effectiveness of this apparent progress. In 1998 justice is as elusive as ever.

In the January/February 1997 issue of *Ms.*, Gayle Kirshenbaum wrote movingly of two heroic women who were among the first to submit testimony to the tribunal. Jadranka Cigelj, who is a lawyer, and Nusreta Sivac, who is a judge, had survived Omarska, a notorious Serb-run prison camp. Their testimony, Kirshenbaum states, "helped convince the court that rape had been used as a military tactic by the Serbs during the war in Bosnia and Hercegovina and should be prosecuted as a war crime."[17] But translation into action has been exasperatingly slow. Very few war criminals have been arrested. At the end of October 1996, four of the men who had been indicted, including Zeljko Mejakic, who had regularly assaulted Cigelj and who was known as the camp commander, were reportedly working openly as police officers. Despite this travesty of justice Cigelj and Sivac "have helped to permanently redefine the crimes for which men like Mejakic will have to answer."[18] Kirshenbaum quotes Cigelj as saying that their effort has been worthwhile, "not just for the former Yugoslavia, but for other parts of the world. There will be more wars."[19] In 1998 the rapists remained at large, as did the commanders who exploited rape as a weapon. Most women survivors of genocidal rape in Bosnia do not trust the tribunal at all. Since it has not charged rape as genocide, it lacks legal accountability. Moreover, there is inadequate protection of witnesses.*

IMPLICATIONS OF THE GYNOCIDAL GENOCIDE IN BOSNIA-HERCEGOVINA AND CROATIA

The atrocities against women in the former Yugoslavia must be seen in the context of escalating worldwide gynocide. Rape and murder of women are part of every war, every genocide. Susan Brownmiller, writing in *Newsweek* in 1993, reawakened the memories and consciousness

---

*Cigelj is reported to have said: "Many, including me, are asking ourselves, 'Should we testify, or not?'... These women are tired. They are disillusioned. They want to move forward." See Elizabeth Neuffer, "Bosnia Rapes Go Unpunished," *Boston Sunday Globe*, January 4, 1998, pp. A1, A12.

of readers by citing atrocious examples from other wars, courageously and uncompromisingly demonstrating that "there is nothing 'unprecedented' about mass rape in war."[20]

The genocide in Bosnia-Hercegovina was a significant plunge further into the phallocratic future because of its focus on atrocities against women (including the use of camcorders to record and promote them) as an integral part of its planned strategy.* This can be a hideous harbinger of things to come in modern warfare and in the wide context of the war against women. As Natalie Nenadic wrote in 1993:

> Croatian and Bosnian Moslem women and girls are being systematically destroyed in Serbian rape/death camps. . . . The outrage that is happening to these women specifically, here and now, should also bring visibility to the sexual abuse and subordination of women everywhere.[21]

The use of pornographic films by the Serbs demonstrates the connection of pornography to sexual atrocities. It especially reveals pornography's inherent function as stimulus for actual rape, mutilation, and murder of women. It may seem absurd that women in the United States and Western Europe would have to look as far as Bosnia to get the point that Radical Feminists—Andrea Dworkin especially—have been making for decades, namely that there are causal connections between pornography and actual rape and torture of women.[22] It *is* absurd. But the fact is that such knowledge and consciousness have been erased in the minds of many women by the pornographers and their supporters. This is especially the case in the U.S., where pro-

---

*Of course, Serb forces also raped Bosnian and Croatian men and boys. It is crucial to keep in mind, however, the obvious fact that the agents of the rapes were men. Naming the agent is required for an adequate analysis of atrocities. As linguist Julia Penelope has shown, agent deletion is a dangerous and common mind-muddying flaw. See Julia Penelope, *Speaking Freely: Unlearning the Lies of the Fathers' Tongues* (New York: Teachers College Press, The Athene Series, 1990), esp. pp. 126–29, 144–79.

pornography and pro–"free speech" propaganda continues to prolifer-ate, spawning endless discussion about the First Amendment. The pornographers and their allies, in the ACLU, for example, intend to prevent the public from recognizing the connection between por-nography and violence against women. Given this cultural climate, it may be necessary for some women to look away from "home" to see the deadly dynamic toward escalation of violence that is inherent in por-nography.[23]

An example of the obfuscation to which American women (and women elsewhere who see American films) are subjected is the highly praised 1997 film *The People vs. Larry Flynt*. The movie is worse than a total lie. It is a whitewash of that infamous pornographer and his vile magazine, *Hustler*. The movie was lauded by film critics, some of whom rated it "four stars" and one of whom intoned, "It makes you proud to be an American." The reason for such incongruous reactions is that in the film Flynt is presented as a great twentieth-century champion of "free speech."*

This movie consists of mind-twisting erasures and reversals of the sort that patriarchal culture commonly uses to batter women's minds, caus-ing many to be unable to see the rot which *is* pornography. *The People vs. Larry Flynt* simply neglected to reveal the truth about *Hustler*, such as the fact that the magazine has featured photos of tortured naked women, women trussed up like dead animals, gang-raped women, mu-

---

*The filmmakers were able to pull this off by referring to a U.S. Supreme Court deci-sion in favor of Flynt and against Jerry Falwell, who had sued *Hustler* for obviously false statements about Falwell in a political satire. This decision was slyly used in the film to make it appear to unsuspecting viewers that the Supreme Court decided in favor of por-nography as free speech. Moreover, Flynt's canonization as a martyr for free speech was achieved despite the fact that his daughter Tonia, whose existence is erased in the film, publicly denounced him for molesting her as a child and teenager. See the excellent and scathing review by Kathi Maio, "The Woman in the Meat Grinder . . . and Her He-roic Champion," in *Sojourner: The Women's Forum*, February 1997, Vol. 22, No. 6, pp. 25–26.

tilated animals, a comic strip featuring a man who stalks little girls, cartoons depicting lynched Blacks and brutally beaten and mutilated women—many of whom are Black and Asian. Viewers are offered one quick flash of the famous cover that portrayed a woman being fed into a meat grinder. This revelation may give viewers a brief and easily forgotten shock, but it functions mainly to bestow credibility upon the film, which might not have passed as "true" if it were one hundred percent sanitized.

The sophisticated technological use of pornography in cyberspace also functions as obfuscating propaganda for the worldwide modern war against women. Cyberspace offers boundless opportunities for pornographers to peddle their wares. To an immeasurable degree it contributes to the spread of the pornographic worldview. It translates into mental, emotional, physical violence by men against women.[24]

Pornographic computer software, pornography in the print media, movies, and television, and increasing objectification of female bodies by fashion and advertising industries produce a climate in which rape, torture, and murder of women and girls become commonplace and even acceptable. The result is that women now live in an escalating state of terror which many are unable to name and acknowledge. Yet it can be exorcised only if we acquire the Courage to Name, confront, and transcend it.

THE ESCALATING STATE OF TERROR
AND THE DIVIDEDNESS/DIASPORA OF WOMEN

The state of terror that is intended to tyrannize women is partially overt and partially subliminal. The knowledge that is the source of terror is the realization that women as women are slated for destruction. When such knowledge is subliminal this can be the result of ignorance. It can also be a consequence of the enormity of the threats now impinging on women, who often repress unbearable knowledge of the conditions of misogynist society. Every day newspapers report murders, rapes, and beatings of women. The economic condition of most women is insecure: jobs are harder to obtain and keep. Fears of sickness abound, and these are fed by the media. The semi-pornographic character of much of advertising adds to the general atmosphere, undermining women's sense of self-worth and safety. Women also feel less able to rely upon and trust other women, who are suffering from the same conditions. There appears to be an exponentially increasing danger of betrayal. This atmosphere is more likely to breed immobility and isolation than to engender Righteous Rage.

Not surprisingly, a primary manifestation of the escalating state of terror is dividedness among and within its victims. The androcratic authors of the state of atrocity contrive to split women apart, to divide us from our Selves and other women. They manage to multiply these divisions endlessly, perverting the richness of our Diversity, which arises from ethnic, cultural, geographic, class, and age differences, into an obstacle to Realizing our Cosmic Commonality. Women thus divided are converted to pinoramic worldviews.

Even Wild Women sometimes feel cut off from our Foresisters, who are Present—even if invisible—and who are clamoring for our attention. We are often oblivious to the Angelic Presences who are Here to guard and guide us. Severed from our own history by phallocratic dispensers of "knowledge," we are sometimes deafened to our own Deep Memories. Frequently rendered speechless, we sometimes feel that we have lost our Powers of Naming. And we appear to have become passive, apparently deprived of our Powers of Acting. Most horribly, we fear that our own Reality is being splintered/destroyed by the agents of dividedness.

Under such conditions, we want to call out to each other, but when we do, we often hear only the sounds of our own voices. We frequently feel abandoned by our most needed Sisters and companions. To Name this state of dividedness and dispersion of women under patriarchy, the word *diaspora* comes to mind. Originally used to describe the dispersion of the Jews, this word, taken in its wide sense, means "exile, scattering, migration" (*Webster's*). *Diaspora* can be applied to the situation of Elemental Women.* I use it here to Name not only our external dispersion, but also internalized oppression—the exile, scattering, and enforced migration of consciousness—which cut us off from deep and focused Realizing of the *Background*.†

The often nightmarish state of dividedness/diaspora is spawned and perpetuated by manmade illusions, especially the illusion of female powerlessness. Such deception flourishes in the *foreground*, the zone/dimension marked by artificiality, lack of depth, of aura, and of interconnectedness with living be-ing.‡

The way out of this zone is Dis-illusioning. Dis-illusioned Women can see through the fundamental strategy of the phallocratic state for breaking minds/spirits/senses. This strategy is dismemberment of consciousness through enormous and often flagrant lies, making acceptable and even invisible the smaller lies that prevail in patriarchy, deadening deep intuitive powers.[25]

Dis-illusioned Women, armed with Outrageous Courage, can reclaim our own Vision and Righteous Rage and move further Out. Given the conditions of diaspora/dividedness, it is imperative that

---

*The word *diaspora* is used in many other instances. For example, there is the African American diaspora, arising from the fact that Africans were forcibly brought by slave traders to America. There have been diasporas of many other ethnic and national groups. The Irish diaspora, for example, involved the dispersion of countless Irish people to other lands, especially after the famine in the 1840s. Forty million people of Irish descent live in North America and millions more in Britain and Australia. As a result of such diasporas, Wild Women are challenged to revel in our Diversity, refusing to sink to bickering over cultural differences or to settle for dividedness from each other.

†*Background*, first Named by Denise D. Connors, means "the Realm of Wild Reality; the Homeland of women's Selves and of all other Others; the Time/Space where auras of plants, planets, stars, animals and all Other animate beings connect." See *Gyn/Ecology*, pp. 2–3, and *Wickedary*, p. 63.

‡By *foreground*, first Named by Denise D. Connors, I mean "male-centered and monodimensional arena where fabrication, objectification, and alienation take place; zone of fixed feelings, perceptions, behaviors; the elementary world: FLATLAND." See *Gyn/Ecology*, p. 3, and *Wickedary*, p. 76.

Dreadful/Dreadless Women Re-member our Elemental connectedness with each other and with all life. We must Invoke our Original magnetizing powers.

MAGNETIC MAGIC AND THE EXPANSION OF HERE

Journeyers expand our Presence by means of magnetism. We are drawn to each other across temporal and spatial divides. Hence Expanding Presence is Magnetic Presence, which is experienced by many Crones and Cronies as Magnetic Magic.

Clues concerning the nature of this magic can be found in one particular definition of the verb *magnetize*, which is "to communicate magnetic properties to: convert into a magnet" (*Webster's*). Thus one Be-Witching Bitch can communicate magnetic properties to another. She/they can continue this process of Metamorphosis, transforming more and more women into Magnets. Together we can Magnetize, radiating contagious Elemental attraction, which is reciprocal and energizing. Rachel Carson wrote often of this reality in nature. For example, in *The Sea Around Us* she explained:

> There is no drop of water in the ocean, not even in the deepest parts of the abyss, that does not know and respond to the mysterious forces that create the tide.[26]

Of course, no Canny Voyager can forget that Elemental Magnetism includes animal magnetism, that is, a Spiritlike force residing within and emanating from animals. Thus the Expanding Magnetic Presence of Time-Traveling Cronies should not be seen as an event isolated from the attractive/attracting activities of other Elemental creatures. All participate in the dynamic drawing powers of the *Final Cause*, the indwelling, always unfolding goal or purpose perceived as Good and attracting one to Act, to Realize her own participation in Be-ing.* This magnetic

---

*The *Final Cause* is the beginning, not the end of becoming. It is the First Cause and Cause of causes, which gives an agent the motivation to Act. *Beyond God the Father,*

participation is Cosmic Concordance. Moreover, it is Be-Dazzling, for it eclipses the foreground world with the brilliance of Background Being.

The Magnetizing Aura of The Fifth Spiral Galaxy summons Magical helpers and companions. Among the helpers attracted into Expanding Here are Words. Some of these can be found in dick-tionaries, while others dwell in various Be-Spelling books. Still others are attracted by these Newly awakened Wicked Words, which have an Urge/Itch to dredge Out their associates from the depths of the Subliminal sea—the Realm of unconscious Memories, where women's buried treasures lie hidden. The latter, in turn, reach out and catch even more profoundly submerged words. The Magnetizing process can go on and on. New/Ancient Words are clues to even more deeply buried Knowledge that Metapatriarchal Pirates continue to Plunder and Smuggle back to Wild Women.

The Force Field of this Galaxy also draws Sister Companions Here. Each bears/wears her own unique Spark of Genius. The Intergalactic Sparking is contagious/outrageous. Each of the Sisters/Foresisters/For Sisters brings along Cronies. We all have our own stories to tell. And so have our Familiars. Our romping, roaring, snarling, squeaking, purring, barking, mooing, oinking, neighing, chirping, gibbering, hooting Friends arrive in style. Their voices are accompanied by swirling of waters, rushing of winds, clapping of thunder, crackling of fire. All are driven by desire—by the Lust to Live and Create Here.

Women who choose to participate in this Momentous event of Magnetizing are overcoming fragmentation and dismemberment. In the process of uncovering our Original Integrity, we reactivate this process in others. We evoke the Quintessential Genius that has been stifled in women.

Chapter Seven, "The Final Cause: The Cause of Causes." See also *Wickedary*, p. 76. *Being* is Ultimate/Intimate Reality, the constantly Unfolding Verb of Verbs which is intransitive, having no object that limits its dynamism. See *Beyond God the Father*, esp. pp. 33–34 and *passim*. See *Wickedary*, p. 64.

ELEMENTAL FEMINIST GENIUS
AND EXPANDING HERE

Australian Feminist theorist Dale Spender has written:

> We need to know how patriarchy works. We need to know how women disappear, why we are initiated into a culture where women have no visible past, and what will happen if we make that past visible and real. If the process is not to be repeated again, if we are to transmit to the next generation of women what was denied transmission to us, we need to know how to break the closed circle of male power which permits men to go on producing knowledge about themselves, pretending that we do not exist.[27]

Brazen Women break the closed circle of phallocentric power and pseudoknowledge by daring to Realize our Selves Here. We break the deadly circle of deception by Spiraling Out into The Fifth Spiral Galaxy. But how do we get Here? We begin to arrive Here by Knowing—by Seeing through the stale males' pretense. When Seers do See through the network of lies we find the Searing Truth. On fire with Rage, women begin to Dis-cover our own Genius.

All Biophilic beings possess Sparks of Genius, which are magnetic. As women become more Radical/Elemental we find that we are profoundly connected with other Biophilic creatures. Since Realizing our Genius requires that we overcome the tyranny of the reigning fools of phallocracy, our own participation in Elemental Genius must logically/Crone-logically be Elemental *Feminist* Genius.

Like Mide, the mythic Fifth Province and notional center of Ireland, which is territorially elusive yet present throughout the officially recognized four provinces of that country,[28] Elemental Feminist Genius is spatially as well as temporally expansive. Existing and acting not only in one individual or in one geographical area or in one era, it is potentially in all women. Voyaging in The Fifth Spiral Galaxy requires spreading the Wild Fire of this Genius. The task for those who have found a Spark of such Genius in ourSelves is to go on actualizing it and Naming its presence in other women—igniting more minds/hearts—so that it can blaze forth Here. The Act of Naming any woman's Elemental Feminist Genius functions as Self-fulfilling prophecy. It is Magical, evoking hidden powers.

On the foreground level, self-fulfilling prophecy can work in a positive or a negative manner. It is useful to read the work of Margaret Wheatley, who applies "the new science" to the mundane world of business management. She notes that if a manager is told a new trainee is particularly gifted, he/she will see genius emerging from that person's mouth. If the manager is told that the trainee is a bit slow, he will interpret even a brilliant idea coming from that employee as a sure sign of sloppy thinking. The employee who is seen as "brilliant" will move quickly through the ranks, having been given more resources because it has already been decided that he will succeed. He is "observed" with expectations of success. However:

> Others in organizations go unobserved, irrevocably invisible, bundles of potential that no one bothers to look at. Or they receive summary glances, are observed to be "dead," and are thereafter locked into jobs that provide them with no opportunity to display their many potentials. In the quantum world, what you see is what you get.[29]

Although Wheatley is not concerned in this work with the situation of women *per se*, the text is suggestive. Canny Women know that the Elemental Genius that can be evoked in women is irrevocably invisible in the "organization" which is patriarchy. Our most brilliant ideas are often observed as sure signs of sloppy thinking. The "managers" have already decided that most women will not succeed—not even by the standards of the tokenizers/tamers, but especially not by Feminist standards, which of course are not really observable by the male-functioning managers.

Only in Expanding Here can Elemental Feminist Genius be Observed. Encouraging Crones can and must Observe the Genius of women Out Loud, that is, Name it. This Genius is not expected of women by the patriarchs. Indeed, the managers of maledom have no idea what to expect. But since Genius *is* expected of women by the Hags who Are Here, it can and will leap forth—in Quantum Leaps, thereby Expanding Here. Consistently and everywhere there are signs of Elemental Feminist Genius in women in all walks of life. Seers Observe such signs.

According to *Webster's, observe* means "to take notice of by appropriate conduct." It also means "to inspect or take note of as an augury, omen, or presage." And it means "to celebrate or solemnize (as in a ceremony, rite, or festival)." Clairvoyant Cronies are learning to Observe the signs of Genius in women in all of these ways, conducting ourselves appropriately in the presence of this Genius by honoring it and recognizing that women's words and deeds can presage great transformations and creations. Ignoring male-odorous patriarchal rituals and ceremonies, we celebrate New Sparks of Elemental Feminist Genius with our own festivals.*

Crones who have retained bleak memories of captivity in the patriarchal "organization" understand that we constitute a political threat and therefore are censored, kept in the dark, and forced to reinvent the wheel, re-creating the meaning of our existence. Having experienced the enervating tedium of having to begin again from square one, we long to escape the patriarchally imposed dead circles of repetition. Hence we are more than ready to soar further into The Fifth Spiral Galaxy.

In The Fifth Spiral Galaxy, a woman comes more profoundly into harmony with her instincts, intuitions, passions. She becomes more consciously connected with all of the Elements. Since she has shed much of her artificial, foreground self, she consciously communicates with other Elemental creatures. Such communication is Quintessentially characteristic of our Elemental Feminist Genius as we find our Roots Here.

---

*For example, the Michigan Women's Music Festival.

ROOTS

Elemental Women surviving the apparent isolation inflicted upon us in the state of diaspora commonly find that as we become more in Touch with our roots we are more profoundly Present to each other. Our Be-Witching powers of communication are enhanced by our connectedness with our Roots. Many women express a sense of identity and/or communication with trees.*

The intuition that women are like trees in our Rootedness was inspired by a letter from Io Ax, in which she commented that trees communicate with each other from root to root.[30] They are Radical! So also women radically communicate with each other.

The closeness between women and trees becomes more evident when we consider other aspects of Rootedness. It has commonly been observed that trees are difficult to uproot when their roots are deeply and widely intertwined with those of other trees. That is, the trees, like Radical Women, are most strongly bonded to each other in their roots. They "hold on to each other."[31]

Another important aspect of Radicalness is manifested in certain trees, whose roots — even after the trees have been cut down — continue to grow/travel. From these traveling roots new trees can continue to sprout. Similarly, Feminist Foresisters who have been cut down by the patriarchs continue to be Radically Here with us — in their writings, in

---

*Zora Neale Hurston, for instance, in *Their Eyes Were Watching God* (New York: The Library of America, Literary Classics of the United States, 1995), p. 181, writes:

Janie saw her life like a great tree in leaf with the things suffered, things enjoyed, things done and undone. Dawn and doom was in the branches.

Moreover, in Alice Walker's *The Color Purple* (New York: Harcourt Brace Jovanovich, 1982), pp. 175–76, Celie alludes to communication from trees when she is expressing her Righteous Rage against "Mister _____," just before leaving him:

Until you do right by me, I say, everything you even dream about will fail. I give it to him straight, just like it come to me. And it seem to come to me from the trees.

the recorded examples of their personal and political Feminist Acts, and through the exercise of their Elemental Presentiating Powers.

Yet another key aspect of Rootedness is enhanced ability to overcome obstacles. The roots of trees produce lateral branches on all sides and these in turn branch themselves, so that a considerable area of soil may be penetrated by the root system. If a stone or other obstacle checks the onward growth of a root, the tip of the root grows around it and then resumes its former course.

Likewise, every Wanderlusting Woman Expanding Here produces roots whose complex lateral branches extend through a considerable area of ground. In so doing she overcomes the obstacles placed in her way by the patriarchs, managing not merely to resume her former course, but also to widen and deepen it. Hence our underground networking continues its Canny/Uncanny Course. Since by creative containment and overcoming of obstacles Wild Women continue to expand our territory, we can triumph over the blockers/blockheads. This is the hidden work of Elemental Feminist Genius, unperceived and unacknowledged by men "pretending that we do not exist."

Clearly, the more Radical/Rooted women are, the more adeptly we can stand our ground, expand our ground. It becomes more and more obvious to those who choose to move in this direction that we can never become "too Radical."

In contrast to this Radical Rootedness, the direction of patriarchal politics remains forever unradical: it can never confront the roots of problems. This is exemplified every hour of every day. A specific example was the apparently self-contradictory position of President Clinton on global warming. In his address to the United Nations environmental conference on June 26, 1997, he stated that "we humans" are changing the global climate. He continued:

Concentrations of greenhouse gases in the atmosphere are at their highest levels in more than 200,000 years and climbing sharply. If the trend does not change, scientists expect the seas to rise two feet or more over the next century.[32]

Despite this admission, he stopped short of the commitment to cutting greenhouse gases that allies have been urging. As John H. Cushman Jr., writing in *The New York Times*, described the situation:

> He [Clinton] satisfied the environmentalists in his constituency on the issue of smog and soot, but deeply disappointed many of them today on the question of climate change. It was a striking disparity, given that the two environmental problems have some important common roots. Soot and smog, like greenhouse gases, come mainly from burning fossil fuels.[33]

As Radical Hags know, politicians are unlikely to see "common roots." They are pulled by conflicting deadlines and constituencies. To fight off the mean-spirited greed of industrialists would require transcendent vision and extraordinary Biophilic Will. This implies Radical Rootedness. Wild Women know better than to expect this of patriarchal leaders, but we can and must cultivate it in ourSelves. Our deepest Hope lies in expanding our own Roots.

In the course of Territorial Expansion it is vital to consider other characteristics that Radical Elemental Women share with trees and other plants: Through our roots in our own rich Gynocentric tradition that has been transmitted by our Foresisters we absorb the nutrients that we need to become stronger and more creative. Our roots, like those of trees, are reservoirs storing materials for future use, enabling us again and again to make a fresh start.[34]

It is not possible to speak realistically about communication between women and trees without facing the horror of what is being done to trees in these times. Trees, like women, are being massacred. In 1996 Worldwatch Institute reported that between 1980 and 1990 the world lost an average of 9.95 million hectares* of net forest annually—roughly the size of South Korea.[35] Kenton Miller and Laura Tangley write movingly of the fact that many of the world's remaining forests are virtually under a death sentence:

---

*One hectare equals 10,000 square meters.

One-fifth of the 12.5 billion acres of forest that once blanketed Earth are already gone. Each second, more than one acre of tropical forest disappears. Scientific theory suggests that at this rate of forest loss, one species of plant or animal dies out every 15 minutes. If current deforestation rates continue, most accessible tropical forests and up to one-quarter of the earth's species could vanish within the lifetime of today's children.[36]

During the past decade most of the world's deforestation has been concentrated in tropical forests, including rainforests. Logging has increased in all three tropical regions—Africa, Asia, and Latin America. The Amazon rainforest in Brazil is 18 percent destroyed. The problems suffered by temperate forests are different but can be equally severe. There has been a major degradation in the quality of these forests, which no longer support a high level of biodiversity.[37]

Forests play an essential role in regulating the amount of carbon dioxide in the atmosphere.[38] The forests of the world are our Goddess-sent benefactors because they *absorb* carbon released into the atmosphere by fossil fuel combustion. Therefore, of course, the necrophilic nothing lovers are perversely *killing* the forests. Their cutting of tropical forests has resulted in sending into the atmosphere 1.5 billion tons of carbon each year.[39] Their killing of temperate and boreal forests can cause billions more tons of carbon to be released. This devastating worldwide deforestation adds immeasurably to the lethal process of global warming, also known as "enhanced greenhouse effect," which results from the introduction into the atmosphere of "greenhouse gases," including carbon dioxide.[40]

What men do to trees mirrors what they do to women. Just as male violence stalks women worldwide, so also it stalks trees. Many Wild Women have understood this intuitively for centuries. An inspiring example of such Female Knowing as source of action is the Chipko Movement of women villagers in India, who were fiercely determined to save their forests from loggers. The Chipko movement gained worldwide attention in the 1970s when peasant women lay down in front of bulldozers and hugged trees to prevent them from being destroyed. As Vandana Shiva explains:

> Basically their lives were at stake. . . . Some of the actions were triggered by enormous landslides after logging operations. In other places, the streams were drying up, and the women were walking longer to collect fuel wood and fodder. Some were disaster situations like villages getting wiped out by floods, and some were ecological disasters.[41]

These protests continued from the 1970s until 1981, when logging was banned from the Himalayas. However, environmental action by women in India has been going on for centuries. Shiva writes:

> Women's environmental action in India preceded the UN Women's Decade as well as the 1972 Stockholm Environmental conference. Three hundred years ago more than 300 members of the Bishnoi community in Rajasthan, led by a woman called Amrita Devi, sacrificed their lives to save their sacred *khejri* trees by clinging to them. With that event begins the recorded history of Chipko.[42]

The same author tells us that in 1977 the Chipko movement became explicitly an ecological *and* feminist movement. She explains that it did not matter to the women whether the forest was destroyed by outsiders or their own men:

> The most dramatic turn in this new confrontation took place when Bachni Devi of Adwani led a resistance against her own husband who had obtained a local contract to fell the forest. The forest officials arrived to browbeat and intimidate the women and Chipko activists, but found the women holding up lighted lanterns in broad daylight. Puzzled, a forester asked them their intention. The women replied, "We have come to teach you forestry." He retorted, "You foolish women, how can you who prevent felling know the value of the forest? Do you know what forests bear? They produce profit and resin and timber." And the women immediately sang back in chorus:

What do the forests bear?
Soil, water and pure air.
Soil, water and pure air
Sustain the earth and all she bears.[43]

OVERCOMING THE STATE
OF DIVIDEDNESS/DIASPORA

The dispersion of Dreadful/Dreadless Women in the "millennial time" is a phenomenon experienced by many—to such an extent that some have felt impelled to ask: "How many of us are still here?" The question thus posed is poignant. This is not, however, the most interesting way to pose the Question.

To introduce an Other way of questioning, Bold Bitches can begin by Re-Calling the fact that *We Are Here!* Each would do well to Roar this proclamation at least five times, thereby expanding our Presence/Here. Each of the many Be-Speakers/Be-Shriekers who are able to Shout Out Loud this announcement can sense resonance with each other. Our Sounding raises a Great Raging Wind, within whose Aura the important ideas and questions are Be-Spoken and Heard.

In order to grasp the possibility of overcoming the diaspora of women, especially of Radical Elemental Women, it is helpful to consider more deeply the distinct meanings of the components/synonyms of the word *diaspora: exile, scattering, migration.*

Exile is defined as "forced removal from one's native country: expulsion from home: banishment" (*Webster's*). It has always been the case under patriarchy that Revolting, Wild Women have been driven into isolation and exile. Yet exile need not be passively accepted as our "fate." Forecrone Virginia Woolf Howled:

> . . . as a woman I have no country. As a woman I want no country. As a woman my country is the whole world.[44]

These inspiring words Name the direction of Wild Women's transformative overcoming of imposed diaspora. We are going nowhere *within* patriarchy. Nor do we want to go anywhere—there. Like the mythic Fifth Province of Ireland, we are Here everywhere in Background dimensions. And in those dimensions we Be-Long everywhere, in "the whole world." Our Be-Longing transcends the manmade embedded need to belong to institutions of patriarchy. It is ontological yearning for active participation in Be-ing, the constantly Unfolding Verb of Verbs. We Long/Be-Long to participate in this Spiraling Ecstatic Movement.*

This Movement implies Journeying, which is also Creating/Building. As our Courageous Foresister Nelle Morton writes at the beginning of her spiritual autobiography:

> Ordinarily a journey takes us over roads that have been well laid out and well traveled, moving steadily toward a destination. But somehow involvement in the woman movement [her expression] appears to have reversed that process and road-building becomes inseparable from the journey itself.[45]

When Radical Elemental Feminists say that our country is "the whole world," we know that this should not be passively taken for granted. Our strenuous project of road-building, which is inseparable from our Journey, brings Wild Women to the recognition that our country, our Home, is "the whole world." Our Journey/road-building *is* Expanding Here. Exile from Here is impossible, unless perhaps, out of fear or perversity, we should exile ourselves.

The verb *scatter* means "to cause to separate widely" (*Webster's*). If we understand *scattering* in a strictly physical sense, this accurately describes the condition of many women who have been compelled to move away to different geographical areas in order to find financial

---

Be-Longing means "transcending the patriarchally embedded need to belong; ontological yearning for participation in Metabeing; Realizing one's Lust for the intensely focused ontological activity which is Happiness." See *Pure Lust*, pp. 336–61, and *Wickedary*, p. 64.

means of survival. Others, in still more dire circumstances, have been forced to leave their countries as refugees.[46]

Again Nelle Morton's words issue a warning: People change:

> One may return yearly to one's roots to find at the same time they are the roots of others also. But soon one is forced to recognize that the branches—the trees—may resemble each other but seem no longer to belong together in the same orchard.[47]

This is a somber reality which we are forced to face again and again as we Journey. Yet it does not negate the possibility of Presence to each other psychically. In fact, it can be a challenge to expand Elemental Sensory Powers. Scattering presents opportunities for communication in many dimensions. We can create New orchards.

A devastating form of scattering is suggested by the common expression "scatter-brained." In an earlier section of this chapter I discussed the internalized diaspora/dividedness of women under the state of atrocity. The backlash against Feminism has effected in many women a split between the deep Background Self and myriad foreground selves, or *personae*, which appear to be required for economic and social survival. To overcome such dismemberment, Dragon-identified Women must reclaim our Fierce Focus, our Purpose.

Intricately related to this scatter-brained/splinter-souled state is the disastrous scattering of Feminist books in the closing years of this millennium. One method employed by monster publishers and chain bookstores is reckless "remaindering," i.e., the selling off of all extant copies of books for a fraction of their list price. Another method is driving women's bookstores—as well as other independent bookstores—out of business.[48]

The Positively Revolting dimension of the scattering of books is that they sometimes reach women who otherwise might not find them, or who perhaps could not afford to buy them at "regular prices." Such seemingly lost books often find their way into used book stores and women's private collections, which we share with our friends. Books too are Moving, Expanding Here. There are many Weird ways of getting our Wicked Words Out and about. Yet none of this compensates for the loss of our books, our words, our bookstores that have been spaces for sharing ideas.

The third word suggested as synonymous with *diaspora*, which is *migration*, is also double-edged. Like the terms analyzed above, it suggests painful separation. However, it also has great potential to express the Hope of women who are experiencing the desolate conditions of diaspora. The verb *migrate* means "to move from one country, place, or locality to another" (*Webster's*). Women participating in Expanding Here can *choose* to move around. One who chooses to Stand her Ground need not always be stuck in one place, or "grounded" (in the sense of being prevented from flying). Indeed, Witches Fly.

Wandering Witches have been obliged to acquire and pass on a Heritage of migratory skills in ways comparable to those of birds as well as some land animals and sea creatures. Realizing our connections with our migratory Elemental Sisters, Daring Voyagers who strive to transmute the deadening/deadending foreground aspects of diaspora into advantages often develop a keen Sense of Direction. Moreover, we are increasingly attuned to stimuli, such as Magnetic Currents. This may be the result of the Hidden Heritage bestowed upon us by our Foresisters. It is also a consequence of our individual acuteness/astuteness (sometimes referred to by Crones as Shrewish Shrewdness) and Elemental cooperation (Sisterhood).

During certain eras and in specific areas of this colonized planet the perpetual diaspora of Elemental Women has been experienced with particularly great intensity. The 1990s are such a period. Yet Wise Women can seize this state of dividedness as an Outlandish opportunity. Migrating women can be like stars in an expanding universe. The ever intensifying Magnetism of seemingly "isolated" Voyagers can draw other stars together, forming New Galaxies of Starlusting Cronies. As more and more Galaxies are formed, we communicate Intergalactically.

Wayward Witches proclaim that the diaspora of Elemental Women must be creatively transformed. Righteously Raging Radical Feminists traveling Here in our own Background can expand our Presence. We see that our exile and enforced scattering can be Goddess-sent opportunities for Massive Migrations. We can Realize Sparks of Elemental Feminist Genius in ourSelves. As the Sparks come together we participate in the creation of Be-ing. We Are Fire.

THUNDER AND LIGHTNING IN THE FIFTH SPIRAL GALAXY

It is axiomatic among those who are swirling into The Fifth Spiral Galaxy that Elemental Feminist Genius is quite common among us. This knowledge, of course, is reinforced by the Presence of countless Fantastic Foresisters who have Migrated into our midst. If this assumption of our Genius seems to some to be Self-congratulatory, the more Loudspoken Lusty Leapers among us Proclaim that it is exactly that! Indeed, many of us jump to our feet to give our Selves Standing Ovations. "Congratulations!" we Shout to each Other. Our explosions of Be-Laughing* crack the manmade pseudoreality that would tame us into timidity. Our roaring Touches the Spirits of women, enlivening Auras, awakening Hope.

The explosions of Lusty Laughter Here blow away much of the foreground debris that the fixers/frauds have used to hide Elemental Genius. Muses Migrating into The Fifth Spiral Galaxy are Howling and Yowling up a Storm.

In every dimension Voyagers experience this Great Storm. Dreadful/Dreadless/Desperate Women who are living and moving through the

---

*By *Be-Laughing* I mean "expression of Elemental humor, carrying Lusty Laughers into the Background: ontological Laughing; be-ing Silly together; Laughing that cracks man-made pseudo-reality; Laughing that breaks the Terrible Taboo. . . ." See *Wickedary*, p. 64.

conditions of diaspora cause violent disturbances of the atmosphere that is contaminated by the vile vapors of the vapor state—the manmade ghostly state consisting of phantoms, delusions, specters intended to terrorize Wildly Witchy Women.

Dispelling these vapors, Dragon-identified Women Be-Stir Storms that are electrical. We produce Lightning. Wonderlusting women are like clouds and like Earth. We discharge atmospheric electricity to each other, communicating Magnetic Light/Knowledge. By so doing, we recall that forked lightning appears as a blinding streak of light. It appears as a sinuous line, usually branched, resembling closely the appearance of a map of a large river and its tributaries, or the branches of a tree.[49] Once again we are reminded that, since we are Radical/Elemental, we are like rivers and trees.[50]

As a consequence of our Magnetic Exchange of Light/Knowledge, we make Thunder, which is commonly defined as "the sound that follows a flash of lightning and is caused by sudden expansion of the air in the path of an electrical discharge" (*Webster's*). Our Thunder is our Be-Speaking.* It is Roaring Laughter. It is Enraged Railing and Wailing. It is Elemental Sounding.

Through our exchange of Lightning and Thundering Energies Elemental Women expand our Field of Force which is The Fifth Spiral Galaxy. Forked lightning flashes in the skies re-mind us of our roots in the Earth and Water. Thunder elicits Memories of Elemental Sounds and thus inspires us to seek out the deepest roots of words. Air, Fire, Water, and Earth, as well as Elemental Sounds, are Realized by us as our own atmosphere. We Breathe more deeply.

The Deep Breath of Con-Questing Voyagers becomes the Breath of Creation. Breathing in harmony with the Elements, we become Con-creators of the Expanding Presence of Be-ing. With each expulsion of

---

*By *Be-Speaking* I mean "1: Auguring, foretelling, Speaking of what will be 2: bringing about a psychic and/or material change by means of words; speaking into be-ing." See *Wickedary*, p. 65.

Breath we expel the demonic necrophilic chokers of life. As ever more conscious participators in our own Magnetic Field of Force, we find our True Course, which is our Magnetic Course. We find that Elemental Genius flows through and pervades all the Elements. As we come more into Touch with our native Biophilic intelligence we can Realize such Genius as the deep unifying principle which is accessible to us—which is in us.

Realizing this Genius can transform the negative condition of diaspora that is enforced upon Radical Women by the foreground foolocrats into Positively Focused Movement that expands Here. In fact, at the very core of Elemental Feminist Genius is power to transform the imposed state of isolation and fragmentation into Magnetic Expanding Presence. Each dispersed participator in such Genius can Magnetize Others, who, of course, are Magnetizing her.

This is the Power most feared by phallocrats, whose aim is to destroy Elemental Life. For this reason they perpetually lie. They try to erase, convert, maim, dismember, assimilate all women and especially all who are bearers of Radical Elemental consciousness. When women Realize our own Genius, the necrophiliac sir nothings will shrivel into the nothingness which is their self-made identity.

Cosmic Comments and Conversations
IN 2048 BE CONCERNING
CHAPTER ONE

by Anonyma

S I WROTE *in the Preface to the 2048 BE Edition of* Quintessence, *when Mary first arrived I bombarded her with questions
about the realities and ideas she Names in this book. The "list"
continues to grow and glow, as does the Light of understanding between us,
which expands to the other members of the Anonyma Network. Our poignant
Moments of Transtemporal Bonding elicit high aspirations, or—as Daly
would have it—"Hopping Hope"—Hope that hops, leaps, jumps intuitively
in harmony with the Elemental world. They enliven our desire for transcendent transmission of our own tradition, which connects us across Time with
each other and with animals, trees, seas, stars, angels, and everyone/every-
thing else that is truly Here.*

*The reader will recall that in my Preface to this work I agreed to write
comments after each chapter. Mary and I agreed to meet and continue our
conversations. So whenever I want to speak with the author I simply Invoke
her, and—unless she is very busy at the Moment—she pops up. And she can
Conjure me as well. When she was lecturing back in the twentieth century
she customarily Invoked her Foresisters, "Past, Present, and Future." Expanding Here and Now is most important to both of us.*

*When I invited Mary to discuss this chapter I asked her how women
managed to communicate their experience of diaspora to each other in the
late twentieth century.*

*She replied that she would like to preface her response by describing the
problem of temporal diaspora as she experiences this in our conversations. She
explained: "From your 2048 BE perspective, Annie, the late twentieth century*

was 'back then.' From my point of view, while visiting you in the mid-twenty-first century, I participate Momentarily in your Present as well as your Presence. So I will speak of the 'period' of the Original edition of Quintessence in the past tense in order to accommodate this situation. But please remember that, according to the linear sense of time that constricts grammatical tenses, I was and still am living 'back then.' In fact, I must return to my work there/then when we finish this discussion. So this is an example of my own experience of temporal diaspora inflicted by patriarchal language with its inaccurate/inadequate constructs of time and space."

Impatiently, I conceded her point, complaining that the old "rules" of language still block communication rather than foster it. "They function to impede our Expanding Here and Now," I said.

"But we seem to be doing rather well!" my visitor replied with a wry smile. "Anyway, in answer to your question: One of the most commonly used words to describe the painfulness of the experience of diaspora was isolation. Over and over again women in the 1990s talked about their sense of alienation. They told me that after they had torn off the mindbindings that prevented them from seeing the horror of patriarchal atrocities against women and nature, they felt alone with their knowledge. Some described themselves as feeling spooked. Often we discussed ways to overcome this condition, and I always advocated Spinning threads that would reconnect Untamed Truthsayers. Together we worked to dispel the illusion that there should be a ready-made 'movement' which we could join. We encouraged each other to keep on Spinning. You might say we managed by mutual Communication of Courage."

I said that our Anonyma Network was the result of such efforts of women to overthrow the state of isolation and bond with each other and all Biophilic beings. I explained that this Network is our response across space and time to the diaspora that affected women throughout the patriarchal era. Looking steadily at my guest I said: "The strength we have Now is largely the result of the Heritage passed on by the Bold Women who survived in the time of patriarchy. We got the message from all of you that we must never accept defeat—no matter what! We thank every one of you for that."

....

My visitor gave me a look of understanding. "Thank you for saying that, Annie," she said. "I'll carry your words back with me when I return to 1998." She rose and walked over to the window of my study. When she returned to her seat her face and voice conveyed deep amazement. "I've just been realizing that the reason why I'm with you Momentarily Now is not just to 'fill you in' about how it was back then, but to bring knowledge of your reality back to my contemporaries," she said. "Maybe knowledge of our Foresisters of the Future can pull us out of the mire of the male-constructed 'millennial time' into the Biophilic Era—which you said we have helped to create. And that might help us to keep on creating it! By the way, you have a wonderful view from your window."

Before I could respond to this my guest continued: "Do you know what else I've been thinking during our conversation? Our connection reaches backward across Time, far beyond the twentieth century, joining us with all our Foresisters Transtemporally in our awareness of Surviving the witchcraze and other patriarchal atrocities that were designed to kill women. This awareness of Surviving is Sparked by the bonding between you and me, Annie. And our overcoming of the temporal diaspora Now hurls us back ever deeper into the Archaic Past, when women had an unbroken Heritage. Our Quantum Leap of Connectedness creates a New Presence of the Past."

Exhilarated by my guest's naming of a Vast Presence that I also frequently sense, I exclaimed, "Our Naming of this reality Here and Now confirms the understanding that we both already possess."

"So, we are Re-Calling together . . . Out Loud!" said Mary.

"Loud and clear!" I agreed. "This is Transtemporal camaraderie as well as confirmation. More than that—it is enspiriting Sisterhood!"

I then suggested that we pick up the thread of "Magnetic Magic." Daly had asserted that Expanding Presence is Magnetic Presence. Now, in 2048 BE, our Anonyma Network is living evidence that this is the case. Ever since its inception, Anonyma has been inspired by the definition of magnetize *in the old* Webster's *dictionary that was available in the twentieth century: "to communicate magnetic properties to: convert into a magnet." We have continued to communicate such properties by Acting as catalysts, awakening the inherent capacity in women to Magnetize others.*

....

Mary commented that by continuing in this tradition we women of 2048 BE must surely have strengthened our Magnetic Connections with all Elemental beings including Fore-Familiars.*

I explained that much of our communicating is done by means of our Third Eye, whose powers we have enhanced by continual practice.

"And we all receive messages through Deep Hearing, as Fore-Crone Nelle Morton taught women to Hear," Mary said. "For this we draw upon the powers of our Inner Ear."

I then asked my guest about her experiences of magnetism in the twentieth century.

Mary responded that she had come to understand that the power of Magnetic Magic among women and between women and animals had been of utmost importance throughout the lives of Radical Feminists. "And Here we are, Annie," she said, "Magnetically drawn to each other across Time."

We began to talk about the doomsday prophecies that had been the object of much attention in the 1990s. I said that my mother, Kate, had told me about a few late-twentieth-century books that dealt with Mayan astrological prophecies. They were interpreted as meaning that the world as it had been known for millennia would end in the year 2012.[1]

Turning to Mary I said, "Kate explained that some historians, scientists, and other investigators of the prophecies declared that there would be a reversal in the Earth's magnetic field and that this phenomenon would be accompanied by a cataclysm."

With an air of agitation Mary abruptly rose and again walked over to the window. After gazing out for a long Moment she spoke. "Well, Annie, certainly you must have guessed that I was planning to ask you about that.

---

*A Fore-Familiar, as defined in Wickedary, p. 125, is "a Super Natural Spirited Background Animal who has gone before; a Graceful friend of a Fore-Crone." Mary told me she would include among Fore-Familiars Gertrude Stein's dog, Basket; Virginia Woolf's cocker spaniel, Pinka; the Irish Witch Biddy Early's dogs, Castro and Spot; Andrée Collard's canine companion, Spinner; Nancy Kelly's golden retriever, Doofy; Erika Wisselinck's Wise-Cat, Adele; Emily Culpepper's Crone Kitty, Kali; and Jeanmarie Rindone's Canny cat, Athalia. I said that we should also include her own fabulous feline Familiars, Wild Cat and Áille Óg.

Having read some of the 'doomsday' material in the 1990s, I wondered whether a cataclysm would occur at some point in the course of the next century. Now, since you have Invoked me, it appears that a catastrophe of such great magnitude still has not happened. In fact, I see no signs of environmental damage here. This place into which you invited me is calm and beautiful. The view from your window is peaceful and inspiring. I can see shimmering green grass, glorious trees, a variety of wild flowers, purple sky, and the aqua surf of the ocean in the distance. And in your time it is 2048 BE! So . . . ?"

I couldn't refrain from smiling. "I'll be glad to explain what happened," I answered. "That is, to the best of my ability. But it's a long story. Before I begin, would you mind satisfying *my* curiosity?" I stumbled on: "I just have to know more about twentieth-century speculations concerning cataclysms! What were they saying about 'the end of the world'?"

Somewhat impatiently Mary nodded her agreement. "O.K. Kate is right about the interpretations of the Mayan prophecies that were around," she said. "On the subject of cataclysms, Immanuel Velikovsky's work Earth in Upheaval *comes to mind. He describes the worldwide phenomena that might be expected to happen if the earth tilts on its axis. At that moment an earthquake would make the globe shudder, hurricanes would sweep the earth, the seas would rush over continents. Volcanoes would erupt; lava would flow from fissures in the ruptured ground and cover vast areas. Seas would turn into deserts. The graphic description goes on and on. His work was used by some prophets of doom in the nineties to support their interpretation of the Mayan prophecies concerning the end of the world.*[2] *In addition, Edgar Cayce, one of the most famous clairvoyants of the twentieth century, had also forecasted drastic 'Earth Changes.'"*

At this point, Mary again looked out the window, thoughtfully admiring the view. "O.K., so the 'worst-case scenario' has not occurred. But I'm still waiting to hear what *has* happened, Annie."

I began: "Both you and Kate agree that a number of twentieth-century thinkers believed the cataclysm described by the doomsday prophets was 'destined' to occur in the first half of the twenty-first century. But we have it on record that many Wild Women fought back psychically. You strove to draw attention away from unrealistic fixation on the prophecies—which sometimes served as distractions—to the real ecological disasters that were actually occurring. We know that a significant number of women combined their Gynergy with the energy of all other Elemental beings at the turn of the millennium and for years thereafter. Well, I can tell you that your Company of Caring Cronies and others coming along later did manage to avert the ultimate catastrophe!"

My visitor was visibly moved. She heaved a deep sigh of relief. Slowly her gaze moved to my colorful ceremonial drums which were prominently displayed on the shelves across the room.

I went on: "Wild Women and other Elemental creatures eventually achieved critical mass and acted to overthrow the moribund patriarchal rule. This Fierce Shifting of energy patterns was achieved with the help of our Sister the Earth, who vomited out many of the poisons that had sickened her. As she cleansed herself, there were many geographic and climatic changes. Over time, women who Survived became freer. Minds and emotions have become stronger and clearer. As we approach midcentury we are becoming able to Act with enormous power. And this self-cleansing of the Earth, accompanied by our strengthening and enlightenment, is a process that moves by leaps and bounds. We are no longer debilitated by patriarchy, which is rapidly crumbling away in our time. Of course, there is still much work to be done . . . "

"Come on, Annie!" Mary interrupted. She jumped up, grabbed one of my drums, and began beating Wild rhythms. "I can't just sit quietly after hearing all that," she said. "Let's celebrate the fall of patriarchy!" she roared. Happy to oblige, I leaped up and snatched another drum. We drummed and danced across the room together. Soon we were out the door.

Mary's feline friends, Wild Cat and Áille Óg, scampered along with us. They had surreptitiously accompanied her on this visit and had been quietly waiting just outside the door, expecting something like this to happen. Then my Familiar,* the Wondrous Wolf I call Fenrir, loped over to us.[3]

---

*A Familiar, as defined in the Wickedary, is "a Super Natural Spirited Background Animal, the Graceful Friend of a Witch." See Wickedary, p. 123.

From every direction multitudes of animals came to join us—squirrels, rabbits, kangaroos, goats, horses, wild cows, elephants, bears, snakes, bees, spiders, robins, eagles, hummingbirds, butterflies—to name a few. We could see in the distance dolphins leaping on the surface of the sea. A pod of seals lumbered up from the beach. Flocks of multicolored birds soared and chattered. Exhausted, we collapsed on the ground, rolling in the rich green grass, laughing joyously.

After this raucous celebration, questions and ideas were Spinning around in our heads. We agreed to get back to work. As we entered the house and prepared to launch into the discussion, I began by emphasizing that, of course, the Changes did not happen "all at once." In fact, they are continuing at an escalating pace.

Mary mentioned the twentieth-century plant physiologist Rupert Sheldrake, who demonstrated the reality of "morphogenetic fields."[4] These are built up through the cumulative behaviors of members of various species," she said. "Such accrued behaviors create forms which reside in the morphogenetic fields and combine with individual energies of species members. Because of this combination, skills and habits are acquired without laborious effort." She emphasized the usefulness of applying these insights to our understanding of virtues, such as courage. She continued: "In the western classical philosophical tradition virtues are described as forms existing in powers of the soul, and are known as 'good operative habits.' This means they are acquired and strengthened by repeated acts. So, for example, we become more courageous by performing courageous acts.[5] By combining this classical understanding of virtues with Sheldrake's insight concerning morphogenetic fields, we can construct a springboard for understanding our remarkable inheritance of virtues from our Foresisters."

When I asked if I was correct in my assumption that a significant number of women in the 1980s and 1990s were aware of such fields and consciously applied this knowledge, Mary replied in the affirmative. "When I wrote of the 'Contagious Courage' of women, I was suggesting not merely that we have Courageous role models, but that a morphogenetic field of Courage is created by Cumulative Courageous Acts of Wild Women over the ages. And here is another important point: Every truly Radical Elemental Feminist

Act of Courage, or of any other Volcanic Virtue—no matter how small it may appear to the individual woman who is performing it—is Momentous and contagious. Its effect is enormous. It helps to create the vast morphogenetic field out of which true Metamorphosis can emerge."

"We Wild Women of the twenty-first century must benefit immeasurably from this inherited field," I said. Jumping up, I quickly went over to my bookcase, picked out a well-worn document, and exclaimed, "Just listen to these words written in the nineteenth century by Matilda Joslyn Gage." I read the following passage with all the passion I felt in my heart:

> *The women of today are the thoughts of their mothers and grandmothers, embodied, and made alive. They are active, capable, determined, and bound to win. They have one thousand generations back of them. . . . Millions of women, dead and gone, are speaking through us today.*

I added: "As you well know—since you often cited this passage—Matilda published it in 1880 in National Citizen and Ballot Box, *the newspaper she founded and edited."*

"I'm excited—in fact it gives me chills—to hear you read it!" said Mary. "Just think of the Wild Virtues that can be acquired and transmitted more easily by you Canny Women of the twenty-first century as a result of your inheritance from Fore-Crones such as Matilda! Your Shrewish Shrewdness, for example, probably has evolved to the point of being almost instinctive."

"I think that's correct," I said. "We seem to know how to be at the right place at the right time. We can assess our situation very quickly and keenly because of that heritage and also because the emotional and mental environment of our thinking is no longer totally infested by the prevailing assumptions of patriarchy. So we've been able to avert disaster and take advantage of the Earth Changes—whose effects continue to occur."

"I'm so glad to hear that!" said Mary. "And now, dear Future Foresister," she asked in a playfully pleading tone, "will you please tell how you arrived in this place? I can't wait to hear!"

"Sure, I'll try," I said with a grin. "A few months before my birth in 2018 my mother and grandmother and many of their Cronies (the Anonyma Network) had premonitions that huge Earth Changes were about to happen. For years these women had been profoundly concerned about the effects of global warming. They were aware of extreme weather events such as droughts and floods, which resulted in diminished food supplies, mass migrations of near starving people, and new wars. They had witnessed the fact that politicians continued to focus narrowly on domestic problems and 'business as usual' while failing to acknowledge destruction of the environment as an essential cause of disaster. These clear-sighted women were aware that the sea level was continuing to rise and at the same time deserts were expanding. They had premonitions that even more catastrophic Earth Changes would occur very soon."

Mary nodded. "Many of the symptoms you describe were beginning to become obvious even before 1998, but it appeared that most people chose not to allow themselves to see what was happening. Please go on!"

"The Anonyma Network was made up of women who steadily refused to close their eyes to reality," I commented. "As the years after the turn of the millennium went on, they continued their activism—especially their psychic activism—and kept their Eyes and Ears open. As their Foreknowing of the coming Changes became more and more focused and clear, they prepared to leave their homes. Some had acquired building skills, and others had became excellent gardeners. At exactly the right Moment, about five thousand of these Foresighted women of all ages and ethnic origins from every part of the Earth (all members of the Anonyma Network) began a Journey. Many brought their young Daughters and their Familiars. The women followed their inspired Sense of Direction. They had packed their essential belongings, including their most treasured books, as well as tools and building supplies. Early in 2018, by a series of multiple 'coincidences,' they arrived here on this beautiful small continent. They built simple homes, growing their own food in this lush and verdant place. Soon after their arrival I was born here. So also were a few other girls."

Smiling quizzically, Mary asked, "Could this be Atlantis?"

I responded that I didn't even know. "Perhaps we'll decide on a better name for it," I said. "My mother and grandmother and their friends were aware of the doomsday prophecies. They knew that Edgar Cayce and others had predicted the 'lost continent' (Atlantis) would rise again. The important point is that we have Dis-covered a New and Ancient world. We are at the Beginning. We are on Lost and Found Continent."

My friend seemed extraordinarily pleased by my response. She guffawed and then exclaimed, "That's an amusing name for it, Annie!" I really didn't get the joke and made a mental note to ask Kate what Mary could have found so entertaining. Maybe I had missed some quirky nuance in my elders' Naming of our home continent. Twentieth-century allusions fly right over my head sometimes.

Mary then told me she had some burning questions. "I have the impression," she began, "that all the inhabitants of this continent are women, girls, and animals."

"That's right. There are no men or boys on this continent," I replied.

My visitor was obviously intrigued. "Is this the only continent left after the Earth Changes?" she asked.

"Oh, no!" I replied. "This is the one that had been lost but then was found." Here I paused, because I thought I saw Mary suppressing a laugh. I was going to ask her what was so amusing, but decided to go on instead. "It was found in 2018 by the Anonyma members. The other seven continents are still around, but they have been altered in size, shape, and location as a result of the Changes. Everything was shaken up quite a bit at that time. There also were shifts in population, including animal population. Wild seas and hurricanes carried people and animals great distances with enormous speed."

"I was interested to see the variety of animals at our celebration a little while ago," said Mary. "The kangaroos were especially surprising, since this place does not resemble Australia. But of course everything is astonishing Now." She gazed off into space, apparently lost in her own thoughts. "Are there men and boys on the other continents?" she asked.

"Yes," I said. "But since patriarchy is essentially finished, the implica-

tions of that change are enormous. Female Presence is powerful, and it is expanding everywhere. The world today is Gynocratic and Gynocentric. Many people have Survived the Earth Changes, and the Quintessential requirement for Survival was and continues to be knowing *and profoundly rejecting the evil of patriarchy and acknowledging one's own part in it. Such knowledge is inherently transformative. The Earth's transformation has required that her inhabitants grow through profound psychic changes. Those who were not able to grow could not endure in the purity and strength of the New energy field. They simply withered away. And the challenge continues. The energy becomes more Metamorphic as we all evolve."*

"Are you saying that men who insisted on clinging to patriarchal beliefs and behaviors became obsolete and 'died off'?" asked Mary.

"Yes, they rapidly became extinct," I said.

"And what became of the patriarchally assimilated women who identified with the roles and rules of patriarchy?" asked Mary.

I answered, "Those women who refused to release themselves from the phallocratic dependencies and habits that had been embedded in them under the old system were in effect refusing to evolve. So they also could not survive in the New energy field."

"If I understand correctly, you're telling me that a New Harmony has been Dis-covered. And I infer that since this is a nonhierarchical order, respect for all forms of Elemental be-ing must have absolute priority," said Mary. "Now I understand better the feeling of complete 'rightness' that I felt when we were frolicking with the animals." She paused and then asked, "Are you sure that this balance can be maintained on the other continents?"

"There is always a danger of slippage," I replied. "We have to remind ourselves again and again of the patriarchal takeover of Gynocentric cultures in the ancient past. That is one reason why Lost and Found Continent is so important. Here we are free of unwanted distraction and the possibility of the draining of our energies by men. Those who choose to live on this continent want to live among women. This is our joyous Women's Space, and it is a Power Center where we generate Elemental Energy. Our Sisters in other places on Earth experience morphogenic resonance with our intensified Gyn-

ergy and are strengthened for their own creation, which in turn also empowers us."

Mary looked delighted but slightly puzzled. *"Will you please explain why you speak about 'the possibility of the draining of (y)our energies by men'? Every woman knows what that was like under patriarchy. But didn't you say that kind of society was a thing of the past?"*

"Sure," I replied. *"But the old ingrained habits are still dormant in most men and in some women. As we become stronger this damage diminishes, but we can't afford to forget the lessons of history."*

"Are you in communication with any of the women and men on the other continents?" Mary asked.

"Of course," I said. *"Some Anonyma members have daughters, sons, sisters, brothers, parents, and other kin as well as former partners and other friends who live in distant places. These women make occasional visits to the other continents. They bring back interesting and up-to-date information about the rest of the world. So we manage to keep in touch. As a matter of fact, I have an item here in my desk that I'm sure will be of interest to you. It was brought to Lost and Found Continent by an Anonyma member when she returned from visiting her brother in North America."* I went over to my desk, took out an official-looking paper, and then turned to my guest. *"This is a copy of a well-known document entitled* Statement from the Biophilic Brotherhood. *It is dated January 1, 2019 BE, and is addressed to all women."* *

"I'm all ears!" said Mary.

So I read the following statement:

....

**We now know that this document was based on an Original text—which was written by a woman, of course! This woman—Jeanmarie Rindone—long ago foresaw the necessity for a Biophilic Brotherhood. The Rindone text was recently discovered by an Anonyma member who was visiting her father in a village named "Providence" in North America. This Anonyma member, who happens to be Kate's close friend Hye Sook, also found evidence that the Rindone text, dated January 1, 1999 (AD), had been found by one of the Brothers in 2019 BE and utilized as a draft for their document—which they have officially described as a product of much discussion and debate among the Brothers, with*

We understand deeply that until all women are free no man can be free. Even when we believe that we've taken everything into consideration we acknowledge that we may be behaving as badly and as snoolishly* as our forefathers. We are learning to recognize this as a culturally inherited blind spot that leads inevitably to the destruction of women and all life on Earth, including ourselves. Moreover:

We resolve to accept counsel when criticism is offered regarding our deficiencies and to make every effort to improve.

We resolve not to unduly burden our Sisters by insisting that they teach us, correct us, and explain to us.

We resolve to respect Women's Space.

We resolve to encourage all women to activate the fullness of their potential and never to stand in the way.

We resolve to take responsibility for our share of domestic chores and childcare.

We resolve to meet together regularly as men to learn how to transform our violent tendencies.

We resolve to eradicate all eroticism that depends upon a paradigm of dominance and submission. We resolve to continue diligently the process of forgetting "how to be a man."

When I handed this document to Mary for her inspection she examined it carefully and commented that there had been few males in the late twentieth century who would sincerely subscribe to such a document. She mentioned

....

no mention of Rindone. When Kate heard about her friend's discovery and saw the evidence, she published an editorial in The Anonymous Observer *(our Intercontinental/ Intergalactic news journal) pointing out that the Brotherhood should explain their failure to acknowledge Rindone as their source. Kate's editorial has been an occasion for much soul-searching among members of the Brotherhood, who now recognize that this act of plagiarism reflected an old ingrained habit inherited from their forefathers—the habit of neglecting to give credit to women for their creative work.*

*The word snool *was defined in the* Wickedary, *p. 227. It means "normal inhabitant of sadosociety, characterized by sadism and masochism combined; stereotypic hero and/or saint of the sadostate. Examples:* Adam; saint Paul; the Marquis de Sade." *The authors of the document were obviously familiar with the* Wickedary.

....

as one notable exception the author and activist John Stoltenberg.* Then she asked, "Have these men followed through on their commitment?"

I replied that all the reports we've received from the other continents indicate that there have been very few lapses and that for the most part those occurred in the earliest years of the Biophilic Era. "The men who survived seem to have figured out how desperately they need to purge the patriarchal residues that corrupted them and everyone/everything around them," I said.

Mary looked relieved. "I have another question. I understand that some of you Anonyma members travel to other continents. I'm wondering whether your families and friends come here to visit," she said.

"Very rarely," I responded. "The Anonyma Network decided quite a while ago that we can't afford the inevitable disruption that even such brief visits cause. But there have been some exceptions, for example, when an Anonyma member has been seriously ill and unable to travel."

"While we're on the subject of 'visits,'" said Mary, "I'd like to digress a little to the subject of my visits to your wonderful Lost and Found Continent. Since you choose to invite me, I assume that these times are not considered disruptions. But our conversation has brought back a question that has been on my mind, Annie. Surely I can't be the only Foresister you've Invoked?"

"As a matter of fact, you are the only one whom I personally have Conjured," said Annie. "That's because I am, so to speak, the local expert on your writings and really have wanted to speak with you. But there are many other individuals and groups on our continent who have 'favorite Foresisters' from various places and times whom they have already brought in and/or plan to invite. This is an ongoing Project."

"I'm so relieved and happy to hear that!" said Mary. "It means our Transtemporal Sisterhood is even more multidimensional than I had guessed. The image for this Sisterhood that comes to my mind is a sort of cosmic rainbow."

We moved on to a discussion of Elemental Feminist Genius. Mary was

---

*John Stoltenberg was the author of Refusing to Be a Man *(New York: Meridian Books, 1990) and* The End of Manhood *(1993; New York: Plume Books, 1994). He was a frequent speaker at colleges and conferences and co-founder of Men Against Pornography.*

quick to point out that the Anonyma members' success in averting the cataclysm and Dis-covering this continent was an amazing manifestation of such Genius. She commented: "Those Quantum Leaps of individual Sparks of Genius and Courage must have evoked such a powerful resonance in other Canny Women all over the planet that many more would want to come to live here."

In response I provided information that supported her supposition, explaining that our original tribe of five thousand is not the only company of women who have immigrated to this continent. "Our magnetic field has expanded to attract many others," I said. "At this time we're aware of numerous groups, each consisting of hundreds—even thousands—of Wild Sisters and their Familiars, who have made the Voyage to this place during the past thirty years. They've raced in from all directions. This phenomenon should not be confused with the occasional short-term visits we discussed a few minutes ago. The immigrations involve a permanent commitment on both sides."

"Would you say there has been a population explosion on Lost and Found Continent?" Mary asked.

"Something like that," I said. "Canny Women attract Kindred Spirits. So our population here in 2048 BE numbers close to fifty thousand Outrageous Hags of every ethnic origin. And the waves of immigration appear to be escalating."

"How do you feel about Wild Women who choose to remain scattered around the world?" she inquired.

"We have enormous respect for the Daring Women on the other continents. Their consciousness has expanded very quickly," I said. "They've learned how to Survive and triumph over the remnants of the necrophilic patriarchal rule, and they're thriving in a Metapatriarchal* society of their own creation. It's thrilling to us to think that Lost and Found Continent plays an important role in relation to all these transformations."

"And do you also benefit from these transformations that are taking place elsewhere?" asked Mary.

---

*I am using the word Metapatriarchal in a slightly altered sense from the original Wickedary definition on p. 82. Here it means "beyond patriarchy, transformative of and transcending that obsolete static state."

"*Absolutely!*" *I said.* "*There's a mutual sharing of information, inspiration, and psychic energy among us Uncivilized Sisters everywhere.*"

"*That's awesome!*" *exclaimed Mary.* "*By the way, have you given much thought to the question of procreation on this continent?*"

"*We're not concerned about underpopulation at this time,*" *I replied.* "*Many of those who come to our Newly Found continent continue to bring their daughters and granddaughters—as Kate and Johanna brought me (in my case,* in utero). *Still, although more and more Wild Women are immigrating each year, and despite the fact that we can expect great longevity in this pristine place, we are thinking about future procreation. We probably will decide to achieve this by parthenogenesis.*"

Mary smiled when I introduced this subject. Her smile was not a signal of incredulity but of gleeful agreement. "*That's a great idea, Annie,*" *she said.* "*My Cronies and I were acquainted with some of the evidence of Ancient Gynocentric Society, with its images and stories of Goddesses giving birth parthenogenetically to Divine Daughters. As you know, myths tend to reflect as well as legitimate the society in which they were generated. So it's plausible that since Goddesses were said to conceive daughters in this way, then most probably women were in fact doing it. But after the takeover by patriarchy, its mythmakers and other propagandists had a strong vested interest in making this threatening possibility an unthinkable thought.[6] And, of course, under phallocratic rule scientists had virtually no inclination to investigate the possibility of parthenogenesis, although there were occasional convoluted admissions of its possibility by patriarchal scientists.* The male wannabe mothers preferred instead to spend their time piddling with 'genetic engineering' and inventing the 'new reproductive technologies' which were so physically and psychically harmful to women.*"[†]

**Robert T. Francoeur, for example, a catholic ex-priest and specialist in experimental embryology, was quoted by Daly in her book* Gyn/Ecology, *p. 84.* He suggests that "*if*" *parthenogenesis occurs in other animals,* "*women may occasionally be* victims *of a* virginal conception" *(emphasis hers, to express her appropriate sense of irony).*

†*A number of Radical Feminists, including Gena Corea, Renate Klein, and Janice G. Raymond, wrote extensively and acted vigorously against the* "*new reproductive technologists*" *in the late twentieth century. As Klein wrote:* "*We exposed the technodocs' new/*

"Members of the Anonyma Network have always been interested in parthenogenesis," I said. "Like you, we are convinced that this mode of procreation was widespread in Archaic times. We don't know how often it occurred in the patriarchal era, but we are convinced that it has happened. In fact, Kate explained to me when I was a young girl that she knows of no other conceivable way, so to speak, that I could have been conceived. I was not really surprised. In fact, I had already suspected that this was the case. And it's clear that Here and Now—with our intellects, imaginations, and passions free to grow and expand, we are Conjuring parthenogenesis on many levels. In fact, it's impossible for us not to see its naturalness."

"The naturalness of parthenogenesis was commonly taken for granted by many Eccentric Women in the 1970s and 1980s," Mary interjected. "But such insights became submerged as the century lurched dismally toward its close. The patriarchy was employing its usual devices for preventing the disclosure of information and undermining women's confidence in our natural insight."

"Well, we've regained that confidence!" I responded. "Besides, we're becoming ever more aware that changing magnetic fields alter our endocrine systems and therefore can affect biorhythmic and fertility functioning. The present condition of the Earth's electromagnetic field may be comparable to its state when our Foresisters of Archaic Times—perhaps Survivors of other Earth Changes—created, procreated, and thrived."

"So are you implying that women everywhere now can and will choose to give birth parthenogenetically?" asked Mary.

"Some Elemental Women on other continents of the Earth may choose to continue to procreate in the way that was believed to be the only possible method

----

old claims of selfless service to (infertile) women as dehumanizing medical violence (and Big Business) aimed at reducing women to their body parts. . . . Concurrently FINR-RAGE (The Feminist International Network of Resistance to Reproductive and Genetic Engineering) established itself as an international lobby group." See her article "(Dead) Bodies Floating in Cyberspace: Postmodernism and the Dismemberment of Women," in Radically Speaking: Feminism Reclaimed, ed. by Diane Bell and Renate Klein (North Melbourne, Australia: Spinifex Press, 1996), p. 346.

under patriarchy; that option is open to them," I replied. "But the Spinsters of Lost and Found Continent choose Otherwise. We live our lives with a specific Woman-identified Fierce Focus. We are expanding our Gynergy in ways that will permit us to carry on our Quintessential and Ecstatic work—transmitting Elemental Power around the Earth and Intergalactically."

Having spent some time discussing the situation in 2048 BE, we returned to the subject of the conditions under which Unsubdued Women managed to carry on in the late 1990s. "Sometimes it was rough," my visitor admitted. "Yet I was impressed by the very positive reaction of many women to ideas that the establishment continually tried to suppress. Outrageous Women didn't succumb to a sense of resignation or to invitations to become assimilated into phallocentric 'reality.'" Mary went on to explain that her Cronies were tough and determined not to accept defeat and not to sell their souls. She insisted that it did not require great effort on her part to elicit Dangerous conversations about Radical Freedom. "Lots of Shrewish Women were fed up with the reversals, the taming, and the systematic crushing of Self-esteem that the sadosociety attempted to inflict upon us," she said. "By Realizing our Sparks of Genius we began to unleash the Creative Rage and Power boiling inside us. So . . . more and more Defiant Women refused the patriarchs' invitations to accept their 'reality.' Once again we began to overturn the lies."

I told my friend that the Self-fulfilling prophecy of Female Genius, as this has been repeated and confirmed by women in the twenty-first century, has helped to bring about a reclamation and expansion of our own culture. "Here on this continent our abundance of Self-confidence and joy regenerates our creativity," I said. "And since our Sisters in other parts of the Earth keep on unleashing their Powers, we've managed together to exorcise most of the insidious toxic residues of past indoctrination. And we're still working on it." I continued almost breathlessly: "And we want you to know that even though patriarchy essentially has been defeated, we've decided to retain the expression Elemental Feminist Genius to signify our everlasting commitment to women and all Elemental beings."

"That's wonderful, Annie," said Mary, "I know you're aware that in *the 1990s the deceptive term* postfeminist *was bandied about quite freely. This reinforced the illusion that Feminism had served its purpose and had become unnecessary. The extent of this deception can be grasped only when one looks at the history of atrocities against women that were actually occurring and escalating on every level during that period."*

"We are all horrified to hear about that gross deception," I said. I asked my visitor to describe the context from her experience.

"It was disgusting!" she exclaimed vehemently. "Obfuscating jargon proliferated in the media and especially in the world of universities, perpetuating the condition which Diana Beguine Originally Named academentia.* *But the Rage of Bitchy Women whose Radical Consciousness had been dormant and diffuse flew in the face of such stupidity. We exposed it to the best of our ability. My writing of* Quintessence *was one act of exposing it and proclaiming that Radical Elemental Feminism would reemerge to become the philosophy and politics of the twenty-first century."†*

"And indeed it has!" I exclaimed.

Mary then described to me the transformation that was brought about by Wild Women of her time who experienced and acted upon what she termed the "Intuition of Rootedness." She explained: "As we became ever more rooted, our deep Underground/Background Bonding with each other and with the Elements intensified and expanded, while this reality remained unnoticed by the necrophilic nothing-lovers. So when we began to spring back, this came as a shock to the tomfools and tricksters who believed that they had beaten us."

The word academentia, *as defined in the* Wickedary, *p. 184, means "normal state of persons in academia, marked by varying and progressive degrees; irreversible deterioration of faculties of intellectuals." The word was suggested by Diana Beguine to Daly in a personal communication in June 1984.*

†Radical Feminist poet, theorist, and activist Robin Morgan called feminism "The Politics of the 21st Century." She maintained that the word feminism *is "inherently and potentially so radical in itself as to make the prefix 'radical' almost redundant." She stated this view in her article "Light Bulbs, Radishes, and the Politics of the 21st Century," in* Radically Speaking: Feminism Reclaimed, *ed. by Diane Bell and Renate Klein, p. 8. Daly preferred to use the adjectives* Radical *and* Elemental *in order to make her position clear and explicit.*

I responded thoughtfully: "Women of the mid-twenty-first century are like new trees that have sprouted from these Roots. As a result of our common Rootedness, the imposed state of diaspora has finally been transformed!" I went on to say that I was eager to comment upon the accuracy of the three synonyms for diaspora *which Mary had found in her dictionary—exile, scattering, and* migration. *"The applicability of these terms to our present condition is Uncanny," I remarked.*

"Please do explain!" implored my visitor.

I launched forth into an impassioned discourse. "I'll begin with exile," *I said. "We in the Anonyma Network have in fact achieved the kind of exile that Virginia Woolf Fore-Named. We are women without a country. We are thrilled to be rid of the patriarchal nations and divides, with their inevitable territorial greed, their instilled pseudovirtues such as patriotism and 'unreal loyalties,'[7] and their cruel and endless wars. We are, as Woolf would say, an 'Outsiders' Society,' and we revel in our nonstatus as Outsiders.[8] We participate in the Race of Women,[9] sharing and adding to all that is good in the cultural diversity we have inherited."*

I continued: "Next there is scattering. *Well, we Wild Women of the mid-twenty-first century, together with the animals and other Elemental creatures, are Positively Scattered—over vast geographical areas. And we've chosen this Scattered State. We've cooperated with the Earth's Changes, and we've found ourselves continually moving on many levels, yet always at Home. While some of us are on Lost and Found Continent, others are dispersed throughout the remnants of the seven other continents as well as on the numerous islands that have emerged from the sea as a result of the Changes. In our worldwide Scattered and Scattering State we continually meet New Sisters, including Animal Sisters, Tree Sisters, Rock Sisters, Star Sisters. Our energies shift constantly. We are Shape-Shifters.* Although we have few possessions, our lives are indescribably richer than the lives of women ever were under patriarchy."*

---

*Shape-Shifting is defined in the Wickedary, *p. 96, as "transcendent transformation of symbol-shapes, idea-shapes, relation-shapes, emotion-shapes, word-shapes, action-shapes; Moon-Wise Metamorphosis."*

Rather impressed by my own lecture, I paused for a few sips of water, looking at Mary to see if I still had her rapt attention. I saw that there was no need to be concerned, so I continued. "Finally, there is migration," *I said. "Our Heritage of migratory skills is impressive. Our Foresisters who for millennia had been forced to migrate passed on to us not only their Stamina, but also their skills for adaptation to new and strange environments. For the Original Migration to this continent Wild Women were aided by their keen Sense of Direction and heightened sensitivity to magnetic currents, developed during the time of diaspora and passed on by generations of Fore-Journeyers. Now, three decades later, we continue to make further Quantum Leaps in our acquiring of migratory skills."*

I added: "We've called upon our Powers of Biophilic Communication, and we've participated in Cosmic Conversation, especially with the Earth. We called out to her as she was cleansing herSelf from the poisons that had been embedded into her. Mercifully she listened and spoke back. We began to understand more about her Changes and where they were occurring and then to move in the best directions. Our conversations with her opened our Inner Ears to the messages of other creatures who were also Migrating."

After speaking these words I paused, noticing that my visitor was being very quiet and dreamy-eyed. "This is A-mazing!" she said in a low voice, as if speaking to herSelf. "Not only have you overthrown the state of diaspora; you have transformed it into Positive Diaspora." Then, in a much louder voice she announced: "This is Metamorphosis! This is Witch-Crafty!" Suddenly there was a loud thunderstorm. My Wolf-Friend Fenrir snarled.

"O.K. Let's get on with 'Thunder and Lightning in the Fifth Spiral Galaxy'!" barked Mary, looking intently at her wrist.

"Why do you keep staring at your wrist?" I asked.

"Oh, it's just an old habit," she answered with some embarrassment. "We needed things called 'wristwatches' in the twentieth century, you know, to, uh, measure time."

Taking up my notes on the last section of Chapter One, I commented that I was most interested in her account of Hags "Howling and Yowling up a Storm." I added that I was impressed by the correspondence between Daly's description of *Wild Women's* explosions of *Elemental* energy and the stories my mother and grandmother had told me when I was a child. Both Kate and Johanna had related their adventurous experiences of the transitional times that reached climactic proportions shortly before my birth.

"Well, that's very interesting," said Mary. "I think all *Canny Women* of the early twenty-first century must have been leaping ahead of that time. We would have had to do this in order to free ourselves from the skewed energy that you told me followed shortly after the millennial era. But keep in mind also that the future is implicitly contained in the present. So it's not surprising that we had presentiments of events that were to occur a bit later. Our prescience would have been aroused even earlier by the fact that signs of the Changes had already begun to occur in the late 1990s."

"Sure!" I interjected. "There must have been hints of these coming events by the turn of the millennium and many more after that. And despite the diaspora, *Elemental Women* would have been extremely sensitive to the beginnings of *Earth Changes*, particularly to *Magnetic Changes*."

"But these explosive realizations seemed to happen among a relatively small number and in a subtle manner back then," said Mary. "The workings of *Elemental Feminist Genius* can be almost invisible at first: One woman *Sparks* insight in another, and so on. The process, seemingly slow at first, is contagious. Then, apparently all of a sudden, it takes cumulative *Quantum Leaps* across Time and Space. That's how our Genius works—by *Expanding Here*."

At this point, my impulsive guest glanced at her wrist again and smiled apologetically. "And now I must dash back to my work at the turn of the millennium. See you in another *Moment, Annie!*"

As I stared at the chair where she had been sitting, Fenrir howled. I felt exhilarated at the prospect of our next visit, and set off for a run with this *Wondrous Wolf* before turning to my Comments on *Chapter Two*.

Chapter Two

Nemesis and the
Courage to Create

IN THE LAST DECADE of the twentieth century it has become abundantly clear that religious fundamentalism of all kinds is on the march. Its impact upon the lives of women continues to be devastating. Islamic fundamentalism has manufactured a world in which women who break religious laws, even when this occurs through no fault of their own, are the targets of legally sanctioned violence. A middle-aged woman can be arrested and whipped with eighty lashes if a lock of hair slips out from under her veil. Prospective brides who are nonvirgins can be killed by male relatives. Rape victims, even very young girls, are imprisoned for "fornication." Islamic extremism has spread through many countries, including Pakistan, Afghanistan, Iran, Kuwait, the United Arab Emirates, Saudi Arabia, Iraq, Jordan, and Egypt. Nowhere is it good for women.[1]

Islamic fundamentalists and the state of Egypt have both targeted as an enemy the world-renowned Egyptian Feminist activist, writer, and physician Nawal El Saadawi. The Egyptian government has banned her many books and articles for almost three decades and has shut down her women's organization (which, among other things, fought to put a halt to female genital mutilation) and her Feminist magazine. Islamic fundamentalists put her on their death list in the early 1990s, but the government of Egypt, which apparently merely wants her silenced but not dead, has supplied her with guard service. Saadawi's publications, which include scholarly works as well as fiction, deal with the oppression of women in the Arab world, especially prostitution and other forms of sexual slavery, female genital mutilation, incest, and sexual diseases.

In an interview with Jan Goodwin, Saadawi addressed the deteriorating condition of women in Egypt, stating that when she was in medical school in the 1950s there was not a single veiled woman there but that in the 1990s close to eighty percent of women in universities and schools are veiled. She commented on the oppression of women by fundamentalism:

> Fundamentalism is why women in the Islamic world are now veiled again. It is why I'm censored, still, after all these years. I cannot speak on television, I cannot be published by newspapers or magazines, and my books are banned. The government is against me and is censoring my voice. The fundamentalists want me dead.[2]

Saadawi is outspoken in making the connections between different manifestations of fundamentalism. She stated in the same interview:

> Women are suffering from state-created fundamentalism, both here in Egypt and in the United States. . . . The American government has also encouraged fundamentalists to oppress American women. The Christian fundamentalists want biblical law to rule in the U.S., and your presidents have supported them in this. Similar movements exist in many other countries, and they are responsible for the relapse of women and the global backlash against them.[3]

Nawal El Saadawi's Naming of the connections between the different brands of fundamentalism is important for Wild Women's understanding of what is happening in the United States and around the world. In May 1997 *National NOW Times* featured an important news article concerning the rise of Promise Keepers, which is described as a product of the leadership of well-financed religious conservative organizations designed to promote their ultra-conservative social and political agenda. As the article's authors (guest writers Alfred Ross and Lee Cokorinos) state:

> Topping its list of priorities: women must "submit" to men. . . . While the leadership of other conservative organizations may well share this

agenda, this is the first time an organization of this size has dared to make this one of their declared pre-eminent goals and been accorded such acceptance from the mainstream media.[4]

Promise Keepers, founded in 1990 and led by former Colorado football coach Bill McCartney, is considered the cutting edge of the religious right and the "third wave" of its political development since World War II. (The first was Jerry Falwell's fundamentalist-led Moral Majority, and the second was Pat Robertson's charismatic-led Christian Coalition.) According to Ross and Cokorinos, Promise Keepers is distinguished from prior waves of religious revivals by its organizational prowess, theological extremism, and the extent to which it wants comprehensively to restructure this country's social order. It positions itself to the political right of the Christian Coalition. "Promise Keepers is attempting to re-segregate U.S. politics, this time along gender rather than race lines, calling for active *male* Christian leadership to set things right."[5]

Promise Keepers organized nearly two dozen stadium recruitment rallies in 1996. The size of the rallies allegedly averaged forty to sixty thousand overwhelmingly white christian men. In the spring and summer of 1997 it was said to have packed eighteen football stadiums. "Never before in the United States have so many political mass events been staged on such a scale."[6] At the same time the establishment of thousands of small groups meeting weekly or biweekly around the country in order to inculcate PK values is a major part of the overall strategy. In addition to the enforcement of submission of women, which is called "Reclaiming Your Manhood," the PK agenda includes anti-abortion as well as anti-lesbian and anti-gay activities.

Promise Keepers is supported by virtually all leaders of the religious right and by conservative secular organizations such as the Heritage Foundation.[7] Its ideology and its strategies are military. McCartney told the Atlanta Clergy Conference in 1996—a rally of thirty-nine thousand clergy—"We're in spiritual warfare." Following a military model, it calls itself a "great army." Breaking into small groups is said to be a "military principle." In case anyone still wonders about the identity of the enemy targeted by this "spiritual warfare," the words of PK speaker Tony Evans on Reclaiming Your Manhood can be enlightening:

> ... sit down with your wife and say something like this, "Honey, I've made a terrible mistake. I've given you my role. I gave up leading this family, and I forced you to take my place. Now I must reclaim that role." I'm not suggesting that you *ask* for your role back, I'm urging that you *take* it back. ... There can be no compromise here. If you're going to lead, you must lead. ... Treat the lady gently and lovingly. But *lead*.[8]

Tony Evans has a habit of taking cheap shots at the Women's Movement. His words reveal that the Promise Keepers agenda is serious backlash against Feminism. In 1996 he wrote:

> Over the last thirty years, this role reversal has given rise to a feminist movement specifically designed to assert the role of women. Now a lot of women don't like to hear me say this, but I believe that feminists of the more aggressive persuasion are frustrated women unable to find the proper male leadership. If a woman were receiving the right kind of love and attention and leadership, she would not want to be liberated from that.[9]

This agenda is not generally revealed, but rather is "well covered" by the mainstream media. PK has succeeded in wooing the media with its superficial righteous image. For example, PK founder Bill McCartney was named "Person of the Week" on ABC *World News Tonight with Peter Jennings* on February 16, 1996. Meanwhile the deceptive and oppressive PK machine grinds on.

At the PK rally in the Los Angeles Coliseum on April 19–20, 1996, Wellington Boone—an African American who has been coopted by the fundamentally racist Promise Keepers* and who "boldly" (his word) af-

---

*PK rhetoric is pseudoantiracist. In line with right-wing politics, it avoids words like *equality*, choosing *reconciliation* instead. PK president Randy Phillips was quoted as saying: "The goal is not integration. ... the goal is reconciliation through relationships."

firms "wormism" as an ideal and Uncle Tom as a role model for the
Black community[10] — reiterated the Promise Keepers dogma that wives
should submit to their husbands.[11] Et cetera.

In one of its documents, the Center for Democracy Studies makes
the following point:

> The cult-like nature of such a system of organizational and personal
> relationships is obvious. This pattern includes, for example, main-
> taining or returning women into a state of "submission" in the family,
> and developing structures through which men will in turn submit to
> leadership [from other men] in even the most intimate matters, such
> as discussing and being held accountable for their personal sexual be-
> havior.[12]

This emphasis on relationships may make the "group" appear to
some to be apolitical, and PK has claimed that this is the case. However,
PK is utterly political in an encompassing sense. McCartney has been a
featured speaker at anti-choice events and active in homophobic
groups. Raleigh Washington, leader of PK's October 1997 rally on the
National Mall in Washington, stated:

> There's no way the group can restrict itself when it comes to public
> policy. We are producing leaders in this organization. They will enter
> the political sphere.[13]

As is commonly the case in the rhetoric of politically motivated "leaders," PK propaganda is filled with deception. In fact its reversals are rampant. Since its "apolitical" intent is political, since its "anti-racist"
agenda is disguised racism, since its "love" for women is oppression, it is
reasonable to suspect other manifestations of reversal.

A case in point is the "anti-pornography" stance of the organization.
At the Promise Keepers rally on the National Mall in Washington on

---

See "Ministry for Men Growing Fast," in Colorado Springs *Gazette Telegraph,* June 18,
1996. Appearing to oppose racism, PK diverts attention from the need for economic and
social change. *Reconciliation* in this context is equivalent to resignation.

October 4, 1997, many men confessed and wept over "sexual sin," which is interpreted to refer in large measure to the use of pornography. It is probable that much of this acknowledgment of guilt was sincere and that it was inspired at least in large measure by the urging of their wives. Yet one logical consequence of sincerity would be taking a stand against the pornographers and their $10-billion-a-year industry. The pornography industry generates images that should not be trivialized as merely "obscene" or seen simply as the source of "impure" thoughts.* Pornography exhibits and promotes the power and sadism of men against women in real life. Pornography dehumanizes women, and it provides stimuli and training manuals for the sexual and social *subordination* of women to men.[14]

The penitent christian men fail to acknowledge any contradiction between their contriteness over their pornography addiction and their acceptance of PK leaders' repetitive insistence upon the ideology of the submission of women which is at the core of PK dogma. Moreover, the National Organization for Women, which performs a very important role by warning and protesting against Promise Keepers—especially for its dogmatic insistence upon the submission of women—has not taken the risk of strongly and consistently denouncing pornographers' woman-destroying propaganda for enforced submission/subordination.

This Radical Elemental Feminist Manifesto declares that the Adequate Protest demands far more than protests. It calls for Great and Daring Leaps of Integrity and Courage to See.[15]

Shrewd Shrews note basic similarities between patriarchs of the left and patriarchs of the right. While the sexual liberals (of the ACLU, for

---

*This trivialization of pornography and the failure to make connections with woman-destroying behavior are repeated and perpetuated in mainstream media's representations of Promise Keepers' confessions. *Time* reports: "They admit to having broken promises, they beg forgiveness–for insensitivity, for infidelity, for abandoning their children, for racial hatred, *for sins as petty as reading pornography to transgressions as heinous as abusing their wives* [italics mine]." See Ron Stodghill, "God of Our Fathers," *Time*, October 6, 1997, p. 35.

example) permit pornographic subordination of women *In the Name of Free Speech*, the right-wing christians promote subordination of women *In the Name of the Father*. The former offer the possibility of mild and impotent rebellion. The latter, PK, for example, offer membership in unpromising groups. Under the rubric "Women of the Promise," there are seductive selections, including "Chosen Women," "Promise Reapers," "Heritage Keepers," and so on . . . *ad nauseam* . . . (boring) . . . (snoring) . . .

Having sojourned long enough as observers in the state of boredom/snoredom, Disgusted Women, refusing merely to react, are eager to Spiral on to Other dimensions of discourse and action. "Let's Go!" we say. And we're off and Away. To The Fifth Spiral Galaxy, of course.

MOVING BEYOND RE-ACTING AGAINST INJUSTICE TO CONCREATING NEMESIS

Voyagers in The Fifth Spiral Galaxy Realize our Powers—especially the power to overcome the negative conditions of the state of atrocity that have been inflicted upon us. We expand our Magnetic Presence. Elemental Women survive and thrive as we work to Concreate* New/Archaic reality and consciousness.

Such transformative action is participation in the work of Nemesis, who is commonly known as the Goddess of Retribution. The acts of Nemesis are profound and complex. She is less concerned with "retribution" in the sense of external meting out of rewards and punishments than with an internal judgment that sets in motion a New psychic align-

---

*I use the word *Concreate* rather than *Co-create* because the rather blunt and harsh prefix *co-*, especially in American usage, suggests a kind of equality, as in *co-author*, or *co-editor*. By using the word *Concreation* I am attempting to Name our participation in the work of Nemesis, who is one "face" or aspect of Be-ing, the Verb in which we Live, Love, Create, and Are who we are. We cannot be "equal" to Be-ing. We can only be equal to the work to which we are called.

ment of energy patterns. Nemesis thus understood is hardly irrelevant mysticism. Rather, this name implies active mysticism which responds to the cries of the oppressed, and which is an expression of our Lust for creative be-ing.[16]

Radical Elemental Women participating in Nemesis are fiercely active. Our acts are Metamorphic and therefore cannot be described adequately by such expressions as "fighting for justice." This phrase, which suggests that there is a commodity to be gained by "struggle," does not Name the *process* as *something that women create*. The problem has to do with the word *justice*, which is not sufficiently Sinspiring/Firing. As I wrote in *Pure Lust*:

> It [*justice*] has the flavor, texture, and odor of a hand-out which women deserve, and which presumably could ultimately be bestowed by or wrenched from the prevailing order. But the prevailing order/ordure does not have the capacity to bestow or even to have wrenched away from it the sought-after treasure. . . . The New psychic alignment of Gynergy patterns associated with Nemesis is not merely rectifying of a situation which the term *unjust* could adequately describe.[17]

The radical implications of the Original psychic alignment which is Nemesis are Named in *Pure Lust*:

> Nemesis moves within a different context, and it creates such a context as it moves.[18]

The foregoing analysis of this movement of Nemesis anticipates the Sense of Direction of Wanderlusting women who are Voyaging away from the foreground/flatland context of these times and into Expanding Here. It forecasts our Metamorphosis of the dismembering dis-ease of diaspora into Elemental connecting.

Yet another essential point:

> It [Nemesis] is about flying through the badlands, badtimes. It is about creating new cacophony, new concord, countering destruction with creation. For such symphonic soaring, a woman needs Outrageous Courage.[19]

Ontological, Outrageous Courage propels a woman into Expanding Here. It gives her Wings, enabling her to Fly Here. Moreover, such Courage is contagious. It is magnetic.

MAGNETIC COURAGE

The Ontological Magnetic Courage of Creative Crones calls forth courage in others. As Millicent Garrett Fawcett put it in 1920: "Courage calls to courage everywhere, and its voice cannot be denied."[20]

As the foreground-inflicted diaspora threatens to break down Crone-logical communication with each other, even women who have Seen and Named our Selves and our Deep Memories can be tempted to slide into a state of discouragement. This is precisely the intent of those who inflict diaspora/dismemberment.

The appropriate response to the dismemberers' scheme is Re-membering. The deadly dividers continually strive to contrive means of cutting Radical Elemental Women from our deepest roots. As Muses dare to Re-member through and beyond the conditions of dismemberment and seeming rootlessness, we can use Magnetic Courage as our Labrys to overcome manmade obstacles to the expansion of our roots. Amazons act with double-edged Magnetic Courage, not only repelling those who try to hinder us, but also attracting powerful allies who can assist us.

Realizing Magnetic Courage reveals more and more about the multifarious methods employed by those who block the natural paths of our roots. Thus the practice of this virtue implies acquiring also the Courage to See, that is, to become Dis-illusioned, to see through male mysteries, to become a Seer envisioning an Archaic Future. This is the *real* Future, which transcends the stagnation of archetypal deadtime. It is reality created by successions of Original Acts/Actions.[21]

As Wild Voyagers see more clearly, we find that we are traveling a difficult road. Since all of the apparently comforting and comfortable deceptions doled out to us in the foreground have functioned as blocks to coming in Touch with our roots and extending our roots, these lies must be seen through, broken through. This is to our advantage, since Courage is a virtue, that is, a good operative habit, and as such it is acquired and strengthened by repeated Acts of Courage.[22] Hence we find our Selves becoming stronger.

By these Acts we are creating a New/Archaic Future. For each Act of Magnetic Courage to See moves us further in the direction of becoming Seers. We see further into the past and therefore into the future, which has its roots in the past. Indeed we Magnetize not only the Archaic Past but also the Archaic Future, which becomes Touchable and attainable by those who dare to Dis-cover our Roots.*

Moreover, Seers/Seekers Concreate a Magnetic field in which we are visible and attractive to each other. Since each Seer is a magnet, our combined Magnetic fields magnify our field of force exponentially, enabling us to attract more visionaries, who also learn to unforget the Archaic Future. We become Augurers, Foretellers, Be-Speakers, speaking of what will be—speaking into Be-ing.

Inevitably, as our vision is strengthened we experience escalations of Female Elemental Rage at the perpetrators of atrocities against women and nature. This spurs us onward. Visionary/Volcanic Women are on Fire with Creative Rage. Hence our Magnetic Courage fans the fires of Nemesis. And we are Stormy, brewing Magnetic Storms.

THE COURAGE TO CREATE—CREATIVE COURAGE

Stormy Women find our Selves whirling further along in The Fifth Spiral Galaxy. We experience ever more vividly what it means to *be* Expanding Here, in our own Element, so to speak—participating in the Elegant Wildness of Quintessence.

It has been recounted that in numerology five is the number associ-

---

*The Archaic Future is briefly discussed in the "New Archaic Afterwords" to the 1985 Edition of *The Church and the Second Sex* (Boston: Beacon Press, 1985), pp. xvii–xviii, xxvii, and xxviii. It is defined in the *Wickedary*, p. 62.

ated with "versatility, restlessness, and adventure."[23] This describes the experience of Voyagers in The Fifth Spiral Galaxy. The more we *are* Here, the more versatile, restless, and adventurous we become. Indeed, nothing/nowhere could be less static than Expanding Here.

The following lines are suggestive:

> People whose names "reduce" to five (when mathematical ascriptions are given to each of the letters) are said to love speculation and risks, and a varied environment. They are fond of travel and resist responsibility or any other factors in their lives that would tend to tie them down.[24]

Wild Women are not concerned about whether our names "reduce to five" in a numerological sense. However, we understand our true Names when we Expand to Five in a Crone-logical sense, by moving on in The Fifth Spiral Galaxy. We Lust for speculation (on many levels) as well as risks and a varied environment, which is precisely Here. We are inordinately fond of Travel, which involves resisting the compulsively tidy foreground responsibilities that are designed to tie us down, and assuming the vast Tidal Response-ability of multidimensional Voyaging.

Our modes of Traveling are tantamount to creating more and more Here. Our participation in Be-ing is at its core participation in Ontological Creation. As we Presentiate ourSelves and others we come into our own territory, not simply by finding something that is "already there" (like the explorers who "discovered" the "wild west" in America) but by creating over and beyond the illusory world. That is, we Realize our own potential. As long as we stay on our true course, we come to Know and Name the fact—as did Susan B. Anthony—that "failure is impossible."

This Leaping/Expanding requires Ontological Courage, which manifests itself as the Courage to Create—to summon out of the apparent void New Be-ing. Daring Women push back the foreground, the nonbeing pompously parading as Be-ing. In New ways Hags are overcoming the anxiety of nonbe-ing/noncreating.[25]

Discerning Women distinguish the Courage to Create, which is characteristic of Elemental Feminist Genius, from the reversal-laden notion of "courage to create" which is sometimes blathered about in patriarchal texts. Elemental Courage to Create breaks through paternal patterns of thinking, speaking, acting. It is Metapatterning—breaking through patriarchal patterns and Weaving our way out of male-ordered mazes.[26]

Lusty Leapers joining the Metapatterning dance of Nemesis sometimes can use the works of phallocentric authors as springboards. These are commonly ridden with reversals. In the process of unraveling them we often find clues that are useful for our own movement.

An example of such a reversal-laden work is a little book entitled *The Courage to Create* by psychologist Rollo May.[27] In response to his own question "Why is creativity so difficult?"[28] May cites a number of texts by male authors. Among these is a playful letter written by George Bernard Shaw to the violinist Heifetz after attending a concert given by that musician. In his letter Shaw wrote:

> If you continue to play with such beauty, you will certainly die young. No one can play with such perfection without provoking the jealousy of the gods. I earnestly implore you to play something badly every night before going to bed. . . . [29]

Commenting on this brief comment, May writes:

> Beneath Shaw's humorous words there is, as there often was with him, a profound truth—creativity provokes the jealousy of the gods. This is why authentic creativity takes so much courage: *an active battle with the gods is occurring.*[30]

This is especially amusing to Cackling Crones who understand that men made up "the gods" in the first place, to resemble themselves. So the "jealousy of the gods" must be the jealousy of men. Perhaps another level of explanation lies/lies in the fact that this is all a cover-up for the reality that so many men lack "authentic creativity" and therefore need courage to risk exposure of this deficiency.

At any rate, to Shrewd Women familiar with the terrain of patriarchal discourse this type of thought can hardly be surprising. We could also anticipate the comment that creativity carries "an inexplicable guilt feeling." And predictably May does make this comment.[31] Of course, such guilt feelings are not inexplicable if one thinks for just a minute about classic examples of the behavior of patriarchal gods/men, for instance, the vengeful and nasty antics of Zeus, Yahweh, Newt Gingrich, and their "handlers." They are always angry, always jealous, and their rivals are forever guilt-tripped/tricked, made defensive, et cetera. Such yawn-provoking repetitious scenarios are of little interest to Wicked Women except as providing illustrations of bore-ocratic behavior.

As Shape-Shifting Witches shift focus back/ahead into our own context, however, our interest is reawakened. We are aware that the gods of patriarchy are pale derivatives and reversals of ancient yet always Present Goddess(es). We suspect that phallocentric writers and artists who have even a glimmer of insight are sometimes made uncomfortable by their own state of deception.[32] Those who have any awareness of the heinous crime of reversal which *is* patriarchy must be in a state of deep conflict and fear of . . . Her.*

Such "creators" are phallocracy's legitimators, who feed upon the stolen energy of Musing Women and whose vampiristic "great art" inevitably perpetuates the reversals of the necrophilic sadosociety. For the godmen, then, "the courage to create" is the "courage" (effrontery) to lie. Indeed, mythically speaking, *an active battle against Goddess(es)*[33] *is occurring.* Ontologically speaking, *an active battle against Be-ing is taking place.* If the patriarchs were to win, this would be the triumph of Nothing, which is ontologically impossible.

---

*This is because they have stolen virtually everything from women. For a brilliant review and/or crash course on this subject see the movie *The Associate*, starring Whoopi Goldberg.

ULTIMATE PSEUDOCREATIVITY:
"CREATION" OF MUTANT SPECIES AND CLONES

The Great Lie and Great Reversal which is phallocracy's pseudocoura-
geous battle against Goddess/against Be-ing is also the supreme battle
against women and all of nature that is occurring at the close of the
twentieth century. This is manifested in the atrocities of biotechnology,
which is necrotechnology.

The nectech reversal mentality was exemplified in a 1984 interview
with a physicist from the Lawrence Livermore Laboratory who was
questioned about the morality of working on "weapons of death." The
scientist, Lawrence C. West, replied:

> I don't think I fall into that category, of working on weapons of death.
> . . . We're working on weapons of life, ones that will save people from
> weapons of death.[34]

In the *Wickedary* I cited the expression *weapons of life* as an example of
a specific kind of reversal (*reversals by redundancy and contradiction*). I
explained the ill logic:

> The genus *weapons* has been fallaciously expanded to include two op-
> posing subcategories, one of which (*weapons of death*) is included in
> the very definition of the genus and the other of which (*weapons of
> life*) contradicts the definition of the genus—that is, it is falsely in-
> cluded. Thus the first subdivision is redundant. . . . The second subdi-
> vision is an absurd contradiction.[35]

The Stunning fact is that at the time of writing the above paragraph I
believed that the speaker was talking about nuclear weapons, since he
was a physicist at Lawrence Livermore. Reading the statement now reveals that he anticipated, consciously or unconsciously, the mentality of
the biotechnologists. In fact, he shared the *same* mentality. It might at
first seem implausible to view life as a "weapon." Now, however, it has
become clear that manipulation and pseudocreation of life—turning

life against itself—is a weapon against life. Its result is gross destruction of life. And, significantly, in the 1990s the national weapons laboratories, including Lawrence Livermore, have impressive genome installations.

At laboratories in the "advanced" nations, genetic engineers are busy rearranging the genetic structures of living beings, working to invent ("create") and patent thousands of novel microbes, plants, and animals. For example, pigs are engineered with human growth hormones to increase their size; tomatoes are engineered with flounder genes to resist cold temperatures; laboratory mice are encoded with the AIDS virus as part of their genetic makeup.[36]

Little attention is given to the fact that there is an enormous amount of killing taking place under the aegis of "biotechnology," "the new reproductive technologies," "genetic engineering," and of course "cloning." When Dolly was cloned by Ian Wilmut in Scotland, it was reported that prior to this "success," there had been 277 "failures." The words *deaths* and *deformities* were not used. The author of an article in *New Scientist* cites Roger Gosden, a reproductive biologist at the Leeds General Infirmary, who stated: "There were an alarming number of miscarriages and abnormalities with the technique."[37] The words *pain* and *killing* were avoided. In fact, the "wise" old adage that "animals do not suffer pain" was dragged out from its mothballs and popularized concurrently with the advent of Dolly's cloning. Clearly, the dissociation which the biotechnologists share with the nuclear weapons builders allows them to be indifferent to the suffering of the animals they "create."

Although most scientists involved in cloning announced in Spring 1997 that human cloning could not and would not happen, public opinion shifted with alarming alacrity from "horrified negation" to "let's do it" about nine months later.[38] Professor Lori Andrews, a professor at Chicago-Kent College of Law, stated: "I see a total shift in the burden of proof to saying that unless there is actually going to be harm, then we should allow it."[39]

And an important question remains unaddressed, namely: "Harm to whom?" If human cloning is the subject at issue, we are talking not only about fetuses but about *women — women's bodies are at risk*. Given the enormous number of miscarriages and abnormalities in the case of cloned animals, the threat to women's lives and well-being is alarming. But this is rarely mentioned.

It is important to notice that a large proportion of scientists involved in animal cloning have a vested interest in infertility clinics. Dr. Donald Wolf, for example, a senior scientist at the Oregon Primate Research Center, who is also the director of Oregon's only *in vitro* fertilization center, "has two federal grants to study cloning in rhesus monkeys. One will involve cloning from cells of an adult."[40]

By late 1997 it became alarmingly obvious that enormous numbers of women in the U.S. were succumbing to the massive propaganda campaign to overcome infertility and, in effect, hand themselves over as (unwitting) guinea pigs to be worked on by technodocs (Male Mothers) at infertility clinics. And this has occurred in a time of population explosion on an already overpopulated planet. Women such as Bobbi McCaughey, by having a "successful" fertility drug–induced litter of seven, served the purpose of inspiring a national paroxysm of pride in Male Motherhood. Few mentioned the fact that multiple births often involve the production of damaged fetuses. The "way out" of the dilemma offered by the "creative" fellows of the medical profession is called "selective reduction," the medical term for the *in utero* destruction of "excess" fetuses.

In January 1998, the twenty-fifth anniversary of the *Roe versus Wade* Supreme Court decision that legalized abortion in the U.S., the voices of Pro-Choice women were drowned out by the pious whining that issued from born again christian fundamentalists and other anti-abortion fanatics.

It would appear that the pseudocreative Male Mothers are winning at the end of the twentieth century. By their nefarious actions they are proclaiming the death of Goddess. By their lies/reversals they sneer: "Ding dong, the Wicked Witch is dead." Frightened little fellows like

Rollo May who fear that "creativity" carries "an explicable guilt feeling" are overpowered by botchers/bullies such as physicist and infertility clinic entrepreneur Dr. Richard Seed (Dick Seed?) who announced that he plans to open a human cloning clinic in Chicago. On January 6, 1998 Seed proclaimed to shocked millions on National Public Radio:

> God made man in his own image. God intended for man to become one with God. We are going to become one with God. We are going to have almost as much knowledge and almost as much power as God. Cloning and the reprogramming of DNA is the first serious step in becoming one with God. Very simple philosophy.

No doubt his more sophisticated colleagues see Seed as a buffoon, perhaps as deflecting attention from themselves as they work on in their quiet ways, destroying the lives of plants, animals, women. All the same, Seed gives the show away, speaking for them, displaying the pseudo-courage to negate.

COUNTERING PSEUDOCREATIVITY WITH THE WILDNESS OF CREATIVE COURAGE

Metamorphosing Women recognize our participation in Nemesis as an active war against the gods, i.e., the impostors. This war is a great series of Acts of Exorcism by Wild Women. It requires Creative Courage, not because the gods (patriarchal men and their myths) are spiritually powerful, but because the lies, which function as masks for ontological impotence, constitute a miasma that functions to hide the Background.

Our Acts of Exorcising pseudoreality are at the same time Acts of Creation. We do not have to cope with any "jealousy" on the part of Goddess(es). That idea is too absurd to contemplate. Goddess *urges* Wild Women to create. Indeed *Goddess* is a Metapatriarchal Metaphor* for the Be-ing in which we live, love, create, and are. The impo-

---

*I intend the expression *Metapatriarchal Metaphor* in the deepest sense. As first introduced in *Pure Lust* and later defined in the *Wickedary* (p. 82), it means: "words that

tent jealousy of "the gods" is not able to stop Be-ing. When we truly *know* this, Radical Elemental Feminists are free to Act with Contagious Courage. Our recognition of the fact that this will not be rewarded by patriarchy liberates Lusty Women to Leap on and on.

Patriarchy is still *there*, of course, whining for our attention, begging for our submission to its ludicrous laws, imploring us to play its games, beseeching us to try to overthrow it. But whenever, wherever women are Wild enough, Wise enough simply to shift our context and our perspective, that state shrivels.

There are rumors that some Wild Women have been disturbed and disgusted by the piteous whimpering of the shriveled gods, who are offering rewards and prizes to those who will return. Most of us, however, are too busy Moving Out to notice this nothingness. We simply are not there.

Spinning Spinsters literally fling ourSelves into the Unknown. Yes, we have Concreating Companions, but we cannot always know when and where they will manifest to us. Our Presentiating powers may sometimes feel weak. Yet we are sustained by Fey Faith* that they are Here and participate also in our Quest for Quintessence.

In order to Name more adequately the Fantastic Reality of this process/progress it is important to grasp yet another aspect of the Courage to Create, which is that it eventually evolves into *Creative Courage*. I am suggesting that this Courage itself takes on dimensions of creativity. It is not completely distinct from the creation that it inspires. It throws us into the throes of creation. It pushes us to Touch the as yet unknown which stirs in the Subliminal Realms, to find its forms and Realize these forms as incarnate, palpable, sensible.

Creative Courage goes/grows by leaps and bounds. It cannot stop

---

function to Name Metapatriarchal transformation and therefore to elicit such change; the language/vehicles of transcendent Spiraling. . . ."

*By *Fey Faith* I mean "the Faith of a woman who identifies with the Fates; Faith which implies the natural clairvoyance of those who reject master-minded mediation of sense experience; the source of the Hope that is characteristic of Hags." See *Pure Lust*, pp. 307–11, and *Wickedary*, pp. 75–76.

short. It participates in the Wildness of the Act of Creation. When the Courage to Create metamorphoses into Creative Courage it becomes Quintessential, that is, it is transmuted into active participation in the Quest for Quintessence. This is not to say that it ceases to be the Courage to Create, but that it also becomes something more. It is not simply the courage to *begin* a work, but to continue the process, daring to forge on.

This Metamorphosed/Metamorphosing Virtue causes New forms to burst forth in and from the maker's mind. It permeates her aura. It is contagious, spreading from woman to woman. It expands our Presence throughout the world.

Creative Courage, then, is the Quintessential ingredient in Elemental Feminist Genius. It moves/stirs creating Crones to Realize in the material world the forms/exemplars that are taking shape in our minds. In this way, our creative Realizing Presentiates Nemesis.

Our Radical Elemental Feminist creations are specific to us as individuals. For one at one time it may be a book, for another a piece of music, for yet another a work of sculpture, and for still another organizing a massive protest against violence. All of our acts of developing friendships are manifestations of Creative Courage. As Concreators we work in harmony. At times this harmony/accord is conscious. Sometimes it is subliminally sensed.

What such Crone-logical creations have in common is that they are works of Elemental Feminist Genius. Insofar as they are fired by Creative Courage, they expand Be-Dazzling Presence/Here. They are reckless works. Smashing in the face/faces of patriarchy they reveal its nothingness—that hideous void, that bloat of nonbe-ing which attempts to insert itself into our Presence.

THE "FIFTH CAUSE" AND EXPANDING PRESENCE/HERE

In *Beyond God the Father* I explained the traditional Aristotelian theory of causality in a straightforward way:

When Aristotle wrote of the "final cause," he intended "cause" to mean that which brings about an effect. Scholastic philosophers followed the Aristotelian theory of the "four causes" to explain change. According to this theory the material cause is that out of which something is made (as the wood in a table). The formal cause is that which determines its nature (as the shape of the wood which makes it a table and not a chair or something else). The efficient cause is the agent that produces the effect by her/his/its action (as the carpenter who produces the table). The final cause is the goal which starts the whole process in motion (as the purpose of having an object upon which to place books, papers, and other items). The final cause is therefore the first cause, since it moves the agent to act upon the matter, bringing forth a new form.[41]

For many centuries this theory provided a framework in western patriarchal philosophical thought for understanding problems of transformation and becoming.* I am employing it here as a springboard for understanding the workings of Elemental Feminist Genius in the process of Concreating Nemesis.

In the schema of "the four causes" of any transformation, as described above, the final cause (purpose) is both the first cause and the last result. It is first "in the order of intention," that is, *in the mind* of the agent of change, causing her/him to act upon the matter (material

---

*As I explained in *Beyond God the Father*, this simple example cannot adequately convey the complexity of the theory. The doctrine of the four causes has many levels of interpretation and meaning. One has only to ask about the "four causes" of the wood itself to glimpse the multidimensionality of this theory. It is particularly important to recognize that there are multiple levels to the meaning of "final cause." Thus, in the example given in the text one would have to go on to ask further questions about purpose. For example, what is the agent's purpose in having books on a table? Perhaps she desires to have a place to study or to write. If so, why does she *want* to study? And so on. Ultimately, according to Aristotle and Aquinas, the purpose of human acts is the attainment of happiness. See *Beyond God the Father*, ch. 7. See Aristotle, *Physics* II, 7; *Metaphysics* I. For a medieval commentary on these texts, see Thomas Aquinas, *In Octo Libros Physicorum Aristotelis Expositio* (Rome: Marietti, 1954), and *In Duodecem Libros Metaphysicorum Aristotelis Expositio* (Rome: Marietti, 1950).

cause). Only then is the purpose achieved. And so the final cause is last "in the order of execution." That is, it is not only a purpose in the mind but it is also actualized as a final result of the whole process.*

For Radical Elemental Women Concreating Nemesis Here and Now there is a glaring deficiency in this system. The purpose (final cause) is already known to some extent by the agent before she/he actualizes it. The system allows for and indeed attempts to explain changes, but it does not open the door to great leaps of imagination. It does not allow for hurling oneself into the unknown. It does not undertake the project of creation, of Realizing genuine Metamorphosis. Like patriarchy itself, Aristotelian philosophy is inherently static. It does not open gateways to something radically Other.

The thirteenth-century philosopher Thomas Aquinas did crack open a doorway to a realm beyond the four causes. Because he was also a theologian, he wrote treatises on creation, which made his philosophical vision begin to reach something beyond itself. However, a problem arose precisely from the fact that he was a theologian, for he was compelled to reserve the power of creation solely to "God," declaring that "God Himself is the first exemplar [idea] of all things."[42] But because he did at least discuss the exemplar, even in this limited context, Aquinas unwittingly provided a leaping off point for thinking about our concreation of Nemesis.

In order to begin the project of Realizing Nemesis in the world Elemental Women can break through the tidy limitations of the schema of "four causes" and encounter the Wild Metamystery† which is the "Fifth Cause." This is the rough, rowdy, untamed Exemplar of Expanding

---

*The scholastic philosophers who were disciples of Aristotle and Thomas Aquinas had an axiom which summarized the role of the final cause quite succinctly: "The final cause is the cause of causes because it is the cause of the causality of all the other causes."

†*Metamystery* means "depths/surfaces that are hidden by man's mysteries/misteries; Wonders of Wild Reality that are behind/beyond the fathers' façades; ever Unfolding reality glimpsed by Seers and announced by Be-Speakers; the Radiant Integrity of Be-ing." See *Wickedary*, pp. 81–82.

Here that roves around subliminally in our intelligence(s), struggling to burst the box of four. It is our Wild Card, our clue to the Way Out of the "divine plan" that designing deadfellows have used for many centuries to keep us stuck in stag-nation. It is our key to participation in the process of creation.

Freethinking women examining the fantastic reality of the Exemplar—the idea/form of our creative work as this exists in our minds as creators—can find it useful to ponder the analysis of philosophers in the medieval scholastic tradition, to whom the exemplar was known as the "extrinsic formal cause." This means that it is the form in the maker's mind, which is extrinsic to the material being used. When the maker does elicit from the matter (material cause) a form imitative of this form in the mind, this is called the "intrinsic formal cause" of the work (e.g., the form of a statue).

Using this description as a point of departure, Elemental creators recognize that when we elicit the form of a work from the matter with which we are working—for example, words, or canvas and paint, or clay, or musical sounds, or organizations—the Idea/Exemplar in our minds is being Metamorphosed into the intrinsic form of the work. But because of the *creative tension* between the form in the mind of the maker and the matter with which she is working, the "intrinsic formal cause" is never entirely identical to the "extrinsic formal cause." There is an element of surprise at the outcome of our efforts. This creative process is at times so magical that it could be seen as comparable to alchemy.*

---

*Some months after I wrote this passage I was startled as I read Andrea Dworkin's description of her creative process in her essay "My Life as a Writer." Her analysis is so beautifully exact that I am citing parts of it here in the hope that her clear voice will confirm and help to explain what I am saying in philosophical terms. She writes:

. . . in the aftermath [of writing] one feels that one has chiseled a pre-existing form (which necessarily has substance attached to it) out of a big, shapeless stone: it was there, I found it. This is an affirmation of skill but not of invention.

Writing is alchemy. Dross becomes gold. Experience is transformed. . . . Nor does form necessarily tame or simplify experience. There is always a tension between expe-

It is important to understand the distinction between the Final Cause and the Exemplar. The latter is, like the Final Cause, an idea in the mind which must be actualized in the external world. But whereas the Final Cause is the general motivating purpose of our creative acts, the Exemplar is the specific albeit inchoate idea/form of that which is being produced in the material world.

The word *form* should not be interpreted in a rigid sense. Its transition from mind to matter is a Be-Dazzling Journey from one dimension to another. As long as the idea/form is still primarily in her mind, the creator does not have exact knowledge of how it is going to come out. This is one reason why creation is sometimes a scary experience, like stepping off a cliff into New Space.

In the writing of this book, for example, I have begun with a general form which has expanded and altered as I have worked with words to bring it into material being. As the misty idea in my mind of *Quintessence* began dancing into words, I was sometimes fighting with them and sometimes "making (them) up." The form/idea nudged me into New places. This Exemplar revealed itself to be versatile, restless, and adventurous. Also it demanded of me that I exercise and further develop these qualities in my Self. Indeed the whole project has been a great adventure. It has made my life more speculative and at the same time riskier. It has encouraged me to Travel—in many dimensions—pushing me into varied environments—temporal, spatial, spiritual. In my creative work I have been roaming in the Realm of Five. It seems that the Idea/Exemplar possesses and engenders the qualities that confirm the appropriateness of Naming it the "Fifth Cause."

When the "Fifth Cause" is seen in relation to the Irish mythological

---

rience and the thing that finally carries it forward, bears its weight, holds it in. Without that tension one might as well write a shopping list.

On the purpose of her writing, Dworkin adds:

It would have to stand up for women—stand against the rapist and the pimp—by changing women's silence into speech.

See her book *Life and Death* (New York: The Free Press, 1997), pp. 14–16.

paradigm of the territorially elusive, mystical Fifth Province known as Mide, we begin to see another manifestation of the four-plus-one pattern characteristic of the design of the Expanding Here. The "Fifth Cause" is vital, Quintessential. It gives specificity (a specific form) to the Magnetizing Idea of the Good which is the Final Cause. It thus coordinates and brings into cohesion the whole array of the other four causes. It is in Touch with them, affecting them all, "coloring" them all. It imbues them with meaning—with the Idea which is their coordinating Form.

This does not mean that the Exemplar supersedes the Final Cause, which is "the cause of causes." The Final Cause (purpose) moves/attracts an agent to act because she perceives her purpose as good. The Exemplar has its own specificity. As the inchoate *form* in the agent's mind of that which is being brought forth, it affects all of her choices regarding her creative work. But the Magnetizing Force that impels the creator of any truly Radical Elemental work to actualize/incarnate the Exemplar is the Final Cause, which attracts her to follow her true course. Empowered by Creative Courage, she Realizes her Idea into material existence.

The Idea that Elemental Feminist Genius strives to embody and expand in any and all of Canny Muses' creative works is nothing less than Nemesis. While each of these works has its own unique form, it is cohesive cosmic Metapatterning which Weaves them together. This Quintessential Metapatterning is, of course, the work of Nemesis Herself.

RE-CALLING THE WORDS
OF ELIZABETH OAKES SMITH

The purpose—the Final Cause—of Elemental Feminist Genius is to Presentiate Background reality through and beyond the conditions of the foreground. The primal way of accomplishing this purpose is Concreation of Nemesis. Radical Feminists have always had some intuition of what this entails. Listen to the words of Elizabeth Oakes Smith at the Woman's Rights Convention in 1852:

> My friends, do we realize for what purpose we are convened? Do we fully understand that we aim at nothing less than an entire subversion of the present order of society, a dissolution of the whole existing social compact?[43]

This powerful Act of Be-Speaking demands of us strong creative action. It summons us to Spin off from these words and Spell Out further the meaning of Nemesis in our lives and work.

Nemesis implies even more than "subversion" of the present order and more than "dissolution" of the whole existing social compact. It requires the Courage to participate Positively in bringing forth New Being. To put this in other Words, the Concreation of Nemesis that is needed Now is Meta-dissolution and Meta-subversion of the patriarchal system. The prefix *meta-* means "occurring later . . . after . . . situated behind . . . change in, transformation of . . . beyond, transcending" (*Webster's*). Meta-dissolution and Meta-subversion of the dead and deadly sadosociety involve putting that "order" into the past, getting behind it into the Background, changing and transforming everything—especially our own lives—and, in sum, getting beyond the vile fatherland, transcending it.

The challenging words of our Foresister Elizabeth Oakes Smith can be heard and acted upon Here and Now in a Positively Revolting sense. As Canny Women move beyond merely reacting to Quintessential Acting, Shrewd Shrews can learn to dissolve and subvert "the existing social compact" without allowing it to drain our energy.

This work of Nemesis is vast and complex. As Inspiring Idea it is one: the plan of inventing another context Here and Now. In its Realization it involves concreation of many New Forms (political, social, philosophical, aesthetic) by multitudes of creators who do not necessarily know each other consciously. The bond that unites such Creative Cronies is our Be-Longing—our yearning for Quintessence.

As we smash through and overcome patriarchal patterns we set our-Selves and each Other on Fire with accumulated sparks of creation. Individually and together we are participating in the work of Nemesis. We are recharging ourSelves and expanding the Presence of the X-Factor/ Faculty which is Elemental Genius.

THE X-FACTOR: ELEMENTAL GENIUS

At a seminar organized by Feminists in Bethesda, Maryland in 1969, a "futurist" who presented himself as an affiliate of a "think tank" authorized by President Nixon addressed the group. He announced that, by the most optimistic calculations, the "X-factor" might survive in human society for another twenty years. By "X-factor," he casually commented, he meant something like what is commonly called "soul" and/or "free will" and/or "spirit." His "explanation" was the growing need for government control of "crazies" who might harm millions of people.

The twenty-year "deadline"—1989—came and went, as did the ominously symbolic year 1984. As this book goes to press, nearly thirty years have passed since that sickening seminar took place. Yet this "factor" still seems to be around. Or does it? Looking at the foreground, the answer would seem to be No. But of course it never was in the foreground. Its absence is noticeable only to those who are Moving Out.

The only conceivable and real locus of this "factor" is in Expanding Here. Springing beyond the think-tanker's explanation, I am employing the expression X-*Factor* to suggest the unpredictable unpossessable nature of Wild Elemental Genius. This is not merely a "factor." It is a power/faculty which enables Elemental, Biophilic creatures to Act out of Original Integrity and to Spring more Wildly in Be-ing.*

---

*In the *Wickedary* (p. 182), X-*factor* is defined as "the Spring of be-ing; the unpredictable, unpossessable Nature of the Wild, which forever escapes the technocrats, medical and scientific re-searchers, 'developers,' and other demonic destroyers of living creatures."

All Elemental creatures possess this capacity and Realize it in their own ways. Every drop of water, every blade of grass, every grain of sand, every animal, every tree, every planet, every star in every galaxy possesses and Realizes the X-Factor/Faculty.

The foreground separation of women from Realizing the X-Factor/ Faculty in ourSelves is our worst impoverishment. It is our most extreme experience of exile. It is at the core of our deadly and desolate sense of diaspora, for it divides us from all Elemental Reality.

A Lusty Leaper, Fired by Rage and Courage, Senses this dismemberment. She Names the agents of the unfathomable atrocities against women and nature. She bonds actively with her Sisters—including her Sisters the Earth, Air, Fire, and Water, as well as the animals and all Elemental beings, overthrowing the static state of diaspora, transforming it into the Daring and Magical Movement that is Expanding Here.

For such a woman, X can be a symbol for the Unknown and Variable Qualities required for her Metamorphic Movement—her Macroevolutionary Leaps that expand sensory and psychic powers repressed and erased in the state of patriarchal paralysis. Such movement is *X-ing*, which is the qualitative leaping of Contrary-Wise Crones who experience Syn-Crone-icities and other "inexplicable" phenomena.[44]

To Be-Spell this out, we need only consider the following facts: First, Weird Women/Witches, like all other Elemental creatures, are Contrary-Wise and therefore opposed to foregrounding/fixating rules and roles. Second, our lives consist of acts of Conjuring Real Presence. Whereas nothing-lovers continually attempt to negate us, to replace our reality with robotized imitations, Witchy Women Presentiate ourSelves and Others. Third, we move in the flow of Tidal Time, in harmony with the Fates, Realizing Elemental encounters, experiencing Uncanny coincidences, Re-Calling Happiness.

Cosmic Comments and Conversations
IN 2048 BE CONCERNING
CHAPTER TWO

....

by Anonyma

IWAS DEEP IN THOUGHT *when I Invoked Mary to discuss Chapter Two of* Quintessence. *When she popped in we hugged each other warmly. "You seem to be in a serious mood, Annie!" commented my friend as I offered her a seat facing the window and brought out a celebratory beverage—fruit punch, this time.*

"My friends and I have been having some disconcerting experiences since your last visit," I began. "Even while we've been discussing our Archaic heritage, we've been distracted during our conversations by surges of hostility toward each other. *We seem to be experiencing new and unexpected lapses into mean-spirited behavior. Even those of us who were* born on *Lost and Found Continent appear to have slipped into what you and your contemporaries described as ingrained bad habits. We've all been shocked and stunned by this regression."*

"I'm sorry, Annie," my visitor responded with empathy. "But don't you think it makes sense that you are still suffering from toxic residues of the patriarchal system? Since the Earth is still cleansing herSelf of toxins from that terrible time, I guess you have to keep on doing the same thing—expelling the emotional poisons that are still around."

"But sometimes we're held back by the old habit of distrust that was subliminally transmitted to us, together with all the 'Good Stuff' inherited from our Foresisters," I said. "We've had to face the fact that there have been fleeting episodes of personal distrust arising from individual histories and differences. And we know this habit of suspicion is also related to old patriarchal divisions of race, class, national origin, and so forth. Intellectually we can see that even though hierarchical systems are obsolete, their destructive

effects sometimes still infect our thoughts and behavior even today. But it's so frustrating!"

Mary gave a quick nod of understanding. "I'm convinced that there were hidden connections in the last century between the toxic invasions of the Earth and the poisoning and fragmentation of women's physical, spiritual, emotional lives. So it's easy to guess that these interconnected evils, even though they must be greatly diminished, would most likely still be hanging around in a sort of ghostly way. Maybe it's a kind of transtemporal spooking."

"You'd better believe it!" I said. "Sometimes we feel really spooked, especially by the remnants of body and mind poisons manufactured by the 'Doctor Frankensteins' of the last century. What a horror show they created! And to think that their 'divide and conquer' brainwashing can still affect us! We work to exorcise patriarchal patterns that still haunt us, but sometimes we find ourselves unable to recognize the enormity of our own powers to do this. And we know that this inability itself is part of our inherited affliction."

"I'm sorry this exorcism is still necessary," said my guest, looking distressed. "But don't forget you inhabitants of Lost and Found Continent—and of the entire newly freed planet, for that matter—have heightened sensory and psychic powers. Since patriarchy has shriveled away, I know that eventually you will be able to eliminate the 'leftover' problems without enormous struggle."

"How do you see that happening?" I asked.

"Well," she replied, "I have a hunch that it would be helpful to consider the possible connections between your Elemental Magnetism and the condition of Earth's magnetic field. In the 1990s researchers working with a variety of techniques came to the conclusion that a 'quiet' geomagnetic field enhanced those powers which they inaccurately called 'extrasensory perception'—and which I have called Elemental Sensory Perception—while a disturbed geomagnetic field interferes with such powers.[1] ESP as we experience it is essential to the workings of our Magnetic powers. The Earth's magnetic field was seriously disturbed at that time by the proliferation of man-made electromagnetic fields, especially those generated by the military establishment. I doubt that this disturbance has entirely gone away."

"So you think we should examine the problem of man-made electromag-

netic fields as these changed the environment in the twentieth century and continue—to a lesser degree—to affect us?" I asked.

"Yes, I do," said my guest. "When I was writing Quintessence *I came to suspect that it was impossible to understand the extreme fragmentation and diaspora of women during the millennial time without considering the harmful effects of electropollution."*

I replied that I would be grateful for any information and insights that she could offer.

"O.K.," Mary said. "The fact that over time women were repeatedly obliged to reinvent the wheel of Feminist consciousness was commonly 'explained' in political, social, and economic terms. Well, undeniably there was a 'backlash' from the patriarchy whenever women began to come into our own power—in the late nineteenth century, for example. But some of us sensed that there was something more *going on in the 1980s and 1990s that almost managed to stop us in our tracks and turn us against each other."*

I asked my guest to be more explicit about this "something more."

Mary replied: "There was fragmentation everywhere in society, and it was especially devastating among women, even and perhaps especially among those who had proclaimed ourSelves to be Feminists and Lesbians. The breaking off of friendships, the abandonments and betrayals were so flagrant and common that many were disheartened and simply withdrew their energies from the cause of women. All of us sometimes felt baffled and confused. The comment that I heard most commonly was 'I just don't understand what is happening!' Wild Women were aware of the Magnetic field of force that could still be Conjured among us. But harsh experiences of foreground diaspora and fragmentation seemed to be characterized either by the absence of Magnetic attraction or—worse—by aversion, a kind of negative magnetism. I could not help thinking that this was connected with abnormal electromagnetic fields."

Mary's comments were followed by a rather long and heavy silence. We both knew that we were obliged to face this grim possibility. I finally said that I supposed Mary followed her hunches by tracking down information on electromagnetic radiation.

"Yes," she said. "I read quite a bit about military and commercial assaults on the environment which were absolutely mind-boggling.[2] Reading such materials heightened my understanding of the difference between the situation of women in my time and that of Foresisters in earlier periods. We were confronted with unprecedented atrocities against our Sister the Earth and all Elemental creatures."

"Will you be more specific?" I asked.

"Annie, after seeing the well-worn books in your library, such as Andrée Collard's Rape of the Wild,[3] I'm sure that you know of the many atrocities against nature that marked the second half of the twentieth century. These included the proliferation of nuclear weapons and reactors and the 'peaceful' uses of nuclear energy, such as the irradiation of foods; the torture and destruction of animals in laboratories and in agribusiness; the spread of pesticides (to such an extent that it became difficult to find healthful vegetables and fruits); genetic manipulation of plants, animals, and humans; cloning of animals and humans; medical atrocities of all kinds; the poisoning of the ocean; the destruction of forests and, in general, the pollution of the material world. To which I must add: the contamination and robotization of the human spirit. The exposure of living organisms to abnormal electromagnetic fields is interconnected with all of the rest, and it is, I think, a hidden source of the spooking experience you and the other women are fighting off."

I felt absolutely overwhelmed, but I managed to respond: "That makes sense to me. But I need to understand better the 'nature' of what we are up against so that we can act more effectively."

Mary nodded in agreement. "Our planet is protected from the full force of the sun's energy by its geomagnetic field. Without this field life could not exist. But there have been changes underneath this 'umbrella.' Robert O. Becker wrote in the 1990s that 'since humanity has learned how to generate and manipulate electromagnetic forces, we have created other forces beneath this shield, the likes of which have never before existed.'[4] He pointed out that 'we swim in a sea of energy that is almost totally man-made' and referred to this environment as 'the electromagnetic jungle that now surrounds us.'[5] Among the phenomena in this 'jungle' in the nineties were the military satel-

lites that cruised by every point on Earth once an hour. Becker wrote that 'from their altitude of only 250 miles, they bounce radar beams off its [earth's] surface to produce images for later downloading over their home countries.'[6] *My point in reciting all of this is to reinforce our understanding that a lot of remnants of this 'stuff' must still be hanging around in 2048* BE. *As you and the other members of Anonyma can see, it will take Earth and its inhabitants a while to find and settle into natural patterns."*

"I like the idea of seeing this as a challenge," I said. "It's encouraging to think that our efforts to obliterate this unnatural electromagnetic jungle and exorcise the remaining patriarchal patterns and demons will help us to further develop our habit of Magnetic Courage. And I'm feeling exhilarated at the prospect of living unencumbered by those intrusive obstacles and free to move into further stages of evolution."

"Compared to the generations of women that preceded you, you are already as free as any proverbial or real bird, Annie!" responded Mary. "So tell me more about what's been going on!"

"Let me fill you in on some of our history which is related to the problems we've just been discussing," I said. "My mother and grandmother told me stories about epidemics of computer viruses, multiple Internet crashes, and the global 'gigalapses'[7] *that struck the whole planet a few years before I was born. They said that many women had used the new computer technology and had established important contacts with each other by that means, but that the Internet became almost obsolete after its great multiple collapses. The Wild Women who initially came to Lost and Found Continent were thrown back, or rather ahead, to Realizing and relying more and more upon their own extraordinary ESP. Having benefited from technology, they had already taken on the challenge of leaping beyond that. Our Wild Sisters elsewhere on Earth made their own decisions about computers and that 'net.' Some were ready to forgo the use of that technology. Others decided to employ it—or what was left of it—in ways they believed served Biophilic purposes in a decentralized, postpatriarchal world. The discussion still goes on."*

Mary alluded to the fact that there were cases of computer crashes and viruses in the late twentieth century, but commented that these were like nothing *compared to the international/intercontinental computer epidem-*

ics and "lapses" that were predicted to occur shortly after the turn of the millennium. "We were told that the things would be having their own kinds of 'nervous breakdowns' on a planetary scale," she said with Wicked grin. "Some anticipated a colossal mess," she continued. "The sleazy snookers and snudges who had been spying on Feminists, invading our space, disguising themselves as women, attempting to turn us against each other, filling the net with pornography, and trying to undermine Canny Crones' Networking at every instant, were destined to lose their control . . . Crashes! Collapses!" she hooted.[8]

"My mother, Kate, who was twenty in the year 2000, told me a lot about what happened," I said. "The hucksters and hackers hacked themselves out of the loop. And they accidentally helped to set us all free of their mal(e)-functioning equipment. The antiprocess of electromagnetic pollution was slowed down, while more and more Wild Women Moved Out and around, full Speed in Spirals."

"I'm sure Kate has seen a lot," said Mary. "I can't wait to meet her. I believe she wrote to me about an article I published in The New Yorker when she was in high school. I could see that she was a promising young woman."

"Yes, she told me you answered her letter, and I know that she is looking forward to meeting you too," I said. "She often speaks about how important the works of Radical Feminists have been in moving women from apathy to action. I remember how she always was saying to me when I was a child: 'We go on moving!' Then we would gleefully recite together: 'Nemesis moves within a different context, and it creates such a context as it moves.' And this is exactly what we of Anonyma are experiencing. The New context we are creating by our acts of courage is a magnetic field in which we are truly visible and attractive to each other. Our combined fields of force magnify this field. In this context we are able to be far more Dis-illusioned than women of previous centuries. We have largely dispelled the illusions embedded by the patriarchs. And our courage continues to be fired by Rage at what was done to our Foresisters over the millennia and at the destruction that is still affecting our world today. We are participating in the creative powers of Nemesis to an extent that could not have been Realized in the patriarchal era."

"I am so happy to hear about all this!" Mary exclaimed. "The possibili-

ties of creation, of Metapatterning, that are open to you are almost unimaginably vast. You are at the Beginning. You and your friends have before you an unspeakably open Future. I've had glimpses of this possibility in Deep Background dreams, and—thanks to you—I'm seeing it continue to unfold Here and Now."

For a Moment we were both "carried away" by excitement and ecstasy. Then I announced: "Our discussion has given me a much better understanding of the context from which the residual disturbances have come! So I'm ready to move on to the next subject!"

"That's a relief," said my visitor. "It's always best not to get stuck wallowing in 'dynamics.' I think you're right to take 'the high road,' forging ahead and following your Final Cause," she remarked.

Taking a deep breath I continued: "The next section in Chapter Two— 'The Courage to Create'—is a topic most relevant to our situation." At that Moment we were interrupted by bolts of lightning and crashes of thunder.

"I guess the Universe is Announcing that we are Be-Speaking into the Ether!" she casually remarked.

"Well, the 'interruption' is appropriate," I commented. "If I remember correctly, the section begins with the sentence: 'Stormy Women find our Selves whirling further along in The Fifth Spiral Galaxy.' I found a lot there that applies. We came to our own continent not simply by blundering upon someplace new to us, but by following our Deep intuitions. We are not at all like mere patriarchal 'discoverers' and colonizers. It was what you call our Elemental Sensory Perception and Courage to Create that brought us to this place. And the process continues. So it is actually the case that our way of traveling is Expanding Here—creating more Here." I hesitated, and then added, "Really, there's something mystifying and, well, Spooky, about these Transtemporal synchronicities."

My guest appeared to be amused.

"Is anything wrong?" I asked, rather self-consciously.

"Nothing at all!" she replied. "On the contrary, everything is so right that I become overwhelmed sometimes. Our Time Travel and Expanding Here and Now are so electrifying! But I can assure you that when I wrote the original chapters I did not know exactly what your experiences would be. In

fact, I didn't even know of your existence—at least, not consciously." At this point she grinned, rather enigmatically, I thought.

"Well, O.K.," I said. "It's a little beyond me. . . . But isn't everything?"

"Sure! I have the same problem," said Mary. "So let's get on with it."

"At the risk of seeming to be an overzealous scholar," I said, "I will admit that I was struck by your description of the Courage to Create as the Courage to summon out of the apparent void New Be-ing. You see, this is how we members of Anonyma experience what we are doing. Since we're without patriarchal 'guidelines'—their rules and roles—we are compelled to hurl ourselves into the Unknown. We are calling forth new forms out of our Archaic Memories—which feels like summoning these forms out of the void. Like you and your Cronies, Mary, we know that our Courage to Create is rooted in far-out faith. In a sense, our concreation of Nemesis is easier than it was for you, because we don't have to cope with the insidious patriarchal assaults. And—besides—we have all of you as forerunners. But in another sense it's more difficult, since we are so free and far out—so obliged to tap into our deep memory."

"Oh, poor Annie!" my visitor responded with mock sympathy. "What a tough life you have, be-ing so free!" She nudged me teasingly. "How you must envy me, stuck back in the millennial dummydom, struggling to write and publish Radical Elemental Feminist books in the predatory state of prickery!"

"Touchée!" I admitted. "But you know what I mean, don't you? Or do you?"

"I'm not sure that I do," said Mary. "To me you appear to be in an absolutely enviable situation. You don't have the obvious enemy to confront every day of your life. You don't have the constant reminders . . . "

"That's what I meant to say," I interrupted. "You see, I think we need reminders of the history of women under patriarchy. That's why I Invoked you! It may be too easy for us to forget."

"That's an interesting point," she conceded. "You've just succeeded in reminding me that Foresisters past, present, and future do all need each other. After all, we are all Spiraling Here and Now."

I continued: "Now I want to discuss the passage in which you explain the evolution of *Courage to Create* into *Creative Courage*. I think I understand this intellectually and experientially. The Courage to Create suggests the need for *Daring* to begin *a New creation*—starting with the blank page, for example, if we're writers. And we're always at the beginning, if we are really creating. But I'm especially excited by the idea of *Creative Courage*, which emerges when *Courage* itself becomes something more, taking on dimensions of creativity and participating in the transformative power of *Nemesis*. This is the Quintessential ingredient in Elemental Feminist Genius. We women of Lost and Found Continent know this from our own experience."

"I would really like to know about your experience," my guest prodded.

"You see," I said, "we of the Anonyma Network actually have been living the evolution of our initial *Courage to Create* into *Creative Courage*. As I told you earlier, after fierce and successful efforts to avert the ultimate cataclysm, the women of Anonyma took advantage of the Earth Changes that were occurring and followed an Inspired Sense of Direction, which drew us to this beautiful continent. Then came the challenge of providing food and shelter and, carrying on from there, creating ways of perpetuating and widening the Magnetic Field of our Network. This involved intense intellectual work, in the process of which we have developed the Creative Courage to push ourselves beyond the bounds of previous efforts. And this process led to my decision to Invoke you." I paused, uncertain about how to pose the question that was haunting me.

"So, Here I am!" said Mary. "You look as if you have something else on your mind, Annie."

I blurted out: "Well, I really have a question that has been Nagging me: Why *didn't* more *Wild Women* of the twentieth century—and of preceding centuries, for that matter—exhibit Creative Courage? I know intellectually how you and many other Crones described the conditions of repression and oppression as well as the erasure by patriarchs of works by women of Genius. Still—on a gut level—I don't fully understand why more women didn't just 'go for it.'"

My visitor looked saddened. "This is a painful question, Annie. First of *all, I must explain to you that neither I nor any other Radical Elemental Feminist whom I have known fully understood this apparent failure of nerve, in ourselves at times, as well as in others. Let's begin by acknowledging that it is sickening to try to face all of the evil all of the time. When I was Searching and reading material on the atrocities against women for* Gyn/Ecology, Pure Lust, *and* Quintessence *there were many times when I was almost overcome by my knowledge of the terrible realities that I was finding and Naming. Yet I also experienced ecstasy in the process of writing, so I just kept on writing. Virginia Woolf explained this phenomenon as she experienced it:*

> *It is only by putting it into words that I make it whole; this wholeness means that it has lost its power to hurt me; it gives me, perhaps because by doing so I take away the pain, a great delight to put the severed parts together.*[9]

"Many women took on this challenge . . ."

"That's exactly my point," I interrupted impatiently. "Some did it. Why not more?"

"Well," Mary continued. "Let's review the tragic predicament of women under patriarchy. First, there were more Courageous women of Genius than either of us can imagine, because men erased and reversed our history. In addition, the potential in many women was crushed from early infancy. I know that you understand this, and I won't try avoid your 'gut-level' question: 'Why didn't more fight back?'"

"Please keep going," I said. "I really want to know."

"You have read about Chinese footmaiming, Indian suttee, genital mutilation in African and Arab countries, the European witchcraze, American gynecological atrocities, female sexual slavery around the world, the proliferation of 'new reproductive technologies,' the worldwide rampant rape, murder, and dismemberment of women. The list can go on and on, accompanied by parallel lists of atrocities against animals and all of nature. There are invaluable works recording and analyzing all of this which are still available to you. Your visceral reaction of astonishment and disgust at the refusal by many women to Name the evil of patriarchy and act against it, even when

it was Named for them, is a Natural and 'right on' reaction. In the face of rampant evil wrought against one's sisters, passive nonresponse seems to you to be, well, the horror of horrors."

"Exactly!" I said. "Could it be that many women did not react because they were incredibly numbed out—psychically 'lobotomized'?" I ventured. "I have read about that operation," I said, with an involuntary shudder. "Of course, I don't imagine that most women were surgically lobotomized."

Mary assured me that the majority of women were not surgically mutilated in this way. "But your question is on target," she said. Then she went on. "The 'procedure,' that is, mutilation, which involved severance of the nerve fibers in the frontal lobe of the brain, can be seen as paradigmatic of what patriarchs have done to women. In fact, a remarkably large proportion of the victims of the lobotomists were women. A famous psychosurgeon, Walter Freeman, known as the 'dean of lobotomists' (who is said to have performed five thousand of these operations),[10] actually stated that lobotomized women make good housekeepers. Such surgery, that is, mutilation, destroyed the capacity for creativity, imagination, and rebellion. Creativity was seen by these men as 'an expendable quality in women.'"[11]

I was not able to control my Sense of Outrage. After I had yelled, sobbed, and paced around the room for a few minutes I made myself sit down. I asked her to continue.

Mary also was visibly shaken. In a fierce voice she said: "It was the intent of the psychosurgeons and of those who permitted them to perform this mutilation on their 'loved ones' that made the 'procedure' such an apt illustration of what patriarchy was all about. A significant 'case' was Rosemary Kennedy, the slightly retarded but feisty daughter of the famous patriarch Joseph P. Kennedy. This much admired father ordered that Rosemary be lobotomized when she was in her early twenties. He did not bother to consult with Rose, his wife. After the operation, the destroyed Rosemary was hidden away for the rest of her long life.[12] This is but one illustration. The intent to destroy Female Freedom, Wildness, and Creativity was a pivotal aspect of patriarchy. It had thousands of different manifestations, thousands of tentacles."

We both were silent for a short while, aching for our Sisters' stunted creative and intellectual lives.

"I understand that you're using this atrocity as one more illustration of a theme that is repeated in your work: In patriarchy all women lived in a state of terror," I said quietly.

"And it was well known that fear and anxiety blunt creativity," responded my guest. *"In the state of terror, even—and especially—because this was not acknowledged and Named, Female Courage and Creativity could not flourish. But it did not die. Elemental Feminist Genius lives in our roots, and it flourishes Here."*

"This brings me to the subject of your analysis of the psychologist Rollo May, whose reversal-laden book The Courage to Create *you dissected in this chapter,"* I said. *"It throws light on his odd and revealing question 'Why is creativity so difficult?' and on his response. If he made any point—whether intentionally or not is irrelevant—it was that patriarchy and its gods discouraged creativity—in men. But he erased the fact that the system did its best, or rather, worst, to* kill *the creativity of women!"*[13]

"But the point for us is to go on and Realize *our own Genius/creativity,"* Mary emphasized.

"And that leads us to the subject of the Fifth Cause," I said. *"I've been discussing it with my mother, Kate and with some of my friends. Many of us are writers and artists of various kinds, so the Exemplar is of great importance to us all the time. Of course, we don't have a Women's Movement as you had under patriarchy. Since our world is Gynocentric it is Women's Movement. Although we have residues to clean up, we have no oppressor. Most of us are not interested in the prospect of drawing up "blueprints" for our society. It has no clear and nameable 'form.' But it is shaping up very well. We all do what we are best at doing and play things 'by ear.' This works out fine, so far. We are happy in our Creative Dis-Order."*

"I guess we're kindred spirits, Annie," my visitor remarked. *"As you may have guessed, I am not interested in 'blueprints for society' either. Personally I find that concept static and boring. But the Fifth Cause, the Exemplar, is not about such dull plans. It is infinitely active and interactive. I am intrigued to to know the role of the Fifth Cause in your development of the Anonyma Network itself."*

"So are we!" I responded. *"You see, the Fifth Cause has always been at*

work in our Weaving of the Anonyma Network, even though it didn't occur to us earlier to call it that. The 'inchoate form,' or rather forms, of our Network have existed in the minds of its members ever since its inception. Over time we have Realized the Idea/Ideas of Anonyma ever more vividly. As I said before, we have been calling forth New forms from our deep Archaic Memories."

"I am impressed!" said Mary.

"And this relates to the words of Elizabeth Oakes Smith," I continued. "It especially connects with your call for 'Meta-subversion' and 'Meta-dissolution' of the 'existing social compact,' which was the patriarchal system. Well, with the help of the Earth Changes and our simultaneous and subsequent enlightenment, that farcical 'social compact' has disappeared. We are in the Here and Now of 'Meta'! We are 'occurring later,' as that prefix implies. We are in the Space/Time that follows the transforming and transcending of patriarchy. Of course we don't believe that we are 'all Here,' with no place to go. We are, as you said, 'at the Beginning.' By the way, I was just thinking as I said these things that 'Meta' might be a good name for our Lost and Found Continent. I'll have to bring that up with my friends. What do you think?"

"Sounds good to me!" said my guest. "Your comment about being 'at the Beginning' brings us to the subject of the X-Factor/Faculty. But unfortunately—to use an odd twentieth-century expression—'time is running out.' I have to dash back to 1998. It's just as well, anyway, because that topic can be more thoroughly dealt with in connection with Chapter Three. See you again soon, Annie."

I sighed as I looked at her empty chair. "Must she always leave so abruptly?" I asked Fenrir, who had trotted over to me in anticipation of a good run. "Is that what life was like back in the nineties—always being in a hurry? I hope that habit isn't contagious!" I ran out the door with my Wondrous Wolf-Friend hoping to work off my frustration before preparing for the next session. "I think I'll ask Kate to come to our next meeting," I said to my loping companion. "That should be very interesting!"

Chapter Three

Re-awakening the X-Factor/Faculty
and Creating the Archaic Future

T HE TWO PREVIOUS CHAPTERS of this Manifesto have Announced that the project of Radical Elemental Feminism,
which is Meta-subversion and Meta-dissolution of the patriarchal order, requires overcoming the state of diaspora. Biophilic Bitches
transform that stalemated state into the Leaping Movement which is Positive Diaspora. Eccentric Women learn to actualize our capacities for
Positively Scattering and Migrating, becoming a true "Outsiders' Society"* engaged in the Metamorphic work of Nemesis.

Our participation in this transformative work requires that we break
out of the dreary state of temporal as well as spatial diaspora. Temporal
diaspora is the state of separation from our Real Present and therefore
from our True Past and Future.† The institutions of patriarchy, most notably the media, foster this separation by embedding deadending archetypal images/molds into women, making us prisoners of archetypal deadtime (a.d.). Deviant Women dissolve these molds by performing Original
Creative Acts, thereby participating in Background Time, which is Orig-
inal/Archaic Time, beyond the stagnation/timelessness of patriarche-

---

*I am Spinning off here from Virginia Woolf's idea of an "Outsiders' Society." See
her *Three Guineas* (New York: Harcourt, Brace & World, Inc., 1938; Harbinger Books,
1966), esp. pp. 106–15.

†In George Orwell's *1984* time control is aptly described: "'Who controls the past,'
ran the Party slogan, 'controls the future: who controls the present controls the past.'"
(New York: New American Library, 1949), p. 32.

types.* By our successions of such acts we create a Real Future, which is an Archaic Future.

Since its beginnings, patriarchy has tried to sever women from such dynamic participation in Archaic/Background dimensions. It is imperative that Original Women examine the methods of those who are attempting to negate our Present, Past, and Future.

THE DIS-SPIRITING STATE OF CON-FUSION

One can say that efforts to rob Musing Women of our participation in Background Time are "nothing new." Virginia Woolf, writing in the 1930s, Named the *timeshed, spiritshed* inflicted upon women.[1] In the foreground "here and now" of the late 1990s, however, we have experienced an escalation of the war against ontological Depth/ Presence.

Crucial to the assault on Elemental Reality are the manufacture and marketing of imitations of this reality, which are designed to evoke pseudopassions.[2] These serve as replacements for genuine, profound E-motion† which can move us out of the fixed state. One result is the banalizing and subsequent erasure from consciousness of Elemental/Spiritual Reality.‡

---

*The word *patriarchetype* was invented by Kelly Ali Greer, personal communication, February 2, 1997. The "feminine" archetypal goddess images popular in various versions of New Age "women's spirituality" sometimes manifest this stultifying timelessness that freezes women into the roles of archetypal deadtime.

†By *E-motion* I mean "Elemental Passion which moves women out/away from the fixed/framed state of stagnation; Pyrogenetic Passion that fires deep knowing and willing, stirring Metamemory, propelling Wild Women on the Otherworld Journey." See *Wickedary*, p. 74. The meanings of this word were Originally developed in *Pure Lust*, pp. 116, 214, 225–26, 375.

‡For example, it is significant that angels, particularly in the 1990s, have been popularized/caricatured as sentimental, cutesy creatures by means of images that fill books, calendars, shelves of knickknacks. They appear to be "everywhere." Even the United States postal service collaborated by issuing a stamp in the spring of 1995 depicting an

The victims of this assault, whose minds/souls are stuffed with pseudointellectual/spiritual junk by hucksters and academic hackers, are pseudosatisfied. Dulled out by dummydom, they are often too depleted to recognize and act upon their own deep longing for Be-ing, their Lust for Happiness. Feeling full-fillment,* they are mixed-up/confused.

To provide a context for an adequate analysis, I am Naming the society which produces such confusion *the state of con-fusion. Con-fusion* is characterized by the merging of Background meanings of words with debased meanings that serve to cover up and caricature the Background.

Con-fusion—a constant characteristic of patriarchy—has spread blatantly in the foreground nineties, a period when tricksters/mind-twisters blend words and images which have opposite meanings, destroying meaning, producing mixed-up meaninglessness. The patriarchal device of con-fusion involves endless blurring of soulless images, signifying nothing. In the foreground, barbie dolls and the Great Goddess are the same. "Feminists" are lauded in the media and academented publications for accepting and promoting pornography. "Feminist" books which hollowly proclaim that sexual harassment does not exist and that there are no societal structures which are oppressive to women are zealously promoted by the rich white men who own and control the media. In a world that is spiritually bankrupt, women seeking Nemesis are offered such alternatives as Madonna. A product advertised as "pure garlic" is labeled and marketed as "Quintessence" by "nutraceutical" hucksters in a New Age magazine.

"angel" as an impudent-looking boy sporting wings. These foreground "angels," pathetically intended to fill the spiritual void that prevails in this time, function as hints, but also as blocks to knowledge of the Background, the realm where powerful intellectual beings, the Elemental Spirits known to ancient and medieval theologians and philosophers as *Angels*, can be Seen and Heard.

*By *full-fillment* I mean "the saddest of the plastic passions: therapeutized perversion of the passion of joy." See *Wickedary*, pp. 201–2. For more on *full-fillment* see *Pure Lust*, where it first appeared, esp. pp. 204–6.

Ultimate con-fusion has manifested its hideous head from a contaminated sea of multiple con-fusions in the late 1990s. The biotechnologists are attempting to convert women and everything in nature they can touch into an ever more touchable caste, not "merely" by cloning, but by frenzied splicing and mapping genes, obscenely matching and mixing cells, con-fusing species. With brain transplants they proudly make chickens sing like quails. "We'd like to know how many and what sort of brain changes you need to make something like song," chirps a neurobiologist.*

Feeling trapped in this wasteland/spiritual void, many still long for the Background, which is unnameable in foreground terms. In the pervasive thought-stopping, speech-stopping babblespheres, some experience the soul-suffocating sense of isolation which characterizes diaspora. It is vital to Search for and find Ways Out of this con-fusing, disspiriting state, and transform it by Creating beyond it.

MOMENTS OF UNFORGETTING
BEYOND THE DIS-SPIRITING STATE

In countless conversations Wild Women have expressed desperation over their sense of isolation. Many describe this as marked by an apparent absence of Other women with whom deep communication is possible. At times the absence is attributed to geographical distance from old friends or to the lack of "new" like-minded women available for real conversation.

---

*This is Evan Balaban of the Neurosciences Institute in San Diego, cited by Phillip Cohen in *New Scientist*, March 15, 1997, p. 16. Chickens are destined to be victimized not only by brain transplants but by one of the nastiest projects of genetic engineering. In the nectech future genetically engineered hens will be headless, featherless, without a digestive tract. Karen Davis, citing Robert Burruss, writes: "Since the chickens won't move, cages won't be needed. Nutrients, hormones, and metabolic stimulants will be fed in abundance into mechanically oxygenated blood to crank up egg production to three per day, maybe five or even ten. . . . The naked, headless, gutless chicken will crank out eggs until its ovaries burn out." See *Satya*, March 1997, p. 10.

One hears comments such as "The nineties are like the fifties."*
These comparisons are often made even by women who are not old
enough to remember the fifties, but who can sense a spooky similarity
between the time that preceded the flowering/explosion of Radical
Feminism—that is, "Before Radical Feminism (B.R.F.)"—and the time
. . . "afterward." The essential question is: Is this era really "after" Radical Feminism? The obvious answer is: On the foreground level of appearances, it would seem so. My Quintessential answer, however, is that
in the Background Here and Now, in the deepest sense, Radical Elemental Feminism is alive and strong, moving in the direction of creating the Archaic Future.

The phenomenon of *spooking*, that is, the fabrication of con-fusion,
disorientation, Self-alienation, and psychic numbing in women
through the tactics of sado-sublimation, is woefully widespread.†

---

*Not every woman who was around during the fifties agrees that there is much simi-
larity between the two periods. The German Radical Feminist writer and translator Erika Wisselinck made the following observation: "The difference lies in the values prevailing in society. Whatever they were in the 50s and however philistine they may have
been, they were still intact (for example, think of American films of that period),
whereas now (at least here in Europe) there is nothing you can rely on anymore. Nobody can. Everything goes. Nobody knows where she/he stands any more. The end of
the Cold War, the final breakdown of the last firm issue, namely the east/west
confrontation—symbolized by the Berlin wall—has a lot to do with this. You can't even
rely on your enemies any more. It's what psychologists call 'the padded wall effect.' And
whereas, as a result of the 50s, for those who wanted change and went for it in the 60s
(Kennedy, Martin Luther King, Willy Brandt, etc.), there was ample hope of achieving
something, in the 90s there are only cynics and disillusioned pragmatists. This can be
seen as a quite logical development, given all the things that happened that made those
who had believed in the possibility of change (especially in the ecological field) disheartened. So the difference between the 50s and the 90s is a very profound change of
quality. Maybe only generations after us—if there still are some and if a sense of history
still exists—will realize this fully." Personal communication, August 31, 1997.

†By *sado-sublimination* I mean "mental manipulation characteristic of the sadosociety, involving deliberate perversion of the natural phenomenon of subliminal perception so that it becomes a tool of the sadostate; the embedding of phallocentric messages
into every product of the patriarchal state . . . e.g., the messages in advertising, films, lib-

Women who are thus disoriented fear being cut off from Realization of Elemental connectedness. At times it seems to many that no matter which way a woman turns, she is blocked from attaining that which she desires. The Spring of Be-ing then appears to have dried up.

Yet, paradoxically, the dis-spiriting state can push us beyond despair. As the divided state becomes more blatant some Journeyers experience an unbearable blockage of our Elemental Lust for connectedness. We long to reverse this reversal of our natural condition and once again participate in the Flow of Tidal Time.

This Be-Longing is so intense in some women that it breaks through the walls that have been installed in our minds to cut us off from Deep Memory. In such cases the extremity of diaspora leads to Moments of Unforgetting. The following account, written by Jeanmarie Rindone, who was a student at conservative Andover Newton Theological School in the early nineties, is a Stunning example.

I visited the virtually defunct Women's Resource Center at Andover Newton in the summer of 1993. The door creaked when I walked into the tiny dorm room where all the belongings of the Center had been left. Pale sunlight was shining through the one dingy window, accenting the covering of dust that had settled over everything. There were books carefully placed on shelves according to topic, but most of them were quite dated and looked as if they hadn't been touched in years.

Although I wondered how and why the Center came to be abandoned, I was energized by the fact that it had been created at all. I felt connected with the authors of the books, the women who read them, who collected and arranged them, and those who used the Center to meet, organize, and act. I sensed the women's presence in the room, and I no longer felt isolated. I realized that some of those women, or others like them, had to be out there somewhere. At last I finally knew that I was not alone.[3]

---

eral and secular theologies, and all the other -ologies." See *Wickedary*, p. 95. For a fuller development of this concept see *Pure Lust*, pp. 153–94.

The magical quality of such Moments is in large measure the result of our Heritage of Memories of the Future, that is, actions that affect/ effect our Future.* The women who organized the Women's Resource Center at Andover Newton more than twenty years earlier, as well as those who wrote the books, were performing actions that would influence the Future. That is, they were creating Memories which could be Realized decades later, not only by themselves but also by other generations of women Lucky enough to find the traces of their Foresisters' Original creation.

In this way New/Archaic transmission of our tradition can and does occur. Wild Women constitute a company of Torch-throwers and Torch-catchers, igniting/blazing trails across Time. Unlike mere "foreknowledge," this is Fore-action, inspired by contagious desiring, which hurls us forward to New stages of evolution of our Elemental Feminist Genius.

So it happens that Metamorphosing Women who perform Acts of Creative Courage generate waves of energy and light extending across the barriers of foreground time and space. We create a field of force in which more and more instances of Fore-action will be possible. We Magnetize women of Future generations and diverse locations into Ex-

---

*Emily Culpepper recounted an Other remarkable experience of Memories of the Future (transcontinental telephone conversation, January 8, 1998). She told me that in October 1997 a group of her students at the University of Redlands in California were preparing for the opening of a Women's Center which they had worked long and hard to create. Over the past ten years a succession of Feminist students and faculty had struggled to regain the Women's Center space that had been taken away from them. Now that they had succeeded, the students were unpacking boxes of books and papers which Emily had kept stored in her office from earlier Feminist student groups. As they held in their hands the documents from those earlier Feminist students, the energy, persistence, and courage of their predecessors' efforts became excitingly alive for them. It was empowering for these young women to see the new Women's Center not only as the result of their own efforts but also as the fruition of those past struggles. The dynamic sense of connection between their (recent) "Foresisters" and themselves was a powerful catalyst for realizing that their own efforts would have significance in the future.

panding Here. We call forth our Selves and Other Women from the deadly state of severance into the farthest reaches of Intergalactic Communication in Archaic Time.* Following this Call requires Acts of Desperation.

ACTS OF DESPERATION

When a woman Senses that she is being tricked and ensnared by the deceivers who occupy the state of staledom she longs to share her insight with those whom she believes she can trust. Not uncommonly, her attempts to Name the situation are met with angry rebuffs and ridicule. Her attempts to escape the imposed condition of patriarchal paralysis increase her awareness of her isolation.

In the nineties—as in the fifties—many women learn to remain silent after such crushing experiences. Like animals caged and tortured in the laboratories of patriarchal "science," women in the state of torture which is diaspora become sensitized to subliminal cues as well as overt threats. There is a general understanding that even more serious punishments will follow if one continues to speak out. Thus women become their own censors and censor each other.

Fearing that she will be ostracized, or fired from her job, or beaten, or killed, a woman may shrink into a living death of quiet—or noisy—despair. Since the condition of despair is the norm for women under patriarchy, she may well appear normal. Being "normal," she rarely acknowledges her despair. Having been subdued, she uses more acceptable terms, such as "depression," to describe her condition, which suggests that she can and should be "treated." The word *despair*, after all, comes close to giving the show away. Therefore it is taboo.

When Contrary-Wise Women have the Courage to Name the real

---

*By *Archaic Time* I mean "Original Creative Time, beyond the stifling grasp of archetypal molds and measures; the measure of Original Motion/E-motion/Movement." See *Wickedary*, p. 62.

condition of women under patriarchy as the *state of despair*, the way is open for Seeing and Naming the Way Out. Since opposites imply each other, and since the opposite of despair is hope, the bold expression *state of despair* subliminally suggests the possibility of hope. Women who see the hopelessness of attempts merely to *reform* patriarchy and who therefore are in despair about this are *desperate,* and that *is* the Hope! Under the dire conditions of diaspora all Leaps of Real/Elemental Hope are deeply intuitive Acts of Desperation which move us beyond patriarchal possession into harmony with the rhythms of the Elemental world.

The dictionary offers among its inadequate definitions of the noun *desperation* "loss or abandonment of hope and surrender to misery or dread" (*Webster's*). This definition focuses on the loss of hope. Women who are Spiraling in The Fifth Spiral Galaxy know that the hope that is lost or abandoned when a woman performs Acts of Desperation is foreground hope/false hope. She *needs* to shed this embedded potted hope,[4] for it blocks her from Realizing Elemental Hopping Hope.

A second inadequate definition of *desperation* is "adoption of a last resource: a seizing on any action or means that offer any hope of success regardless of consequences: extreme recklessness"(*Webster's*). Canny Women will note that this also is merely a description of foreground desperation. This definition negates the Deep Background Thoughtfulness that characterizes Wildly Hoping women, whose Acts of Desperation require intense focus on our Final Cause. We are not only getting *out* of something (the stuck/divided state of diaspora), but Leaping *toward* and *into* something—active participation in the Spring of Being.

By Courageous Acts of Focused Desperation Wild Women can dispel the demons who block the Passages of our Otherworld Journeying. Giving voice to Original powers, intuitions, memories, we transmute the diaspora inflicted upon us into the Creative Movement of Diaspora. In Other words, we Spin.

A woman who overcomes the state of severance and blockage which is diaspora Naturally becomes a Spinster, a woman whose occupation is to Spin. She becomes a whirling dervish participating in the Spiraling movement of creation.[5]

Desperate Daring Women who have Survived the diaspora of the 1980s and 1990s are hereby invited to Hear more Deeply than we could ten or twenty years ago the meaning of words which were first Discovered in the late 1970s. For the thread of connectedness has been broken and apparently lost again and again, and yet Clairvoyant Crones have continued to repair the remnants left to us. And we are learning to be more astute and agile, knowing better when and how to Spin quickly on our heels, away from the necrophilic patriarchal processions.

Dreadful, Dreadless Women are the ones who have never stopped trying and who have continued to Hope. Our Hope is vigorous and active, and it is sustained and continually inspired by the Outrageous Courage of our Sisters/Foresisters who are ever more intensely Present to us, beckoning and Daring us to move further into The Fifth Spiral Galaxy. They are Calling us to continue our work of Metapatriarchal Metamorphosis Here and Now. This will require a New/Archaic Awakening.

RE-SURGING OF ELEMENTAL FEMINIST GENIUS

The expression *Elemental Feminist Genius*, as I have shown, Names the ability of Shrewd Women to Be-Speak and Act from a sense of Original Integrity and Leap more Wildly into Be-ing, which is the wellspring of creativity. Further development of this analysis derives in part from focusing attention on two very different books published in the year 1971, which was a time of explosions of psychic/intellectual daring.

One of these books is Colin Wilson's *The Occult: A History*, which continues to survive in libraries and in recorded history. As far as I know, few women have ever read it. The Other* is *The First Sex*, by Elizabeth

---

*By *Other* I mean "outside the parameters of patriarchal predictability; Wicked, Wild, Strange." See *Wickedary*, p. 87.

Gould Davis, which was received, or rather neglected and rejected, by the heterosexist literary world with contempt and ridicule. It went out of print after a short time and is difficult to find. Many Radical Feminists, however, have been electrified and lastingly inspired by this work. A comparison of these books, both of which are concerned with the past and future of human evolution, is enlightening.

The central thesis of Wilson's *The Occult* appears to be that there exists in "man" a "paranormal" potential that he calls "Faculty X." The meaning of this potential is described in various fragmented ways. He explains it in his Preface as follows:

> One day man will have a sixth sense—a sense of the purpose of life, quite direct and uninferred. . . . We need to develop another kind of consciousness that is the equivalent of the telescope. This is Faculty X. And the paradox is we *already possess it to a large degree* [italics his], but are unconscious of possessing it. It lies at the heart of all occult experience.[6]

He elaborates further:

> Faculty X is simply that latent power that human beings possess *to reach beyond the present* [italics his]. After all, we know perfectly well that the past is as real as the present. . . . *Yet my senses do not agree* [italics his]. They assure me that this place, here and now, is far more real than any other place or any other time. Only in certain moments of great inner intensity do I know this to be a lie. Faculty X is a sense of reality, the reality of other places and other times, and it is the possession of it—fragmentary and uncertain though it is—that distinguishes man from all other animals.[7]

Wilson's bland assumption of "man's" vast superiority over animals is revealed in other passages. For example:

> It is man's biological destiny to evolve Faculty X. All living creatures on the surface of this planet have been trying to do this throughout their history. Man is more than halfway there.[8]

The book concludes with a chapter entitled "Glimpses," in which the author asserts that "man's future lies in the cultivation of Faculty X."[9]

Wilson's own glimpses of "Faculty X" were fuzzy and blighted by his foreground assumptions of the inferiority of women and nature. His exclusive use of the pseudogeneric *man, human beings,* and so on might be overlooked by overgenerous Crones. After all, one could say, it was "only" 1971, and consciousness about "false inclusion" of women in such generics was just getting out and around. But his androcentric bias is on display throughout the work.

Wilson was a patriarchal scholar, unaware of his own blinders, attempting to write about the hope for future evolution of life on this planet, while barely noticing the existence of women. While apparently trying to move consciousness ahead, he did not manage to glimpse the crucial role (or for that matter, even the existence) of Female Creativity. He was unable to recognize even the possibility that it is women who are the Memory-bearing group capable of Realizing an X-Factor/Faculty and of Leaping into an Archaic Future.

For an enormous blast of fresh air, or, more accurately, a strong wind that can clean and clear the air, after reading Wilson's limp discussion of "Faculty X" I turn to Elizabeth Gould Davis, who, over a quarter of a century ago, made her case for the Past (and therefore Future) primacy of women.*

---

*I have chosen to cite Elizabeth Gould Davis, not because she was always the most accurate or most circumspect of scholars, but because of her timing, her influence, her visionary daring, her bold Naming. Davis was like a comet. She was the first to bring to the attention of women of the Feminist movement's "second wave" the good news that we were and therefore are The First Sex. She deserves to be honored and remembered for her work, which sounded the clarion call that awakened a generation of women to a vision of our history. Other scholars who later wrote of the origins of patriarchy and the beginnings of Feminist consciousness include Gerda Lerner, whom we can thank for her scholarship and brilliant insights and analyses, especially in *The Creation of Patriarchy* (New York: Oxford University Press, 1986) and *The Creation of Feminist Conscious-*

Whereas Wilson merely surmised and rambled on *about* a time-transcending "sixth sense" that "man will one day have," Davis broke through to *Realizing* an Extraordinary Transtemporal Sensory Power and communicating this to her readers. She made something happen. She brought her readers face to face with the X-Factor/Faculty, displaying it through her Act of Courage to Write of things that have been hidden/concealed (made occult) by the erasures and reversals that pervade patriarchal history.

By her Act of Writing Davis evoked a true Past. She Spanned Time. She backed up her theory with impressive evidence supporting two streams of thought: "the first, that the earliest civilization we know was but a renewal of a then dimly remembered and now utterly forgotten older one, and the second, that the impelling and revivifying agent in what we know as civilization was woman."[10] The evidence led her to the insight "that modern man was a *repeater*—that every discovery he made and every invention he conceived had been discovered and invented before, in a forgotten past civilization of tens or even hundreds of thousands of years ago."[11]

Davis states her case succinctly:

> The tradition shared by all early peoples, but glossed over by later historians and myth-interpreters, that it was woman who had preserved the germ of the lost civilization and had brought it into its second flowering was too insistent to be ignored. The primacy of goddesses over gods, of queens over kings, of great matriarchs who had first tamed and then reeducated man, all pointed to the fact of a once gynocratic world.[12]

The criminal takeover of Gynocentric society by patriarchy is clearly described:

---

ness (New York: Oxford University Press, 1993). It would be unthinkable to overlook the scholarly achievement of Marija Gimbutas, especially as represented in *The Goddesses and Gods of Old Europe, 6500–3500 BC* (Berkeley and Los Angeles: University of California Press, 1982).

He [patriarchal man] has rewritten history with the conscious purpose of ignoring, belittling, and ridiculing the great women of the past, just as modern historians and journalists seek to ignore, belittle and ridicule the achievements of modern women. He has devalued woman to an object of his basest physical desires and has remade God in his own image. . . . Worst of all, he has attempted to transform woman herself into a brainless simulacrum, a robot who has come to acquiesce meekly in the belief in her own inferiority.[13]

"The fact of a once gynocratic world" is supported by the evidence from mythology, archaeology, and anthropology.[14] It is also embedded in the Deep Memory of Archaic Time. Women who have not had the opportunity to look carefully into the scholarly sources *can Sense* intuitively the truth of our origins. As Monique Wittig wrote in 1969:

There was a time when you were not a slave, remember that. You walked alone, full of laughter, you bathed bare-bellied. You say you have lost all recollection of it, remember. . . . You say there are no words to describe this time, you say it does not exist. But remember. Make an effort to remember. Or, failing that, invent.[15]

Davis, who was Wildly in touch with her Elemental Genius, did remember and she Re-membered. Her convictions about the Past brought her to knowledge of the Future, enabling her to bring her argument to a Be-Dazzling conclusion:

The rot of masculist materialism has indeed permeated all spheres of twentieth-century life and now attacks its very core. . . . The ages of masculism are now drawing to a close. Their dying days are lit up by a final flare of universal violence and despair such as the world has seldom before seen. . . . In the new science of the twenty-first century, not physical force but spiritual force will lead the way. Mental and spiritual gifts will be more in demand than gifts of a physical nature. Extrasensory perception will take precedence over sensory perception. And in this sphere woman will again predominate. She who was revered and worshipped by early man because of her power to see the unseen will once again be the pivot . . . about whom the next civilization will, as of old, revolve.[16]

This passage represents a major Shape-shifting. It was written during a period of re-awakening and boldness that had begun to emerge in the 1960s. Since then, there has been much great Feminist productivity, but more recently it has been followed by tameness, timidity, and tiredness. Perhaps this should have been anticipated, since we knew then that the taming of Wild Women is an unstated goal of all the institutions of patriarchy. But the prevailing spirit of exuberant optimism enabled many Feminists to overlook the ominous signs of encroaching backlash. We were having such a Great Time!

THE TAMING OF FEMINIST GENIUS
BY ACADEMENTIA

The toning down/tuning out of Female Creative Genius in academia/academentia, particularly in the 1990s, is an atrocity that requires attention. Nothing less than the spiritual/intellectual life of women is at stake.

Specifically, the taming of women's thinking by much that parades as "feminist theory" undermines Female Elemental integrity and power. One manifestation of this is the intrusive and con-fusing imposition of "gender" jargon by "postmodern feminists." For example, some insist that the word *women* is "essentialist" and should be replaced by constructs such as "persons gendered as feminine." Of course, women who live and breathe in the (real) world outside the walls of academentia might not guess that this bizarre construct refers to them. So they might not know how to answer if they were thus addressed.* But postmodern

---

*Their probable reaction could be something approximating the words of Lily Tomlin, the telephone operator in the memorable TV show *Laugh-in*, who asked, "Is this the party to whom I am speaking?"

theorists need not bother their heads about the (real) world, since for them it does not exist.

For one who takes such a construct as "persons gendered as feminine" seriously enough to examine it, important questions surely would include "What does 'feminine' mean?" and especially "'Gendered' *by whom?*" But the theorists who use such constructs have evinced no interest in *Naming agents*. In fact, they hide agents, especially when these are male oppressors. For decades linguist Julia Penelope has repeatedly warned against deceptive agent deletion, and her readers got the message.[17] It seemed that such a lesson could never be unlearned. Ah! But we did not foresee the invasion of Feminist theory by minions of postmodern masters.

Wild Women who have been awakened to Radical Feminist consciousness by classics such as de Beauvoir's *The Second Sex* and Davis's *The First Sex* were first shaken into a wakeful state by the *titles* themselves of these works. Even the thought of fitting them into the corsets prescribed by postmodern linguistic fashion designers is a chilling and repulsive joke. These books Name the agents of women's oppression. Should we "update" them by substituting thrilling new titles such as "The Second Gender"? Or "The First Gender"? One senses that this operation would be a semantic castration of their authors' Genius. Castration of Feminist Genius and capacity to Act is a logical result of agent deletion coupled with gender jargon. For it is impossible to Name and Act against oppression if there are no Nameable oppressors.

In order to achieve the goal of mental castration, oppressors must have access to the minds of their victims. Women's Studies provides an arena in which such access can be assured. Feminist theorist Renate Klein has written eloquently of the invasion of Women's Studies by postmodern theorists:

> From Freud to Foucault (a veritable cult hero), Nietzsche to Merleau-Ponty, Deleuze to Derrida, Lacan to Lyotard, Barthes to de Man (no order or affiliation implied) and many many more, it is MEN who colonize the pages of supposedly feminist writers. Their ubiquitous presence tries to invade the reader's self—mySelf—I feel assaulted.[18]

Wild Women can hear Virginia Woolf Howling in the Background: "The cat is out of the bag; and it is a Tom [read: Jacques]."[19]

One may object: "But it is *women* who are ardently promoting this kind of theory." To which I reply: So what else is new? Women under patriarchy have always been assigned to be carriers of woman-negating ideologies. And we should be familiar, by now, with the mechanisms of backlash, including erasure, reversal, and intimidation, and subsequent attempts by the institutionally powerless to obtain approval and rewards from those in power. But recently there has been a serious escalation. Many women in academia have truly become tongue-tied in their efforts *not* to name the agents of their own (denied) oppression or even the fact of oppression. How did it get this bad?

It may be helpful to look at the history of Women's Studies in the past few decades. For many years, Wild Women have dreamed of a Feminist University/Diversity. In the early seventies, we thought we could at least try for "Feminist Studies" within—or rather on the Boundary of—the usual universities. It rapidly became clear that this would be unacceptable to the misters/masters who held the purse strings. So we settled for "Women's Studies." That began as promising, but already in the mid-seventies it became noticeable across the United States that odd patterns were developing. It seemed that very few colleges could manage to offer a major in Women's Studies, ever. For some reason or other, they just "weren't ready yet," and this "unreadiness" has continued literally for decades. For those of us traveling around the U.S. it was astonishing to hear students at a variety of institutions of "higher education" intoning year after year: "No, we don't have a major in Women's Studies yet, but we do have a minor." (In some cases, very minor.) They seemed sincerely to believe that this was progress. And then in the late eighties and nineties there came the newest device of assimilation—"Gender Studies" (blender studies).[20] Again we may ask: But how did it get *this* bad?

Shrewd Women can turn to Foreseeing Fore-Crone Virginia Woolf for insight. She was fully aware in the 1930s that women were coming to a point in history when they would manage to join the processions of the professions. And she wrote:

For we have to ask ourselves, here and now, do we wish to join that procession, or don't we? On what terms shall we join that procession? Above all, where is it leading us, the procession of educated men?"[21]

She knew that the outcome would not be unequivocally good:

Before us lies the public world, the professional system, with its possessiveness, its jealousy, its pugnacity, its greed.[22]

Anyone who has read her great work *Three Guineas* will remember that Woolf advised the "daughters of educated men" who choose a professional career to follow four "teachers": poverty, chastity, derision, and freedom from unreal loyalties.[23] Particularly to the point are her warnings to avoid "adultery of the brain," or "brain prostitution."[24]

We have come to a place in history, just sixty years after the publication of *Three Guineas*, when Virginia Woolf's words and her vision are of more crucial importance than ever. Concerning the uselessness of colleges and universities that foster brain-selling, her Passion inflames the reader:

Set fire to the old hypocrisies. Let the light of the burning building scare the nightingales and incarnadine the willows. And let the daughters of educated men dance round the fire and heap armful upon armful of dead leaves upon the flames. And let the mothers lean from the upper windows and cry, "Let it blaze! Let it blaze! For we have done with this "education"![25]

Many Radical Feminists of these times are inspired by that Fire. Disgusted Searchers who have longed to teach and study our own Heritage, feel done in by this "education." Indeed, as Kathleen Barry writes, there has been a "defeminism of women's studies" and widespread de-funding of analyses of racism, sexism, and classism.[26] Within this context Feminists who have attempted to radicalize Women's Studies have been derided and denied adequate salaries. Many (read: all) Radical Feminists have been driven out of academia or squashed into improbable situations.[27] Hence Wild Women working on the Boundaries of such institutions are understanding more deeply than ever that we must heed Woolf's Howl and set Fire to the same old hypocrisies, many of which are currently garbed in the emperor's new postmodern clothes.

As I was writing these words one Wild Woman I know well (mySelf) made the following statement to me:

"It's such a *relief* to hear you (me) say that! Let me tell you a secret. I've *always* found postmodern writings unspeakably boring. It is brain torture for me to read them. The question that puzzled me at first was: What's wrong with me? Then, after discovering that most of my friends had the same reaction that I had, I wondered: Why have the convoluted and sterile texts of postmodern men been received with such reverence in certain areas of academia? A lightbulb switched on in my head when I read a text by a 'postmodern feminist theorist' expressing her fear of the 'conceptual sloppiness' that she perceived in Feminist thinking. She contrasted this with the 'intellectual rigor' she believed could be found in male-authored postmodern theory.[28] Aha! Those old patriarchally embedded feelings of women's intellectual inferiority were at work."

I thoughtfully agreed with mySelf and then flashed back to my memories of spending years studying Aristotelian philosophy and medieval theology, specifically that of Thomas Aquinas. This intellectual work nourished my soul and was deeply satisfying. It was a "karate of the mind" and was rooted in a deep intuition of be-ing. Even the overt misogynism and other flaws in these entirely male-authored works fed my mind, giving me overt and subliminal knowledge of reversals and erasures that I would later decode in the process of creating my philosophy. In contrast to that invigorating experience, reading postmodern writings has felt like attempting to force down ashes garnished with shredded newspapers. It's depressing and dryasdust. I choke.

After this internal dialogue (monologue?) I pondered the condition of young women who are being eaten alive by dust mites which they have been taught to revere as authorities. Who will be there to remind these students that—despite book burnings—we Now have a visible Heritage of hundreds of thousands of pages of brilliant theorizing by women? We have proven ourSelves many times over. We just need to keep on Moving. Who will be there to inspire students to *respect their own Genius?* Must they turn to phallocentric necrophiles who will reinforce the Self-doubt which generations of forefathers have already embedded into women? Certainly it can be worthwhile to study male-authored philosophy. But why select such un-philosophical (speci)-mens? What is wrong?

I re-turned to the article by Renate Klein cited above:

> But within the context of the academy that has never stopped resisting the development of strong women-centered Women's Studies that *discusses women qua women*, such (resurrected) prominence of men is understandable; it might well be one of the reasons why feminist post-modernism, so utterly unthreatening to male hegemony, is allowed into the academy and even seen as the only legitimate feminist theorizing in many places.[29]

"Of course!" I thought. "We need to exorcise this academonic[30] invasion of women's psyches." And at that Moment I Re-Called the "Sado-Ritual Syndrome," which I first Dis-covered in *Gyn/Ecology*.[31] The Sado-Ritual Syndrome is a set of interconnected components of sado-rituals* which can be recognized by Searchers as links among seemingly unrelated atrocities. I will experiment with applying this analysis to the invasion and taming of Feminist thought by "postmodern feminism."

---

*By *sado-rituals* I mean "rituals which recreate and reinforce the primordial patriarchal mythic event—the murder/dismemberment of the Goddess within women and all be-ing; rituals devised to accomplish and legitimate the dis-spiriting and devastation of the Wild; rituals designed to destroy the integrity of Life and creative divine powers in women and all Elemental creatures. *Examples*: Chinese footbinding; hindu suttee and dowry murders; the systematic rape of Black female slaves in america; the ongoing murder and mutilation of women by sex killers . . . throughout the United States and the world; the normalized, routinized use of 'pesticides' (biocides) in agriculture." See *Gyn/Ecology*, pp. 130–33, and *Wickedary*, p. 94.

There are seven components of the Sado-Ritual Syndrome:

(1) *In the Sado-Ritual we find, first, an obsession with purity.* "Postmodern feminism" is an oxymoron, a mind-rotting deception. It purifies women's minds of the capacity for Feminist thought. As Denise Thompson has written:

> The concept of "post-modernist" feminism is a contradiction in terms because, while feminism is a politics, post-modernism renders its adherents incapable of social commitment. . . . While feminism needs to be able to identify domination in general, and male domination in particular, in order to challenge it, post-modernism refuses to identify, and hence cannot contest, relations of domination and subordination.[32]

Add to this the problem of "timeshed/spiritshed" that was so Cannily foreseen by Virginia Woolf. Thompson makes the case clearly, stating that texts identified as postmodern "are frequently characterized by a cryptic inscrutability which demands investments of time and energy unjustifiable in feminist terms."[33] The seductive elegance of style of postmodern musings is con-fusing, luring Feminists into an inescapable house of mirrors, brain drain, and betrayal of our own kind.

In sum: Preoccupation with and by "postmodern feminism" is a source of Self-contradiction. Postmodern theory is a cause of paralysis; it stops activism dead. It functions/malefunctions to purify women of our Deep Memory, our Deep Selves, our Radical connectedness with other women and with nature. It works to purify women of the Courage to See, to Name, and to Act.

(2) *Second, there is total erasure of responsibility for the atrocities performed through such rituals.* The men who colonize the pages of "postmodern feminist writers" appear to be absent from the scene of the crime, and some even repudiate postmodernism itself:

> Foucault rejected the category [postmodern]; Guattari despises it, Derrida has no use for it; Lacan and Barthes did not live, and Althusser was in no state, to learn about it; and Lyotard found it in America.[34]

Erasure of responsibility has been a remarkably Byzantine process. The name "French feminism," often used to refer to what is called "postmodern feminist theory," is defined by Christine Delphy as

> a body of comments by Anglo-American writers on a selection of French—and non-French—writers: Lacan, Freud, Kristeva, Cixous, Derrida and Irigaray are the core group. But there are others. "French feminism," then, is an Anglo-American strand of intellectual production within an Anglo-American context.[35]

The plot thickens. Delphy states:

> The main reason its [anglo-American] inventors invented their brand of feminism as "French" was that they did not want to take responsibility for what they were saying. And in particular for their attempt to rescue psychoanalysis from the discredit it had incurred in feminism—but not only in feminism, as this discredit is general throughout the social sciences. They pretended that *another* feminist movement thought it was great—that in fact it was all the other, admittedly strange, movement was interested in.[36]

The Anglo-American "French feminists" managed to turn the word *feminist* into a meaningless label, which is happily applied to feminists, nonfeminists, and antifeminists. (The fact that Kristeva and Cixous are outspoken antifeminists is high-handedly dismissed.) Antifeminist male authors are also welcome. Furthermore, Alice Jardine, a major manufacturer of "French feminism," suggests that the antifeminist women are the authors of the most important writing for feminist work and that since their thinking is derived from men, the women themselves need not be considered.[37]

Delphy explains this "admittedly strange" scenario:

> As in all colonialist discourses, there's a mixture of both fake respect and condescension for the culture. Enough respect to warrant the attention of the American reader: "French feminism" is important, we

must listen to what it has to say. But that respect is really condescension: for what sort of feminists can feminists from France be if they take as their major theorists women who not only are anti-feminist but are men's parrots?[38]

Delphy deftly makes the point that the inventors of "French feminism" could not get away with saying that the most important writers for U.S. feminism today are Katie Roiphe or Camille Paglia or Philip Wylie. But with the "French" smoke screen they (especially Alice Jardine) can pull off the ruse. The goal of reinstating men as the colonizers of Feminist knowledge was achieved.

And that is one true story of contemporary erasure of responsibility for atrocities against the minds of women in academic circles.

(3) *Third, gynocidal ritual practices have an inherent tendency to "catch on" and spread, since they appeal to imaginations conditioned by the omnipresent ideology of male domination. Moreover, since the patriarchal imagination is hierarchical, there is a proliferation of atrocities from an elite to the upwardly aspiring lower echelons of society.* "Postmodern feminist theory" has had a tendency to catch on. It is "catching," and the (academic) carriers of the disease appear to have an ideal environment for contagion within "the academy." The academic system, with its hierarchical structure, its self-styled professional elite, its upwardly aspiring fear-filled faculty and students (particularly graduate students), its manipulative and exploitative administrators, and its national and international networks of publications and organizations, is a perfect carrier for this disease. One appeal of this theory to academic bureaucrats surely must be the fact that it gives the appearance of being intellectually "challenging" (frustrating) and elegant (the emperor's new clothes) and at the same time discourages risk-taking and real challenge to the hierarchical status quo within academia and elsewhere. Even those who have no appetite for the theory are subdued by the pervasive climate of con-fusion and blandness that it legitimates. As Somer Brodribb summed up the vacuousness in the title of her eloquent critique of postmodernism: *Nothing Mat(t)ers.*

(4) *Fourth, women are used as scapegoats and token torturers. . . . This masks the male-centeredness of the ritualized atrocity and turns women against each other.* In her incisive article "(Re)-Turning to the Modern: Radical Feminism and the Post-modern Turn," Kristin Waters skillfully applies my analysis of "token torturers" to "feminist" versions of postmodernism. Waters refers to "the use of women who are supposedly in sympathy with other women to perform the sadistic tasks of excising female genitals." She then comments:

> In this case, it is not the clitorises but the hard-earned theories resulting from radical and socialist, Black, Asian, Native, and Latina feminist work, to name only a few that are undergoing excision.[39]

I could not agree more with this comparison. To which I would add that there is also a castration taking place in both cases. In the case of female genital mutilation women's bodies are castrated. Sterile forms of "feminist theory" castrate women's minds.

(5) *Fifth, we find compulsive orderliness, obsessive repetitiveness, and fixation upon minute details, which divert attention from the horror.* Postmodernism does all of this perfectly, and thus succeeds in diverting attention from the horrors of patriarchy. As Kristin Waters summarizes the details:

> In a post-modern world, theories become discourses, words become signifiers, both books and bodies become texts to be read, studied and dissected, criticisms become deconstructions; and people and groups become fragmented selves, reason becomes desire, and substance becomes style.[40]

And that style is "elusive and obscure, ungrounded and apolitical."[41] Postmodern theorist Judith Butler, drawing upon Freud and Lacan, maintains that the phallus is transferable. She thereupon devotes thirty-four pages to the lesbian phallus.*[42]

---

*Commenting on Butler's "lesbian phallus," Emily Culpepper wryly remarked: "Oh, we've had a name for that for a long time. . . . It's called 'the prick in the head'" (trans-

(6) *Sixth, behavior which at other times and places is unacceptable be-comes acceptable and even normative as a consequence of conditioning through the ritual atrocity.* The behavior in question here is "feminist" Self-abnegation. Women are reduced to groveling for rotten crumbs of "theory." Somer Brodribb responds forcefully:

> As for the idea that feminists should be ragpickers in the bins of male ideas, we are not as naked as that. The notion that we need to salvage for this junk suggests that it is not immediately available everywhere at all times. The very up-to-date products of male culture are abundant and cheap; it is one of life's truly affordable things. In fact, we can't pay not to get it, it's so free. So what we have is a difficulty in refusing, of *not* choosing masculine theoretical products.[43]

(7) *Seventh, there is legitimation of the ritual by the rituals of "objec-tive" scholarship—despite appearances of disapproval.* Postmodernism is the ultimate in patriarchal scholarship. Therefore it is perfectly dead. It has produced a monster, "postmodern feminism," which, like itself, is a dead thing and can be legitimated only by postmodernism. There can be no Future in this postmodern setting because there is no Life—no Present and no Presence.

Phoenix-identified Women set Fire to the corpse/corpus and Soar on. Refusing to be pulled into the academonic deathtrap of pseudofeminist theory with its endless lies and reversals we summon the Courage to Dis-cover our Elemental Feminist Genius and Realize the Archaic Future.

METAMORPHIC LEAPING
INTO THE ARCHAIC FUTURE

Timidity is a consequence of the taming process and terrible tiredness is the end result. Do we have to trudge, drudge on in the same paths?

---

continental telephone conversation, January 8, 1998). Obviously, in Radical Lesbian Feminist parlance this has never been considered a good thing. It is an invasion of a woman's mind by phallocratic images and attitudes that negatively affect her life and need to be dislodged.

Do we do it all over again? Unthinkable. Desperate women have no Time for that.

Outrageous, Contagious Courage impels Wild Women to Break Out from the domain of deadheads, which is marked by the need to please. We Speak Out, Act Out. It is not good enough to drop out, as Valerie Solanas valiantly Pointed Out.*

The way up and Out is true New Archaic Fore-action. It is re-awakening of our Genius. Elemental Genius does not simply repeat. As Davis wrote, repeating is the role of "modern man," who cannot Re-member. Fore-actors can Unforget and Spiral on.

So *who* will help us? I suggest that those who can pull us ahead may be our Foresisters of the Future. For millennia women have been creating Memories of the Future. By performing actions and generating works that can affect/effect the Future, Wild Women have been creating Memories that will be Realized in the minds and actions of those who will come after us. We have been storing treasures of our own creation in the Treasure House of the Future. These wonders await us. And they have not been passively gathering dust as do the "treasures" in the museums of patriarchy. They have influence on Wild Women Now. They encourage us and give us hope for the Future because we know that these treasures will one day affect women of the Future, who will then Re-member us. Thus our knowledge of the effects of our work upon Future Foresisters attracts us into the Archaic Future, where we are welcome, where our work is appreciated.

It may seem that my Act of claiming to have such Foreknowledge of Future acceptance is rash. Why not simply say that I have hope that

---

*"Dropping out is not the answer; fucking up is. Most women are already dropped out; they were never in. Dropping out gives control to those few who don't drop out; dropping out is exactly what the establishment leaders want; it plays into the hands of the enemy; it strengthens the system instead of undermining it, since it is based entirely on the nonparticipation, passivity, apathy, and noninvolvement of the mass of women. Dropping out, however, is an excellent policy for men, and SCUM will enthusiastically encourage it." See Valerie Solanas, *SCUM Manifesto* (1967; San Francisco: AK Press and Freddie Baer, 1996), p. 44.

there will be such enlightened Future Foresisters? The point is well taken that such knowledge is also hope. It is, in fact, Desperately Hopeful knowledge, and it is rooted in an understanding of our history, our Past.

A startling example of such Desperately Hopeful knowledge is the preservation by Fore-Acting Foresisters of fragments of Sappho's poems. These were copied on wadded strips of papyrus used as mummy wrappings in Oxyrhyncus, Egypt, and were discovered between 1897 and 1906 in the course of an archaeological expedition.[44] Sappho herself had such Foreknowledge, when she wrote the following:

> You may forget but
> Let me tell you
> this: someone in
> some future time
> will think of us.[45]

We witness the phenomenon of re-discovery over and over again. Matilda Joslyn Gage, who was erased by her contemporaries, towers as an intellectual giant over meanspirited "sisters." The works of Virginia Woolf, who was driven to suicide by the oppressors of her Life, Live Now.

Our knowledge that we are creating great Memories of the Future becomes more substantial, more real, as we come to recognize *who we are* and the value of what we are doing. As we Realize our Genius and grow in Self-confidence we can *know* the value of our work to Future Foresisters and therefore be invigorated and spurred on to Hopeful, Courageous, Creative work Now.

The better we can Re-member our history, the better we can provide for our Future Foresisters. And our anticipation of their Future Thriving draws us forward.

The better we know who we are, the greater can be our Leaps. The doors are open. We ourselves have been opening them. We have only to remove the blinders imposed in the pseudoworld of the foreground to See that these Future Women are Here Now. Not only do the treasures of our own creation attract *us*. They attract the Future Foresisters who receive the Memories of the Future we have created. Mutual Magnetic attraction brings us together.

This is indeed Intergalactic Travel. It is Transtemporal Diaspora that transforms foreground temporal diaspora. Our Exile, Scattering, and Migration create an Outsiders' Society that is outside anything imaginable to microscopic/telescopic (re)visionaries. And it is Re-membering that makes it Real.

Cosmic Comments and Conversations
IN 2048 BE CONCERNING
CHAPTER THREE

....

by Anonyma

WHEN I LOOKED *for Kate with the intention of inviting her to join the next Transtemporal conversation I found her working in her vegetable garden, pulling up weeds. As soon as I asked her about the possibility of her participating with us in a discussion of Chapter Three, she stood up, her eyes twinkling.*

"I thought you would never ask!" she exclaimed. "Couldn't you see that I was almost jumping out of my skin with impatience every time you mentioned your Transtemporal Conjuring? I thought I would have to make some excuse to break in during your next conversation if you didn't invite me. Of course, I would have restrained myself, but . . ."

I began to explain, "Well, Mom, I was totally focused on my new experience of exchanging ideas with an author who had spent decades writing and living Feminist philosophy. Besides, I knew you two had corresponded 'back then,' and I wanted to sort of make a fresh start, rather than just come on as 'Kate's daughter.' You know what I mean, don't you? I felt like a newcomer on the scene."

Kate laughed. "I really understand, Annie. I'm just eager, especially since Mary and I always just missed each other 'back then.' When she was in one city I would be in another. It was frustrating. And, by the way, don't you think she feels like a 'newcomer' when you Conjure her? These visits must be quite a shock to her. After all, she's just popping in and out from 1998."

"She does seem to be in a spacy state when she arrives. I feel the same way. And she's rather shy, anyway, I think."

"And how would you describe yourself?" Kate asked. "You wouldn't exactly be at ease at a cocktail party."

....

"At a what?" I asked.

"Oh, that's just an obsolete expression of the last century for a sort of pretentious gathering involving alcoholic drinks to provide fake stimulation and empty name-dropping babble," Kate replied, tossing some weeds onto a pile.

"You mean a boring party preoccupied by cocks?" I asked.

Kate guffawed. "Something like that," she said.

"Well, our conversations aren't boring, and there are no cocks involved," I said. "And I think we're both quite at ease in the course of our Sparking discussions. But that doesn't preclude our feeling a bit giddy, you know, flying between Time/Space zones. And we don't need 'cocktails' to do that."

"Just tell me where and when," said Kate, brushing disheveled "pepper and salt" locks off her forehead.

"How about right here, later this afternoon?" I suggested.

"In the garden?" Kate looked around. "Actually this would be a great place to visit with Mary. Count me in! Are you sure she'll show up?"

"She always has," I said. "We seem to have a clear line of communication. I've told you the gist of the earlier conversations. In Chapter Three, as you know, Mary focuses on our favorite subjects—re-awakening what she calls the 'X-Factor/Faculty' and creating the Archaic Future. And then there's the stuff on the late-twentieth-century attempts to tame Feminist Genius in academia. It'll be interesting to see how your memories mesh with her experience and analysis of 'academentia.' After all, you were just eighteen and in your first year of college when Quintessence was first published in 1998!"

"Sure, I'd be interested in discussing that," Kate replied. "As I explained to you when you were growing up, I've blocked many of my memories of the time before 2018 BE. The Earth Changes and our struggle for Survival were so traumatizing that partial amnesia concerning events that happened 'back then' is a common phenomenon among us immigrants to Lost and Found Continent. But I'm sure a lot will come back to me. I'd also especially like to talk about Memories of the Future and how the creation of these has continued to move our Anonyma Network on its Spiraling Voyage.

"This is going to be fun!" I said.

"I'll be right back!" Kate called over her shoulder as she hurried toward the house.

After I had drawn a couple of benches and tables together under one of our beautiful apple trees along the edge of the garden, I sat down to Conjure Mary. When she didn't come immediately I began to worry. Unable to sit still, I went for a short stroll around the garden, and when I got back to the tree, there she was, sitting on a branch, enjoying a juicy red apple. "Hello, Mary," I said. "I see that I don't have to invite you to make yourself comfortable."

"Sorry to be a bit late," she said. "I was in the middle of writing a paragraph, and I couldn't stop until I got the wording just right. What a luxuriant garden!"

"This is Kate's garden," I said. "She's joining us this afternoon. Am I glad to see you!"

At that Moment Kate came sauntering over to the table, carrying a bottle of wine and three glasses. She had spotted Mary in the tree. "It's great that a Crone can be a 'tomboy,' to use the old-fashioned twentieth-century term. Shall I join you in the tree or would you deign to come down with us?"

"Oh, I'll come right down," said Mary obligingly, as she hopped down onto the table, slid off onto a bench and then stood solidly on the ground. "Your arrangement makes tree-climbing easy, even for a klutzy Hag. I hope I haven't scratched the furniture. Apples, anyone?" Mary gestured mischievously toward several apples that had been shaken from the tree in the course of her acrobatic maneuver.

Kate and I laughed and we all exchanged hugs. No introductions were necessary. "You seem to feel quite at home," said Kate. "I'm so happy to meet you, at last!"

"The happiness is mutual, Kate," said Mary. "I remember the letter you sent me when you were a senior in high school. That certainly was a boost to my hopes for the 'new generation.' And, yes, I do feel at home. After all, this is my fourth trip to your Found Continent. Annie may have told you that we were both a bit stunned during earlier visits. But this Time travel becomes

easier with practice. Overcoming our separation by temporal diaspora and transforming this into Transtemporal Communication is an invigorating experience!"

"You can say that again!" said Kate. "I'm feeling positively charged already, and look forward to a heady discussion."

The three of us were huddled on the benches around the table, which was strewn with books and papers I had brought for this event. We were munching our apples. "It's consoling to know that these wonderful apples are 'organic'!" Mary said, winking at Kate.

Kate grinned. "And they don't cost more, either," she said.

"I don't get the joke," I said. "Aren't all apples organic? Could they be 'inorganic'?"

"They're all organic here," said Kate. "But most fruits and vegetables were laced with pesticides 'back then,' and those that weren't poisoned were called 'organic,' while the poisoned ones were called 'conventional.' So there was a concomitant mind-poisoning."

"Oh, so that's what they did!" I said. I added that I don't always "get" these details about life in the late twentieth century, since I never experienced them firsthand. Then I realized that the "organic" thing was part of the "state of con-fusion" Mary wrote about, and I blurted out: "What a scrambled mess you had to deal with!"

Both Kate and Mary laughed loudly. Kate said to Mary, "Do you remember the articles on 'Quintessence' that were coming through on the Internet when you were writing this book? My friends and I did a 'search' on the 'net' when we heard you were writing a book with that title. We found recipes for brewing 'Quintessence,' ads for enterprises such as 'Quintessence Software Foundry,' and some occult treatises. It was a con-fusing glut of irrelevant foreground stuff which functioned to hide the deep meaning of Quintessence."

I interjected that I couldn't quite picture the foreground "angel" images that were all over the place at that time. I explained that I have never seen any such "cute" pictures.

Kate responded that she would attempt to draw an example of such a

*caricature. "You would understand immediately if you could see them, An-
nie," she said.*

*I replied that I would appreciate a sketch of a "Barbie doll" as well. I
said I knew that they were not like "baby dolls."*

*Mary and Kate groaned in unison. "No, they functioned as role
models," said Kate. "What a creepy phenomenon that was! When I was a kid
there was quite a fuss in the media about the tape-recorded voice of a 'Teen-
Talk Barbie' lamenting that 'Math class is tough.' Because of protests against
this sexist propaganda, the manufacturer (the Mattel Corporation) discon-
tinued that particular line of Barbies. But they kept expanding and increasing sales. I wrote a paper on the subject for an English class in high school and
was disgusted at all I found out. 'Barbie' had been invented in 1959, and
Mattel celebrated the thing's thirty-fifth 'birthday' in 1994. I read that in
1994 Mattel made over 3.2 billion dollars in worldwide sales. It was reported
that the typical American girl at that time owned an average of eight Barbie
dolls and that they were sold in more than one hundred and forty countries
around the world."*

*"It would be hard to overestimate the subliminal influence of those de-
structive 'toys' on little girls," said Mary. "Girls were indoctrinated with the
idea that they should look like 'Barbie'—which was an unattainable goal.
The doll probably contributed immeasurably to the spread of unnecessary cosmetic surgery, anorexia, and bulimia, which reached epidemic proportions."*

*"Speaking of cosmetic surgery," Kate added, "I recall that there was a
well-known photographer, Cindy Jackson, who actually had nineteen operations to make her look like Barbie."*

*"But that's just one aspect of the horror show," said Mary. "The Barbie
phenomenon was an appalling illustration of American exploitation of
women and children who worked in factories outside the U.S.—in Thailand,
China, and Indonesia, and—as globalization progressed—all over the
world. Just before this, uh, trip, I was reading about the subhuman conditions in a factory called Dynamics, located just outside Bangkok, which manufactured Mattel's Barbie dolls, as well as Disney products such as 'Lion
King.' A journalist who visited there described the sick and dying women and*

children working in the factory, which in 1997 had 4,500 employees.[1] Most were in terrible shape. This is not surprising, since Barbie contained polyvinyl chloride, a substance that released carcinogenic dioxins into the environment whenever the doll was made or incinerated.[2] I read that most workers had respiratory infections because their lungs were filled with dust and chemicals, and many had chronic lead poisoning. Some suffered from pains in their hands, necks, and shoulders, while others experienced nausea, dizziness, and hair and memory loss. The air was so bad that even the managers didn't come in for fear of being contaminated. As one journalist explained, most of the workers in this plant came from northeastern Thailand, where the poverty was abject and where it was common practice for parents to sell their daughters (frequently not over eleven or twelve years old) into sexual slavery or as cheap labor. Those not sold into slavery outright were often sent to cities like Bangkok to work in factories like the one I've just described."[3]

"So Barbie reveals volumes about patriarchy!" I said. Then turning to Mary, I continued: "I'm beginning to understand the significance of the comment that 'the nineties are like the fifties.' I remember reading that after World War II there was a huge backlash against women, who had gained a measure of freedom when 'the boys' were away at war. For example, there were subliminal messages embedded in the illustrations in magazines for 'ladies' telling them to leave their jobs and return to their role as full-time house-wives. I think it was no coincidence that 'Barbie' was spawned in 1959 and then continued to spread like creeping fungus while the Women's Liberation Movement was flowering. So when the backlash against Feminism came, in the late eighties and nineties, Barbie was everywhere, and her popularity increased." I couldn't contain my disgust, so I added impetuously: "I wish I had one of the rotten things, so I could smash its ugly head!"

Then my companions laughed and began telling me how fortunate I've been because I was never subjected to such brainwashing. I almost "lost it." "All right, you two," I snapped impatiently. "I really don't need to hear any more about how lucky I am. That's not very enlightening! I'm trying to learn and understand things that I have never experienced."

Looking toward Kate, Mary said, "Annie's right, of course. Both you and I experienced the state of the world before the beginning of this Era. You've known the world 'before' as well as 'after' the Great Transition. With the exception of these brief encounters, I know experientially only how it was before. But Annie and her generation as well as those who are following can have no direct knowledge of the horrors we are talking about. She has a right to know. And as you know, Kate, you are 'the link.'"

"When you put it that way, I am reminded of my essential, albeit fast disappearing, role," Kate replied. She folded her hands and stared ahead with exaggerated solemnity. "I must learn to become an adequate 'link.'"

"And, to round off our moralizing digression," added Mary, "it is extremely important that I learn from you both, so that I can convey an accurate understanding to my own contemporaries."

"Oh, do let's move on!" I implored. "I'd like to know more about the backlash—for example, the pseudofeminism that served the purposes of the male establishment by denying the reality of women's oppression. It must have been almost unbearable to have to deal with such widespread and malignant denial."

"It certainly caused a lot of con-fusion at my college when I was a student," groaned Kate. "Self-righteous pseudofeminist authors were sometimes invited by con-fused committees to give lectures during 'Women's Month'— which was March—supposedly because they were 'controversial,' which meant they were trying to erode Feminism. We found out that conservative groups of rich white men, such as the Heritage Foundation, often promoted phony feminists as speakers—like the author of the reversal-filled book Who Stole Feminism?—and even funded their 'research.' In effect, conservative foundations were hiring these women to indoctrinate students with backlash b.s. I was a 'freshman' when this infiltration of the Speakers Series was taking place at my college. My friends and I protested this, and we won!"

Spontaneously Mary and I applauded and cheered. Kate stood up and took a bow. "Yeah, we had some Wild times!" she responded, smiling mischievously. "I guess they thought they'd break us or convert us or something. They certainly tried." Then she added: "Besides the overt attacks on Radical Feminism there were more subtle means of undermining that occurred under the rubrics of 'gender studies' and 'postmodern theory.' I get a headache even re-membering it."

"So that sort of deception must have caused con-fusion among the stu-dents who didn't know the meaning of the word feminism," I mused.

"Sure, that was the plot," said Kate. "In some circles it was even consid-ered an insult to be called a feminist. That was derided as 'the f-word.' And if you Named the plot for what it was, you were called 'dated,' or 'paranoid,' or dismissed with the ultimate labels of late nineties pop culture, like 'male-bashing' and 'sexist.'"

"Sexist?" I asked in alarm. Then, a second later, I said, "Oh, I get it. You were supposedly oppressing men, and worse than that, women who didn't agree with you. You see, I understand the concept of reversal intellectually, but it's so alien to my own experience! I suppose they accused you of 'reverse discrimination' as well. It must have been boring and draining to deal with that dull stuff over and over again. No wonder so many women gave up. There you have it—an important condition of the diaspora of women—ex-haustion."

"Let's not bore and exhaust ourselves with it any longer," pleaded Kate. "Remember, our guest has to go back to 1998."

Mary groaned lugubriously. "I'm so glad I have these Time Trips to look forward to," she said. "I'm relieved to get a break from the 1990s when I can. But there is a bright side—I know Now that a better Future is coming!"

"And that brings us back—and ahead—to Quintessence," I said.

Mary, looking far off into Space, continued, as if speaking to herself: "And these visits give whole New dimensions of meaning to the idea of 'Mem-ories of the Future.' I'll be carrying my Memories of these experiences of the Future back with me. I can't even comprehend it. Wow!"

"Sorry, but I can barely hear what you're saying. You're muttering," I complained. "What did you say?"

Embarrassed, Mary answered: "Just thoughts too New to frame into words. They're about something I haven't quite figured out yet." Pulling her-self together, she asked me: "What do you think about the stuff on Memories of the Future?"

"It's very thought-provoking," I said. "And it ties together so many things. I think of the students who created a Women's Center in the 1970s at that school—what was it called? Oh, 'Andover Newton'—and how they were creating Memories which would be Realized decades later by Jeanmarie Rindone (author of the Original text of the Biophilic Brotherhood's statement), who later went on to create another library for women at the Women's Center in Providence, Rhode Island. And then I think of the three of us Here, Now. We are creating Memories of our Future, which will affect women who follow us."

"Yes, we are," Mary said softly, staring off into Space.

"She's looking and sounding funny again," I thought, but I kept it to myself this time. Aloud I said, "And Memories of the Future are connected with Acts of Magnetism. When you wrote 'We Magnetize women of Future generations and diverse locations into Expanding Here,' did you have any inkling that you were Magnetizing us?"

"Perhaps I had a subliminal inkling," she answered.

I continued: "And was that Act of Magnetizing an Act of Desperation? I ask this because right after that sentence you wrote: 'We call forth our Selves and Other Women from the deadly state of severance into the farthest reaches of Intergalactic Communication in Archaic Time. Following this Call requires Acts of Desperation.' So I suspect that your Magnetizing of us was a Desperate Act. And this throws some light on my Act of Conjuring you. Maybe it was the force of your Desperation that Magnetized and Inspired me to Conjure you, and that made it work."

"That might well be," Mary agreed. "I was really eager to get out of the 1990s—Momentarily, at least." She gave me an appraising look. "You're sharp, Annie," she said forcefully.

I thanked her for the compliment and then moved on with my train of thought. "I'd like to proceed further with my interpretation of your text as it applies to our situation. I understand that you recognized despair over reforming patriarchy as a condition for Real, Elemental Hope. Well, such Hope generated the 'Leaping Acts of Desperation' that brought the members of the Anonyma Network to Original Dis-covering of this continent. I think this same Hope brought you here too."

....

"I think I have to agree with that," said Mary, looking at me very intently. "It was similar in some ways to my Desperate Leap across the Atlantic at the end of the fifties to study thirteenth-century theology and philosophy for seven years in the medieval city of Fribourg in Switzerland. I just had to get out of the fifties. Then my Time Travel was into the Past, but it eventually contributed to my Future work and travel."

Then Kate, who had been listening attentively, chimed in: "We're all Desperadoes Here. Welcome!"

"I am deeply honored to be welcomed Here," said Mary.

Kate then opened the bottle of wine she had brought from the house. We toasted each Other and all Transtemporal Desperadoes. As we savored the wine, she said, "Talk about Time Travel—How about Elizabeth Gould Davis writing The First Sex when she did! I was so moved by that book! It changed my life."

"What was it that impressed you so deeply, do you think?" Mary asked.

"First, there was the utter boldness of her message, which was announced immediately in the title, The First Sex," Kate responded. "I read it with a group of my friends when I was in college. We felt like outlaws reading it. After a 'near death experience' of boredom from dryasdust theory it was like a refreshing swim in the ocean. We were all familiar with Simone de Beauvoir's historic work The Second Sex. De Beauvoir's title stated clearly the foreground fact—which she convincingly and elaborately demonstrated in the book—that women have been socialized and subdued into being 'the second sex.' But unfortunately I think it also conveyed the subliminal message that women are and have always been 'the second sex,' almost by definition. And de Beauvoir herself overtly stated that this has always been a man's world. Davis transmitted something like an electrical jolt by proclaiming and daring women to realize that we were and are and will be 'the first sex.' Those three words 'rang a bell,' and they blasted away the wall that kept women from knowing what was already known, at least unconsciously. This brings me to the second part of my answer to your question. I was deeply impressed by the massive array of evidence and clues she brought together to support her thesis. As you have written, other scholars and thinkers had already made this point in various ways over and over, but the evidence they presented *had largely been ignored and erased. Davis brought it back and with power-ful focus. To borrow a well-known phrase from Virginia Woolf, she 'put the severed parts together.'"*

"The Timing of the publication of The First Sex *seems to have been just right," said Mary. "De Beauvoir's book, with its powerful analysis of fore-ground history, myths, biology, psychoanalysis, et cetera, combined with its limitations, seems to have paved the way for* The First Sex.*"*

I interrupted: "I see what you mean by saying her foreground exposure of patriarchy 'paved the way' for Davis. But I'm not sure that I know why you think its limitations *moved things along."*

"That intuition came from my experience," Mary replied. "You see, Annie, we were not only excited but also frustrated *by de Beauvoir's analysis. Her unquestioning supposition that patriarchy had always existed just didn't feel right. By the early seventies we wanted something more, and many of us were ready for it, although it was not clear what we needed. Davis sounded a Call and provided fuel for further Great Leaps of Daring. This seems to be the case with books that Leap ahead, pushing back boundaries."*

"And even though I arrived on the scene later," Kate said, "my friends and I also needed that special push. Of course there were scholars, notably Marija Gimbutas, who came along after Davis and brought us more spe-cialized data. But I know what Mary means. There was bold Originality and Fire in The First Sex.*"*

"Many years after Davis's book had gone out of print," Mary said, "one of my students made a number of photocopies of The First Sex, *and we passed these out in my class. It caught on like Wildfire."*

"This is helping me catch a glimpse of something that is needed on Lost and Found Continent Now," exclaimed Kate. "We need once again to Dis-cover Fire. And for this we need to communicate Memories of Desperation, Sparking the imaginations of our Sisters. Some of us can recall the Despera-tion we experienced before we Found this continent. The Acts that it enabled us to perform then can Now be Realized as Memories of the Future. They can inspire us to ever greater Desperate Acts."

"But the question is, can we really feel Desperate, since we are no longer in the state of despair which was patriarchy?" I said.

....

"I think you can if you look beyond the foreground meanings of desperation," replied Mary. "Great Desperate Acts are triggered essentially by Hope, not merely by despair. Precisely because you have moved out of the crippling state of despair you are able to be totally Desperate. Since you are not distracted and forced to reckon with brain-draining by bullydom you are free to practice Thoughtful Focused Recklessness. So, in this Time of Transcendent Diaspora why not cultivate Transcendent Desperation? Why not perform ever more Dreadful, Dreadless Desperate Acts/Leaps of Hope?"

Kate jumped in. "As the 'link' between you two I can describe what I have learned from my experience. When the Members of Anonyma made our Great Leaps—separately and together—which brought us to this place in 2018 BE, we were Fired by the mixed Desperation that marked that time. We had to get away—fast—from the state of despair, but we were also pulled by Real, Elemental Hope that was qualitatively beyond the hope any of us had experienced before. I remember the New and Wild Desperation I felt then, and the ever Wilder Desperation I learned later—which came from total loss of false hope and the subsequent experience of Freedom to Create. I came to understand this New Desperation as the pure expression of unbounded Hope. You might say it is the Leaping quality that characterizes Great Hope. And that brings us to the subject of the X-Factor/Faculty."

"Kate," said Annie, "as you were speaking I felt that you were communicating a Memory of the Future to me. I felt that I was in touch with those experiences you and other women had before I was born. It was as if I could remember something of what it was like before and during the Great Transition. So maybe the 'Wildfire' you spoke about a Moment ago is beginnng to spread among us right Now. Perhaps we've been preparing for a Re-Surging of the X-Factor among us."

"That's interesting," said Mary. "Strangely enough I was having a different but perhaps somewhat parallel experience. I felt pulled ahead into the Future, as if Kate's words were Positively Reversing the gross sensation of being sucked backward in foreground time that marked the 1990s. You know, the feeling of having lost so much of what we had gained? And I am confirmed in my intuition that our Fore-action back then is fueling your Leaps of 'unbounded Hope' Now."

....

"We are sounding like a Transtemporal 'mutual help society'—perhaps a therapy group," Kate quipped. "Remember that bad old song 'Lean on Me'?" Then she roared in exasperation, "I want to get on with our discussion of the X-Factor/Faculty!"

"But that's just what is happening," I said. "I have Sensed being pulled back and Mary told you she was being pulled ahead by your words. That sounds like Spinning, Spiraling movement to me. Maybe it's like a Witches' Dance. There's an intense transmission of Gynergy among us. We are Whirling! This must be the way the X-Factor warms up."

"I can Sense it too," said Mary. "Kate, since you are the link in Time you are in some sense the center. We're caught up in a Cyclone, and you are its central calm, its Eye. Maybe that's why you don't feel it with the same intensity as Annie and I at this Moment."

"Yes, I am in a Strangely calm state," said Kate. "But I do experience a kind of vertigo, with you two swirling around me. I can see and feel that the movement is Counterclockwise."

"That's as it should be," said Annie. "We are moving in Fairy Time, Tidal Time. Look! Mary is finally taking off her watch. Hooray! Oh, I can hear the Storm we are Brewing!"

"Our Mutual Magnetic Attraction is making this happen," called out Mary over the sounds of the Storm. "I can feel that we are being lifted into the air. Where do you think the Storm is carrying us?"

"I can't quite see, but we seem to be heading east," Kate cried out. "Maybe we'll catch a glimpse of other parts of the Earth. This is exciting!"

After a couple of Moments I could feel the Storm subside. There was a slight jolt, and we knew we had landed. Looking around, I said, "What a Strange place! Where are we?"

"And when are we?" Kate asked.

Mary was looking "transported" with delight. "We're in Fribourg, Switzerland!" she exclaimed. Then she pointed upward. "Look over there! You can see the cathedral on the hill. The river we're standing beside is the Sarine. We're in the basse ville (literally, the low city)—the original old city, which was built down on the river's edge. When I was studying in Fribourg *in the 1960s the university was located way up beyond the cathedral. That area was called the 'high city' or the 'new city.'"*

We walked around for a while, staring at everything and everyone. No one seemed to notice us, however. Kate said it was like the pictures of medieval towns she had seen in history books. "But," she quickly added, "it's so much more. This is real. It makes me think of my own trips to Europe when I was a student and how exhilarating they were. I could never understand from books what I learned from my own travels. But this *trip is something else! Even the air is different. I can feel the aura of the place, the time, everything! I wonder if we actually have moved into the Middle Ages!"*

I was gaping around—literally dumbstruck. Then I noticed Kate and Mary staring at me. "What's wrong?" I asked.

Kate laughed. "We'll have to take you out more often!" she exclaimed.

"It's so great to be back," Mary said. "You know, it's different from the basse ville *as I knew it in the sixties—which may mean that Kate is right in thinking that we've moved into the Middle Ages. But I can still recognize it, and I can feel the same powerful aura."*

"I feel so connected with the women of the Past, even of the very ancient Past!" I said. "It's as if everywhere I look I can see them peeking out at me from nooks and crannies. I can even hear them cackling. They seem to be as invisible to the townspeople as we are. In this time and place I feel closer to the ancient Gynocentric world than I ever could have imagined."

Suddenly we began to feel again the Sensation of being caught up in a Cyclone. "It's Time to go," I said. We were pulled up into the air, just as before. In No Time we were back on Found Continent.

We found ourselves sitting at the table under the apple tree. After we had all finally caught our breath, I exclaimed, "We three certainly are a powerful combination! I can hardly believe we did it!"

"Positively Potent!" responded Mary. Then she asked, "Why do you think we Time-traveled to medieval Fribourg?"

"I think it had something to do with the Magnetic pulls between you and Annie," Kate answered. "There was a sort of 'tug of war,' perhaps, between Past and Future. But maybe it was especially the intensity of your de-

sire to revisit Fribourg that drew us to that specific place. Were you trying to reawaken something?"

"Yes, I think you're right, and that 'something' was the X-Factor/Faculty. Our trip to Fribourg was a good move, at least for me," said Mary.

"But that surely was a patriarchal time and place!" I said.

"Oh, sure," Mary replied. "But I think it was not as far gone as the late twentieth century in the U.S. There were still Deep Archaic Memories embedded in the architecture and in the atmosphere of the place. And even though that particular cathedral was dedicated to saint Nicolas, most of its great sister-cathedrals of the Middle Ages—Notre Dame in Paris, for example—were really built to Goddess, who was represented, in a tamed way, by 'the Blessed Lady.'" The whole aura of the town with its cathedral was like a window opening into the Background. And, despite their contradictions, so also were the theology and philosophy I studied there in the 1960s. I'm glad that our visit together helped reawaken Archaic Memories for both of you also. Anyway, it was not a fully conscious decision, you know."

"I thought it was a great trip!" I said.

"I'll be thinking and dreaming about it for a long while," added Kate. "We had to start somewhere. And besides, I think it was a sort of unconscious collective decision. Having read Outercourse, Annie and I both had enormous curiosity about Fribourg. We knew it was a magical place for you, and I suppose we wanted to experience some of that magic."

"Mary," I said, "I'm curious to understand why you were 'pulled back' into the Past, despite the fact that before our trip you said Kate's words about New Desperation and unbounded Hope made you feel 'pulled ahead.' That could seem to be a contradiction, don't you think?"

Mary nodded. "Sure, Annie, it could seem self-contradictory, but it isn't, really. As you know, being pulled ahead in this dimension is not just linear movement. You yourself described the intense transmission of Gynergy among us as 'Spinning,' 'Spiraling,' and 'Whirling.' Returning to Fribourg was integrally connected with being Magnetically attracted by the Future. Touching that medieval time and space opened the way further into the Past than the medieval period because the cumulative riches of that period are derived from a more distant Pagan Past. And therefore it can awaken imaginative powers to take Great Leaps not only into the Past, but also into the Future—the Archaic Future that we are creating together. Those cumulative riches, which subliminally opened doorways into the Pagan Past, provided exactly the Archaic atmosphere I needed to prepare for writing books that might one day affect women in the Future."

"The trip we just took together was a kind of illustration and 'lived experience' of the last part of Chapter Three, wasn't it?" I commented.

"You could say that," replied our visitor. "I think we needed each other's Transtemporal companionship to take that trip and follow through on its implicit meaning for our Concreation of the Future. You see, just as Kate is a link between you and me, Annie, I seem to be connecting both of you with medieval times. Somehow, it's all about opening doors into the Archaic Pagan Past and Future."

"I'm thinking of the sentence in Chapter Three: 'Those who can pull us ahead may be our Foresisters of the Future,'" I said. "Well, we ourselves in 2048 BE are performing Acts that can attract our Future Foresisters, who will receive the Memories of the Future we are Concreating Here and Now. And our hopeful knowledge that this is true pulls us all further into the Future."

"I'll drink to that!" said Kate, pouring the rest of the wine into our three glasses. As we lifted the glasses we toasted our ever expanding Outsiders' Society and the X-Factor/Faculty in all of us.

Chapter Four

The Fifth Element
and the Fifth Direction

D ARING WOMEN who enter the drastic movement of Metamorphic Diaspora are Crones who have been around—and
around—Spiraling along Momentous paths.

Crones are not afraid to be Alone. We cherish the solitude in which we
can Spin. "Isolation" can Now be seen as insulation from a world of babble and compromise—the endless lies—that would hold us back from
Hearing.

In our Aloneness Spinsters Rage together. Hearing each other into
Speech, we shout out New Thought-Forms, breathe out New Word-
Storms. Weird/Wise words flow as we break through the blocks that were
built to keep us apart. No longer subdued by the system in which we
never belonged, Wild Women moan, groan, howl, growl. Furies sever
ourSelves from the state of severance, breathe Fire, and fly into freedom.

Cronies cry . . . "Out!" And Here, in the Fifth Element, Nemesis hears
our sounds of Rage, Grief, and Laughter. Together with us and through
us she rails and wails and howls.

Sirens are Sounding in unison. Our former desolation is Now sympa-
thetic vibration. Wild Women Name the basic/base deadly sin of the
lords of the sadostate: they *lie*.* Their lies are laced with doublethink, the
nonthought process by which patriarchal reversals are generated and
which makes belief in these absurdities possible.[1]

---

*In *Gyn/Ecology* I Named deception as the first among the Eight Deadly Sins of the
Fathers: "It is significant that in the traditional listing of the 'Deadly Sins,' Deception is

UNVEILING THE REVERSALS
OF PATRIARCHAL "SPIRITUALITY"

The woman-destroying reversals of western religion—most specifically christianity—have been exposed widely by Canny Women, who recognize and Name the more subtle variations of these reversals as well as the obvious instances.[2]

In order to escape the tyranny of christianity, some have turned to other forms of institutionalized spirituality. A number of women have been attracted to eastern religious traditions because they appear to pay homage to strong, autonomous Goddess figures and have some women in leadership roles. Are they sometimes jumping from the proverbial frying pan into the fire? I suggest that the answer is yes, there is danger of being deeply deceived . . . and, consequently, burned.*

All patriarchal religions sap female energy. Such "divine" vampirism,

---

not usually named. This . . . is an indicator of the pervasive deceptiveness of male-constructed 'morality,' which does not name its own primary Deadly Sin. Deception is in fact all-pervasive. It keeps us running in senseless circles. It sedates and seduces our Selves, freezing and fixing Female Process, enabling the fathers to feed upon women's stolen energy. The Paternal Parasites hide their vampirizing of female energy by deceptive posturing, which takes the form of Processions (religious, military, judicial, academic, etc.). For this reason, I choose to use the term *Processions* to name the deception of the fathers." See *Gyn/Ecology*, pp. 29–31.

*It is thought-provoking to read the stark and simple definitions of *nirvana* in *The American Heritage Dictionary of the English Language:* "1. a. *Buddhism.* The state of absolute blessedness, characterized by release from the cycle of reincarnations and attained through the extinction of the self. b. *Hinduism.* A similar state in which reunion with Brahma is attained through the suppression of individual existence." This dictionary adds the following etymological information: "Sanskrit *nirvana:* 'extinction (of individual existence).'" While extinction of the individual self may appear desirable to many men, Wild Women question whether it is really something that women would consciously desire—in any context, but especially in a gynocidal, biocidal world in which women, animals, and plants are targeted for extinction. Conversation with Hye Sook Hwang, February 27, 1998.

as it operates in the context of eastern spirituality, can be subtle and virtually invisible to one who is seeking escape from christian woman-hating. Myths, symbols, and practices of these other traditions also seductively transmit demeaning and misogynistic messages.

This problem of seductive deception has been analyzed and illustrated by the Scottish Feminist theorist June Campbell in her book *Traveller in Space*.[3] As a very young woman in the 1960s Campbell became a buddhist and went off from her native Scotland to a nunnery run by Tibetan exiles in the foothills of the Himalayas. There she studied the Tibetan language and buddhist philosophy. A few years later she traveled throughout Europe and North America as interpreter for her lama-guru, Kalu Rinpoche. In the course of this intellectual and spiritual relationship the idealistic and unsuspecting convert to Tibetan buddhism experienced a profound shock:

> Subsequently he requested that I become his sexual consort, and take part in secret activities with him, despite the fact that to outsiders he was a very high-ranking yogi-lama of the Kagyu lineage who, as abbot of his own monastery, had taken vows of celibacy. Given that he was one of the oldest lamas in exile at that time, had personally spent 14 years in solitary retreat, and counted amongst his students the highest ranking lamas of Tibet, his own status was unquestioned in the Tibetan community, and his holiness attested to by all.[4]

Campbell points out that the imposed secrecy of her own situation was not unique. She maintains that such secret sexual practices were widespread over the centuries and that unsuspecting Tibetan women immersed in the culture had found it almost impossible not to agree to these "requests." Moreover, the secret role into which these women were drawn "bestowed a certain amount of personal prestige," despite the fact that there was no public acknowledgment of what was going on. Also, "by participating in intimate activities with someone considered in her own and the Buddhist community's eyes to be extremely holy, the woman was able to develop a belief that she too was in some way 'holy' and that the events surrounding her were karmically pre-disposed."[5]

Campbell explains that in her own case "it was plainly emphasized that any indiscretion in maintaining silence over our affair might lead to madness, trouble, *or even death*."[6] To say the least, she was terror-ized. Such fear was also imposed on other consorts of "celibate" lamas.[7]

Emotional and spiritual mutilation is inflicted upon women in this kind of situation:

> The imposition of secrecy therefore, in the Tibetan system, when it occurred solely as a means to protect status, and where it was rein-forced by threats, was a powerful weapon in *keeping women from achieving any kind of integrity in themselves* [italics mine].[8]

Violation of Female *integrity* is pivotal in patriarchal religion's effacement of women, for women whose realization of their own integ-rity has been blocked cannot actualize their deep powers, and unin-tentionally collaborate in their own Self-defeat. My own analysis of the material presented by Campbell is as follows: In the case of Tibetan buddhism, all three components of enticement into secret sexual part-nerships, described above, combine to undermine the integrity of the compromised woman. First, the phony "prestige" allotted to the bam-boozled woman by those who know about her "secret" role but do not openly acknowledge it, while appearing to validate her position, is in fact Self-invalidating because it encourages her complicity in decep-tion. Second, her internalized illusion of "holiness" by association with her "holy" seducer (un)naturally reinforces the doublethink that is al-ready embedded in her thought processes by the enforced deception. Therefore, it is confus-ing and Self-diminishing. Third, the fear which is embedded into the consort of the "celibate" lama in order to prevent disclosure is thought-stopping, speech-stopping, action-stopping. Such stoppage/inhibition of Self-Realization inevitably prevents women from bonding deeply with each other and from creating and transmitting a woman-identified understanding of reality.*

Although there are variations among patriarchal religions, there is also a tedious sameness. It is therefore instructive to consider other aspects of Tibetan buddhism, which, although it may on the surface appear utterly unlike christianity, manifests a woman-effacing syndrome that is startlingly recognizable to those familiar with christian symbols and practices. I have Named this syndrome "male motherhood."[9]

Examining the word *lama*, Campbell remarks that the syllable *la* means "superior," while the syllable *ma* is the word for "mother." Literally, then, a "lama" is a superior mother.[10] Moreover, Chandra Das's *Tibetan-English Dictionary* acknowledges that the literal translation of the word *lama* is "soul mother," or "the all-sustaining mother of the universe."[11] Several lamas confirmed to her that the explanation for this title is that the "lama" is viewed as naming the highest form of motherhood.† She comments that if there were a word that was originally

---

*The similarity of this spiritual corrosion to the corruption of women tokenized by other institutions, most specifically academia, is not hard to detect. First, the phony prestige bestowed upon women for "brain-selling" (Virginia Woolf's word, which appears in *Three Guineas*) and for selling out each other may be a secret that is repressed into almost unconscious realms. It is Self-invalidating. Second, the illusion of academic accomplishment and "success" that is consequent upon "brain prostitution" (again, Woolf's expression in *Three Guineas*) is Self-diminishing, Self-negating. Third, the craven fear of being caught, by others and especially by herSelf, committing acts of adultery of the brain, is ultimately Self-undermining. A woman in this situation cannot bond deeply with other women, because she fails to be Present to herSelf. Having chosen not to Realize Elemental Feminist Genius in herSelf, she may (ill)logically work to block and destroy this in others.

†Such illusions are not dissimilar to the phallic fantasies of christians. When I was writing *Beyond God the Father* a quarter of a century ago I Dis-covered "The Looking Glass Society," in which the priests of the highest of higher religions (christianity) continue the Looking Glass tradition of Mother Adam, the first of history's unmarried pregnant males, their teacher and model: "They devised a sacramental system which functioned magnificently within the sacred House of Mirrors. Graciously, they lifted from

meant to refer to a member of a male priesthood, it would surely have been *lapa*, using the male ending, *pa*, and argues that "the word [*lama*] was in use in Tibet before the hierarchical theocracy of 'lamas,' and referred possibly to the female Tantric priests of ancient India or to the shamanistic practitioners who worshipped the Great Mother in pre-Buddhist times."[12] The carryover of the female term suggests the significance of the Female at an earlier time in Tibet's history.

My interpretation of this information is that a semantic transsexual operation has taken place and that this signifies an actual historical evolution, or rather, degeneration, in the course of which Pa tried to become Ma by draining the energy of the original Ma, robbing her of her power, erasing her history, and assuming her name and identity.[13] In this process women have been and continue to be deceived and diminished. The logical conclusion of the story is the ultimate annihilation of women.

MYTHIC FORESHADOWINGS OF CLONING AND THE ANNIHILATION OF WOMEN: EAST AND WEST

Further light is shed on the widespread male motherhood syndrome by considering the astonishing Tibetan tulku system. *Tulku* is defined as "a child chosen to be enthroned in a position of religious power, in the belief that he (rarely she) is the reincarnation of a lama who has died, or of a divinity."[14] In this system, the lama is his own successor. The tulku is

---

women the onerous power of childbirth, christening it 'baptism.' Thus they brought the lowly material function of birth, incompetently and even grudgingly performed by females, to a higher and more spiritual level. Recognizing the ineptitude of females in performing even the most humble 'feminine' tasks assigned to them by the Divine Plan, the Looking Glass priests raised these functions to the supernatural level in which they alone had competence. Feeding was elevated to become Holy Communion. Washing achieved dignity in Baptism and Penance. ... The Looking Glass priests made it a rule that their members should wear skirts. ... They thus became revered models of spiritual transsexualism." See *Beyond God the Father*, pp. 193–98.

"self-born," a "complete son." The woman who bore the child and sur-
rendered him to the system is absent, her role of giving birth and moth-
ering having been symbolically usurped by the system. The mother is
downgraded to the rank of receptacle for the holy tulku, who on a symbolic level is a clone.[15]

The tulku system, then, is a very explicit enactment of the patriarchal
male dream of excluding (insofar as possible) the need for females. In
western mythology this dream also reveals itself. In Greek myth, the
story of the birth of the god Dionysus is an instructive example. Jane
Harrison points out that "the word Dionysus means not 'son of Zeus'
but rather 'Zeus-Young Man,' i.e., Zeus in his young form."[16] As Robert
Graves explains, when Semele, the mother of Dionysus, was six-months
pregnant, Zeus struck her with thunder and lightning and she was con-
sumed. Hermes saved her son by sewing him up inside Zeus's thigh, to
mature there for three months longer, and in due course of time delivered him.[17] As I wrote in *Gyn/Ecology:*

Thus Dionysus's mother was already dead long before he was born.
Zeus dispenses with the woman and bears his own son. But there is
more to the convoluted plot than this. For some of the myth-masters
held that Semele had been impregnated by drinking a potion prepared by Zeus from the "heart" (probably meaning phallus) of Dionysus, who had pre-existed her. . . . Thus Dionysus is his own father, reborn and self-generated. Since he (Zeus–Young Man) is identified
with Zeus who bore him, he is also his own mother. Thus Semele can
be seen as epitomizing the patriarchal ideal of mother as mere vessel.
Moreover, the apparently contradictory aspects of Dionysus—his self-
fathering and his femininity—coincide. In the "light" of these elements of the Dionysian myth we can well be suspicious of male fasci-
nation with the all too feminine Dionysus, for his mythic presence
foreshadows attempts to eliminate women altogether.[18]

Such patriarchal mythic foreshadowing of the elimination of women
is carried over into christianity:

To anyone aware of the meaning of Christ ("the Word incarnate") in christian myth, the parallel [with Dionysus] is inescapable. Christ is believed by christians to be the incarnation of the "Second Person of the Trinity," and thus consubstantial with the father. Therefore, Christ, too, pre-existed himself and was simply a later manifestation of "Zeus (Father)–Young Man."[19]

The plot further unfolds: Enter Mary, the Archaic Goddess who was taken over, made over, and diminished by christianity for that religion's own patriarchal purposes.

In order to become the Goddess, the male god, manifested in Christ, had to be reborn. This theme was of course present in the story of Dionysus, who pre-existed himself and was reborn from the thigh of Zeus. However, this was a cruder story than that of Christ, who did not even require a paternal thigh from which to be reborn, and whose mother (Mary), unlike Semele, did not need to drink a potion containing his "heart." In the christian myth, the second person of the eternal trinity pre-existed his own incarnation as Christ. The holy ghost, the third person, who was consubstantial with him, impregnated Mary spiritually. So spiritual was the whole affair that Mary remained a virgin, according to christian theologians, before, during, and after his birth.[20]

Helen Diner has pointed out that the christian myth of the Virgin Birth of Christ is actually the opposite of real parthenogenesis, for in this myth Mary does nothing, whereas in parthenogenesis the female accomplishes everything herself. She writes:

Thus the Virgin, in the extreme spiritual religion called Christianity, means only the vessel waiting in purity for the bearing of the Savior.[21]

It cannot be stressed strongly enough that myths function as self-fulfilling prophecies. It is clear that patriarchal males are attempting to act out the myth of the pre-existing divine male giving birth to himself, while simultaneously working to eliminate Divine Female Creative and Procreative Power. The recent developments in cloning coupled with

the new reproductive technologies, which are leaping toward their catastrophic conclusions as the twentieth century comes to an end, are
manifestations of this megadestructive pattern.*

Dionysus has been glorified as "boundary violator" who by his femininity breaks down cognitive boundaries in women, driving them
mad.[22] This strategy has had some success through the invention of
what Janice G. Raymond has Named and analyzed as "The Transsexual
Empire."[23] The invention of "Gender Studies" has been another Dionysian pseudotriumph over Feminist clarity. Postmodern theory also
has been a massive Dionysian plot to destroy Feminist knowing of
reality.

Physical boundary violation has always been familiar to women under patriarchy. Sexual molestation, rape, and battering of women are
commonly discussed. But recently Dionysus has violated the boundaries of women and nature with insidious force. Jeremy Rifkin has
written:

> The new gene-splicing and cell-fusion techniques allow scientists to
> cross virtually all biological boundaries. Species are no longer viewed
> in organismic terms as indivisible entities, but more as mainframes
> containing programmed genetic cassettes that can be reedited, rese-
> quenced, and recombined by proper manipulation in the laboratory.[24]

As Janice Raymond and others have shown, the new reproductive technologists, continuing the medical violation of women that came into
force with the invention of gynecology in the nineteenth century, and
employing the new methods of genetic engineering, increase their

---

*Anne Dellenbaugh has described important associations between parthenogenesis
and cloning. She points out that a deliberate effort is being made to remove creativity
from women and reestablish it in the realm of male domination and control. Thus the
christian version of the "Virgin Birth" is a link between Primordial Mythic Parthenogenesis and technological attempts to establish the "father" as the one "true parent"
through cloning. See "She Who Is and Is Not Yet: An Essay on Parthenogenesis," *Trivia:
A Journal of Ideas*, Fall 1982, pp. 43–63.

probing, manipulation, and experimentation on women while sending out the seductive message that they are bestowing a great gift upon "infertile" women.[25]

At this terrible time it is important to pay attention to similarities between eastern and western patriarchal myths and behaviors such as I have described in order to reinforce women's awareness of our universal history of oppression and to reawaken Memory of our Common Heritage of an Archaic Past.

For this analysis of mythic foreshadowing of cloning and the annihilation of women I have chosen to focus not only on western myth but also on Tibetan buddhism, in part because the women-erasing intent of the latter is so startlingly manifested in its imposed secret sexual arrangements and its tulku system. Another reason is that its extraordinary expansion in recent decades can contribute to the erasure of women in the western patriarchal imagination.

Since the Chinese invasion of Tibet in the 1950s Tibetans in exile have spread their religious tradition across the world. They have established hundreds of *dharma* centers around the globe, and their assets have accumulated to billions of dollars. As a result of this geographic shift, their previously hidden culture has been dislodged from the isolated area of Tibet and at least indirectly has affected millions of westerners as well as inhabitants of many developing countries in Asia. This relatively new geographic proximity of Tibetan buddhism presents an incentive to Canny Women in the west to examine this tradition. It can challenge us to reinforce and widen our own Sense of our Archaic Past as well as sharpen our understanding of the means by which women's history has been distorted and covered over. In this sense the Tibetan arrival "in the neighborhood" is important for the enhancement of our Feminist consciousness.

The magnificence and grandeur of the Tibetan landscape—even when experienced only "secondhand" (for example, through conversations, books, or films)—has evoked in westerners nostalgia for something far away and yet recognized and remembered. For Wild Women it is crucial not to stop short when such Be-Longing is experienced. For us, the Quintessential "something" to be Re-membered is an Archaic Time and Space of Female Elemental Power of Presence.

The Space was in many areas of the world. The poignancy of the images of Tibet's beauty can sharpen our sense of Grief and Rage for all that patriarchy has robbed and continues to rob from women. In the midst of such Elemental splendor the beauty of Elemental/Female Integrity has been negated by a religious system which is even now the object of uncritical adulation, as it spreads its misogynist con-fusion throughout an already misogynist world.

Glimpses of an Archaic Past, implying an Archaic Future, are Moments of awareness of the Background, sometimes seen through the windows of patriarchal religion's most revealing reversals. Roman catholicism, for example, masks and distorts the Background, while sometimes also unintentionally revealing that Realm of Wild Reality—through its rich traditions, its haunting music, its majestic cathedrals, its shrines to Goddess (deceptively guised as Mary, the "Mother of God"). It works its con-fusing and mystifying magic by means of its sacramental system, especially the Eucharist—which is its colossal but not entirely successful attempt to hide the Body and Blood, Soul and Divinity of Goddess—the Quintessential *Female* symbol of the integrity, harmony, vitality, and luminous splendor of the Universe.*

---

*As Robin Morgan has written:

> What have they dared,
> sucking at man's wounds for wine,
> celebrating his flesh as food?
> Whose thirst has been slaked by his vampire liquor,
> whose hunger answered by his ghostly bread?
> *Who have they dared to hang on that spine instead*
> *and then deny, across millennia?*
> *Whose is the only body which incarnates creation everlasting?*

Robin Morgan, from "The Network of the Imaginary Mother," in *The Lady of the Beasts*. Originally published by Random House in 1975. Reprinted in Robin Morgan, *Upstairs in the Garden: New and Selected Poems* (New York: W. W. Norton, 1990). Printed here with permission of the author.

Wild Women can glimpse through the shoddiness and horror of fore-ground reversal religion to the magnificence of our own Heritage that was robbed from us. Reversal religion tries to vampirize that boundless Source of vitality, the Background, tricking women into remaining "hooked" by doling out starvation rations from the richness that is right-fully ours. Hooked women have pseudo-options. They can spend their energies endlessly struggling for change within a particular patriarchal religion, or they can switch from one religious death-trap to another— which is comparable to changing from one bad hospital (school, insur-ance company, etc.) to another.

Or . . . we can Break Out. In this case, we will break the phallocentric Taboo against Touching our own Elemental powers. Speaking and Seeking for ourSelves, we can acquire the Courage to See and Touch the Background without the "aid" of phallocratic religion's blindfolds.

Some Weird Women do choose to use symbols that have been taken over by patriarchal religion. The point to keep in mind is that all patriar-chal symbols have a way of seductively disguising the woman-erasing/Goddess-erasing messages they convey. Sarasvati, hindu goddess of elo-quence, for example, might appear attractive to one who struggles to ar-ticulate her longing for Elemental connectedness. But the problems as-sociated with this symbol are not hard to find. The following passage is revealing:

> Inventor of all the arts and sciences, patron of all intellectual en-deavors, Sarasvati is the very prototype of the female artist. She in-vented writing so that the songs she inspired could be recorded; she created music so that the elegance of her being could be praised. In her identity as Vach, goddess of speech, she caused all words to come into being, *including all religious writings* [italics mine].[26]

This description may seem inspiring, but the concluding sentence dis-plays con-fusion. Shrewd Shrews are not particularly enamored of "all religious writings." All patriarchal religion is, by definition, woman-hating, and is built on reversals and lies so that it can serve its purpose of legitimating patriarchy. Canny Women sense something suspicious about the praise doled out to Sarasvati in hindu religious tradition. Would a great Goddess, a symbol of strong, autonomous female divine power, cause misogynist propaganda to come into being? We conclude that Sarasvati, like so many other goddess-symbols, is a tamed derivative of the Original Goddess whose image has been distorted and used by the patriarchs to legitimate their pronouncements. *

It is commonly believed in hinduism that Brahma the creator needs Sarasvati for the world to come into being.[27] In fact, every hindu god must have a *Shakti,* or enlivening female force. It does not take an extraordinarily complex work of decoding to notice that in such religious myth the draining of female energy by the gods is essential for their godly "creativity." Such myths both reveal and subtly justify the behavior of those gurus who sap the psychic and physical energy of their female disciples, thereby becoming "pure" and "spiritually powerful" masters who are revered by their followers. Some masters/gurus, using miasmic charisma as well as psychological intimidation, coerce female disciples into lengthy abusive relationships. Wild Women can act to prevent such deception by Naming the setup and encouraging others to stay away from spiritual lechers. Searchers set an example by avoiding gurus of all kinds and proclaiming the need to escape the unhealthful realm of gurudom.

Elemental Women sometimes independently choose to invoke an-

---

*Barbara G.Walker has written:

Male writers through the centuries broke the Goddess figure down into innumerable "goddesses," using different titles or names she received from different peoples at different times. If such a system had been applied to the usual concept of God, there would now be a multitude of separate "gods." . . . Perhaps one should take more seriously the ancients' often-repeated opinion that their Goddess had a thousand names. Every female divinity in the present Encyclopedia may be correctly regarded as only another aspect of a core concept. . . .

See *The Woman's Encyclopedia of Myths and Secrets* (San Francisco: Harper and Row, 1983), p. 346.

cient Goddess Names, when these evoke Deep Memories and elicit real resonance for us. Re-membering our own Archaic heritage makes it possible for us to Hear these Names in our own Original context. Crones Re-Call the Sarasvati behind the tamed and possessed "Sarasvati," as well as the Isis behind "Isis," and the Athena behind "Athena." Such Naming is reclaiming what has been stolen from women. By Be-Speaking the stolen names Wicked Women Erase the erasers' lies. Our Elemental sounding Be-Stirs waves of re-cognition. The task that remains is Spelling it all out. And this we can do because we are coming into our own Element.

THE FIFTH ELEMENT

Raging Women, propelled and summoned by the Wrath of Nemesis, come Storming into our own Element—our heritage of creative Genius, which has been stolen and hidden from us, silenced in us.

Men have always mourned the massacre of men's genius, represented by the destruction of books. In his *Areopagitica*, for example, John Milton argued for the liberty of unlicensed printing. In a passage that must be thought provoking to Searchers, Milton wrote:

> [A]s good almost kill a man as kill a good book: who kills a man kills a reasonable creature, God's image; but he who destroys a good book, kills reason itself, kills the image of God, as it were, in the eye. Many a man lives a burden to the earth; but a good book is the precious life-blood of a master spirit, embalmed and treasured up on purpose to a life beyond life. . . . We should be wary, therefore, what persecution we raise against the living labors of public men, how we spill that seasoned life of man preserved and stored up in books; since we see a kind of homicide may be thus committed, sometimes a martyrdom; and if it extends to the whole impression, a kind of massacre, whereof the execution ends not in the slaying of an elemental life, but strikes at that ethereal and fifth essence, the breath of reason itself, [and] slays an immortality rather than a life.[28]

It can be an A-mazing experience for Searchers to attempt a comparison between the alleged spilling of "that seasoned life of man preserved and stored up in books" and the martyrdom and massacre of women's minds/souls. In reality, there can be no comparison between the piddling offenses of men against men and the unspeakable erasure of women's creativity, as represented in women's books. Throughout its ages/stages patriarchy has struck at the Ethereal and Fifth Essence. The rulers of snooldom have stifled our Creative Genius, our breath/ breadth of reason itself, attempting to slay our immortality as well as our physical lives.

Milton could express outrage over the destruction of books—all or most of them presumably written by men. How Utterly Unmeasurable, then, is the Rage of Crones, who See multiple Outrages against women, which of course are unrecognized by the patriarchal establishment. Books by women are being destroyed in the contemporary massacre/ bookburning by megalithic/monolithic publishers and booksellers. In an astonishingly revealing issue of *The Nation*, Mark Crispin Miller wrote:

> ... the giants [megabookstores] have also shrunk the culture actively—by dumping, or red-lighting, any book that offers revelations irksome to themselves.[29]

And *what* could be more irksome than books by women who are Radical Feminists? Given the prevailing backlash—we have reason to suspect that books by Feminists are *especially* likely to disappear, not only from publishers' catalogs and from bookstores, but also from libraries.[30] "Accidentally," of course. But that is only the tip of the unacknowledged iceberg.

To understand more deeply, we need only recall that for thousands of years women all over the world have been prevented from writing books and even from learning to read. And when women have read books, for the most part these have been authored by men. When books written by women have been published, their authors have usually been numbed into silence about the taboo subject of the atrocities of patriarchy. When Female-authored books, particularly Feminist books, have been successful in their time, they have more often than not been erased from history. Elemental Genius—most specifically, Elemental Feminist Genius—has been massacred, over and over and over.

The reason is simple. Deviant Women with Big Ideas—especially Radical Feminists—are a threat to jock-ocracy. Therefore Websters are censored. Our Webs of communication/information/inspiration are broken again and again in the foreground, and each generation must Re-Weave as best we can.

The X-Factor/Faculty has been slain and slain again. Yet it refuses to die. Why? Because without it there would be no spiritual life on Earth. And Spirit demands to Live.

Wild Women, whose immortality—our Heritage—has been targeted for destruction, Rage at the would-be perpetrators of this massacre. Our Raging lights the Fires of Impassioned Knowing and hence brings us Here, to the Fifth Element/the "Fifth Province" of our minds, where we are in Touch with Elemental Genius, which informs all the Elements.

Our Rage enables us to recognize the reality which is hidden by the foreground. It triggers our Breakthrough to seemingly esoteric, yet utterly available knowledge. It is useful to read the following passage from Alfred North Whitehead:

> When you are criticizing the philosophy of an epoch, do not chiefly direct your attention to those intellectual positions which its exponents feel it necessary explicitly to defend. There will be some fundamental assumptions which adherents of all the various systems unconsciously presuppose. Such assumptions appear so obvious that people do not know what they are assuming because no other way of putting things has ever occurred to them.[31]

Whitehead's passage itself contains such an assumption, which is masked by the pseudogeneric term *people*. He assumes that there is no class of "people" (no cognitive minority) who know about the prevailing assumptions, which, as Whitehead fails to acknowledge, are the assumptions of patriarchy. Many women have known and transmitted insightful analyses about these assumptions. However, such analyses, brilliantly developed in books and articles by women, have repeatedly been erased.[32]

Continuing to expose the prevailing assumptions and to pursue their implications is both manifestation and expression of Elemental Feminist Genius. The purpose of the backlash against Feminism is to stop Fiercely Focused Women from unveiling the lies. Such women are dangerous! Touching the Fifth Element, Truthsayers are alive with the Creative Transformative Power of Nemesis!

Recalling that the Fifth Element traditionally is known as Ether, Searchers note that Ether has been called the ground or field from which the other Elements arise or "the one river from which the other four rivers arise."[33] Moreover, its chakra center is said to be located at the throat and the neck. The Ether center, then, is a place of interconnection and communication.[34] In addition, Ether is associated with the sense of hearing. This refers not just to hearing external sound, but also to a deep sense of knowing.[35]

It is helpful to return once more to the idea of the mystical Fifth Province of Ireland, called Mide. Mide has been described as the "expanding centre" of Ireland. As Michael Dames has written: "In ancient Ireland, Mide was 'Here' to everyone."[36] Of course, this could appear to be problematic:

> The Irish word for province, *cóiced*, also means a fifth; yet the ancient and continual division of the island into the *four* provinces of Ulster, Munster, Leinster and Connacht seems to leave no room for a fifth part.[37]

Dames refers to Mide as "territorially elusive, yet vital to the cohesion of the whole sacred array" of provinces. There is, then, a four-plus-one pattern. Moreover: "As a national 'head and brain,' it [Mide] coordinated intelligences from the other provinces."[38]

The likeness of Mide to the Fifth Element is striking. The relation of Mide to the four provinces as "Fifth Province" is analogous to the relation of Ether to the other four Elements. The role of Mide as "head and brain" or "notional center" coordinating intelligences from the other provinces is comparable to the role of Ether as coordinating and en-Spiriting the other Elements.

Knowing the central place attributed to Ether in some traditions, Searchers are intrigued to read that it "governs the emotions in general and combines with the other elements to create the various qualities of emotion" and that "it governs the specific emotion of grief."[39]

Women Voyaging in The Fifth Spiral Galaxy are all too familiar with the Passion of Grief. We grieve for our Foresisters and our contemporary Sisters who seem to be lost in the diaspora over time and space. We grieve for those burned alive, in the European witchcraze, for example, or in the rite of Indian widow-burning (*suttee*), and for those whose books were burned even before they ever had a chance to write them. We grieve for our Sisters who have been raped, sexually abused and harassed, beaten, driven insane, mutilated, murdered.

We grieve for our Sisters the Animals who have been tortured in laboratories, hunted down, destroyed by agribusiness. We grieve for our Sisters the Trees who have been slaughtered and for our Sisters the Seas, the Lakes, the Rivers that have been polluted. We grieve for our Sister the Air that has been filled with poisons and for our Sister the Sun that has been turned against us. We grieve for our Sister the Earth, who will survive the assaults of the patriarchs long after they have shriveled into oblivion.

Our Grief is not passive. We do not consume our Time in depression. Our Grief combines with Rage. Our Wailing *is* our Railing.

Knowing that Sound is a Potent Force, we Sound Out our Naming. We Name. We Blame. We do not settle for sitting in ashrams chanting an OM. Preferring to OM as we Roam, we Wander the Galaxies, especially the Fifth, Re-Claiming our Home.[40]

Be-Speaking is Speaking into Be-ing. With Words we Concrete

New Vortices of Force. By Naming what we know, we bring forth New Be-ing. We Are more and more Here . . . But where is Here?

THE FIFTH DIRECTION

Chinese and Toltec astronomy both divide the world into five directions, with the center as the fifth.[41] It is increasingly clear to Voyagers that our Sense of Direction in The Fifth Spiral Galaxy guides us to our Center. Our Dis-covering of Expanding Here is uncovering Elemental Realities that have been hidden by frauds, and finding the treasures of women's Memory/Knowledge/History that have been buried by the grave diggers of patriarchal re-search. The Focus/Center/Core of our Search is Unforgetting these treasures—Righteously Plundering them and making them accessible to women.

On the foreground level, it might appear that we are not going anywhere. In fact, from a Background perspective Voyaging women are Moving profoundly into our Core/Center—into participation in *Powers of Be-ing*, that is, Be-ing the Verb, which can be understood in multiple and diverse manifestations, e.g., Knowing, Creating, Loving—and through diverse Metaphors.[42]

Wild Women are Centering, Balancing, Focusing, regaining our Original Integrity, which appeared to be shattered in the state of diaspora. We are refinding our Elemental connectedness, which opens the possibility of expansion.

As Voyagers become centered, we become more and more like trees, spreading our branches over vast territory, and spreading our roots, which intertwine with those of other Elemental creatures. Like migrating birds Voyagers are Magnetized to our home. Deep Memories are awakened.

In the Center, which is Here, Seers Sense a falling away of the fragmentation inflicted under patriarchy. At the same time, we blast away the con-fusion that is intended to confound us. This process is in accord with the nature of Ether (Akasha), whose qualities include conjunction

and disjunction. That is, we bring together—conjoin—Elemental realities that have been artificially split off, and we distinguish and separate—disjoin—the ideas, images, and realities that the mind muddiers
of the media have deceptively blended/combined. Our minds/imagina-
tions are clarified.

Wise Women understand ever more deeply the magnitude of the
mind-deadening atrocities inflicted by sadosociety. Such understanding
can be enhanced by contemplation of an ancient Metamysterious Image—the Sphinx.

THE SPHINX

Just as Be-Speaking certain Words and arrangements of Words has tremendous power, so also Re-membering and decoding certain myths
and images can conjure vortices of force. In this process ancient energy
forms are reclaimed by Wise Women. The Greco-Egyptian Sphinx is an
embodiment of such energy forms.

Of the Sphinx, Barbara G. Walker writes:

> It is rarely pointed out that the classical tragedy of King Oedipus was
> brought about by the curse of the Goddess in her Sphinx form, a deri-
> vation of Egyptian Hathor as the lioness-destroyer. Trying to overturn
> the matriarchy in Thebes and preserve himself as permanent king,
> Oedipus threw the sacred statue of the Sphinx off a cliff and broke it.
> He defied the Goddess by guessing her famous riddle. The Sphinx
> had her revenge. Some said Oedipus was not only blinded but also
> slain in the Goddess's sacred grove by her avenging Furies.[43]

There are clues in this passage. It is significant that in order to triumph
over the matriarchy Oedipus threw the sacred statue of the Sphinx off a
cliff and broke it. The breaking of the statue was an ominous, blasphe-
mous act. It was a foreshadowing of the shattering, scattering, splinter-
ing of women and nature that was to come. It was an omen of diaspora.[44]
Crones can See the depth of the horrible intent when we recall that the

Sphinx was typically represented as a Monster having the body of a lioness, wings, and the head and bust of a woman. In the symbol of the Sphinx, the body of the lioness represents the profound connection of Elemental Women with animals. Her Wings suggest our connection with birds, and especially with divinity.[45] Hence, the smashing of her statue by Oedipus was a symbolic enactment of patriarchal breaking of women's Elemental Integrity and Connections. The Sphinx is Roaring to us that we must reclaim this Integrity and these Connections.

Seers See the reductionist deception in patriarchal versions of the myth, which drone about the Sphinx's inane "riddle," guessed by that bright fellow Oedipus.[46] The riddle can be recognized as a manmade mask for the truly Metamysterious nature and message of the Sphinx.*

Having broken through the fathers' façades, Furies Announce: "The Sphinx will have her revenge." When we decode the tale of Oedipus guessing the riddle of the Sphinx, we begin to grasp the intent behind all such propaganda, that is, to hide Metamystery. Avenging Furies work ever harder to expose the prevailing assumptions and lies.

The Sphinx is often described as a monster. The word *monster* is said to be derived from the Latin verb *monere*, meaning "to remind, warn," and akin to the Greek *mnasthai*, meaning "to remember"(*Webster's*). The Sphinx is indeed a Monster. She reminds us of the patriarchal takeover and its reign of deception. She warns of its poisonous reversals and mind-mutilating made-over myths. She encourages us to Re-member our own Monstrous Archaic Heritage.

Patriarchal authors stop short in their analyses of the Sphinx. For example, J. E. Cirlot writes:

> Being the supreme embodiment of the enigma, the sphinx keeps watch over an ultimate meaning which must remain for ever beyond the understanding of man. . . . It is, of course, a symbol which unites, in the midst of the heterogeneity of existence, the four Elements . . .

---

*According to *Wickedary*, *Metamystery* means "depths/surfaces that are hidden by man's mysteries/misteries; Wonders of Wild Reality that are behind/beyond the fathers'

with the quintessence or the spirit (signified by the human part of the figure).[47]

As history demonstrates, the Sphinx indeed keeps watch over an ultimate meaning which remains forever beyond the understanding of patriarchal authorities. Cirlot interprets the Sphinx as embodying/manifesting the unity of the four Elements with Quintessence, which he equates with spirit. I propose a different interpretation: I suggest that the Sphinx manifests the unified integrity of all Five Elements. The function of the Fifth Element—Ether—represented by the head and bust of a woman—is to unify the other Four Elements. The unifying of all Five Elements then opens the possibility of conscious participation in Quintessence, which is Universal and Cosmic Harmony that transcends and includes this integrity of the Five Elements. It is Integrity beyond the integrity represented by Ether. It is the music of the spheres.

My interpretation of the Sphinx, then, is that she is a symbolic message, or lesson, summoning us to participation in the Transtemporal and Trans-spatial Presence of all creation. She invites us to Realize expanding Integrity, Harmony, and Splendor of form/forms across Time and Space.

Soothsayers Announce that the Sphinx can inspire our Quest for Elemental and Cosmic connectedness. The Sphinx invites us to Dis-cover the Quintessential and therefore Unifying nature of Goddess under her many Names. The Egyptian Lioness-Goddess, Hathor, for example, is clearly associated with the Sphinx, and therefore with Quintessence. And Isis superlatively manifests Quintessence.[48]

There can be no question that Nemesis, too, is Quintessential. In union/unity with her Sister/Self, the Sphinx, she cries out to Metamorphosing Women to Realize our Sphinxlike Selves, our Cosmic interconnectedness, and thereby transform the world.

---

façades; ever Unfolding reality glimpsed by Seers and announced by Be-Speakers; the Radiant Integrity of Be-ing." See pp. 81–82.

Cosmic Comments and Conversations
IN 2048 BE CONCERNING
CHAPTER FOUR

....

by Anonyma

I WAS RELAXING *after an intense discussion with my friend Anowa, when I suddenly realized that it was Time for me to Conjure Mary and talk about Chapter Four. Anowa and I had been ruminating about the patriarchal state of deception and trying to imagine how hard it must have been for women to be constantly struggling to unravel the lies— especially the reversals—that were all-pervasive throughout that era. The very thought of that struggle was exhausting and unnerving. Anowa decided to go for a walk by herself and mull it over.*

I hurried over to Kate's garden to announce my intention to Conjure Mary. But Kate had already Sensed what was about to happen and was arranging a jug of cider and mugs on the table.

It was a glorious fall day, and I anticipated that our visitor would enjoy sitting outside and strolling around. As it turned out, "enjoy" was too mild a word to describe her reaction.

Mary came sauntering into the garden, displaying greater exuberance than she had shown previously. After hugging us both she breathed in the sweet aromatic air with a look of bliss. Walking directly to the section where herbs had been planted, she sniffed in ecstasy. Kate had planted lavender, yarrow, mint, oregano, and thyme, and these all seemed to be vying with each other for the attention of eager noses. "What fragrance!" she exclaimed. "It's like coming home, but it's a thousand times more real, more home than 'home.'"

Kate and I were drawn into her mood. We both knew that "back then" in 1998 she lived in a world of sensory deprivation, in which the air was pol-

luted and fragrances and colors were muted. And this was all the worse because most people seemed not to recognize the tragedy. Here Now, on Lost and Found Continent, our senses are alive.

We strolled together down the paths of the garden. When we came to the little brook that runs beside one of the paths we all threw ourselves on the grass and gulped the delightful fresh water. "We can actually drink the water!" Mary gasped. "We don't have to be afraid that it's poisoned! And it tastes like nectar!"

Kate interrupted her with a laugh. "Mary, it just tastes like real water!"

"Right!" responded our guest. "It tastes like Super Natural water." With that remark she plunged her head down to the brook again and drank for such a long time that I was alarmed. Just as I was thinking of grabbing her feet and dragging her away she pulled her head up and flopped on the grass, smiling with contentment.

We decided to begin our discussion right there, as we sat on the grass. "My friends and I have been discussing the problem of how you and other Hags survived in the state of deception," I began. "We were wondering how you managed to sustain a vigorous intellectual life, when so much energy was drained by the necessity of reversing reversals and erasing erasures and simply surviving in such a hostile environment."

Mary was joyously feeling and smelling the grass and clover. I could sense her reluctance at being dragged back into speaking about that dismal period, and was about to suggest that we go for a walk, but she quickly rallied to the task. Inhaling deeply she spoke patiently. "At first we managed to take the massive system of deception as an intellectual challenge. A tremendous amount of Gynergy went into the undoublethinking process. But patriarchal 'education' denied young women access to the knowledge we had already uncovered. So we had to repeat the process over and over for each new generation. That was sometimes draining. Like other Bitches, I sometimes became impatient. I was starving for intellectual stimulation and communication."

"We hope you can find plenty of that Here," Kate said. "I haven't entirely forgotten that state of intellectual oppression. When I remember that suffering, combined with the all-pervasive sensory deprivation, I'm amazed that some of us Wild Women managed to stay alive. It was especially hard when so many around us had been dulled into not noticing what they were missing."

Somewhat hesitantly I interrupted. "So far only one other woman besides Kate knows about our visits. Her name is Anowa, and she's deeply interested in the subjects you discuss in Chapter Four. She and I both were born here in 2018 BE, and we've played, studied, and argued with each other ever since then. She's especially good at weaving connections among apparently unrelated phenomena. I was hoping you two could meet, but of course it's up to you."

"Another Wild Woman can add another dimension to our discussion. So why not?" Mary answered. "I'd be happy to meet your friend. I seem to remember a play called Anowa. Is your friend by any chance Named after the African mythic ancestress whose daughters are the women of Africa?"*

"She sure is!" I replied. "Anowa chose her name, of course. I'll run and get her." Jumping up and starting to run, I called over my shoulder, "We'll be right back!"

We were slightly delayed on our return because Anowa insisted on bringing her notebook and pen, which she had to go find in her study. When we arrived Kate and Mary were engaged in an animated discussion. Not wishing to interrupt them, we sat a few feet away, obviously eavesdropping.

Kate was telling Mary about her trip to Found Continent in 2018 BE. She had already explained that she made the voyage with her friend Sophie, who is Anowa's mother, together with my grandmother, Johanna, and several other Cronies. Kate was in the process of comparing that Original Voyage with the Time/Space traveling adventure that the three of us experienced recently when we went to Fribourg.

"Both trips involved traveling in Tidal Time as well as Intergalactic

---

*A play called Anowa, based on an old Ghanaian legend, was written by Ama Ata Aidoo and published, together with another play, in a book entitled The Dilemma of a Ghost and Anowa (Essex, England: Longman Group U. K. Ltd., 1965, 1970, 1985). It was part of a series of books called Longman African Classics. We have a copy in our Archives.

Spatial movement," said Kate. "Both were fueled by Desperation. The Original Voyage of Anonyma women to Lost and Found Continent was inspired in part by Desperation to get out of the state of despair. Essentially, though, it was a convergence of Desperate Acts catalyzed by Hope. Our Fribourg adventure was triggered by a new Desperation. As you know, there was a surging of the X-Factor among the three of us. We were eager for something more. We wanted to expand our experience of Freedom to Create."

Mary noticed that we had arrived. "Hello, Anowa!" she called over. "Why don't you two come over and join the party?"

Since we both were too impatient to bother with the formality of introductions, we moved closer, plopped ourselves on the grass, and began asking questions. Anowa's eyes were alive with excitement and anticipation. Looking directly at Mary, she jumped into the conversation. "I'm really absorbed in attempting to understand the state of deception that you name in your books. I'm trying to imagine how all-pervasive it was. And now, after eavesdropping while you and Kate were talking about the X-Factor and Freedom to Create, I'm eager to explore the connections. I'm wondering how the patriarchal omnipresence of lies inhibited the emergence of the X-Factor. I understand this in a general way, but I'd like to know more about your experience, Mary, especially when you were writing Quintessence. The atmosphere then must have been deadly."

"Here's one experience I vividly recall that may be suggestive," Mary said. "I remember going out one evening in 1997 to meet my friend Abbie after she finished a book signing in one of those monster bookstores situated in a shopping mall. We went for an evening snack in a 'chain' restaurant that was also in the mall. After we left the restaurant we came upon a locked doorway over which hung a darkened sign that said 'Mall Entrance.' (It looked a bit like 'Hell Entrance.') Peering in, we saw an empty, bleak, filthy passageway that appeared to be endlessly leading nowhere. As we stared through the dismal door we experienced a shared feeling of horror. Abbie commented: 'This is our time.' Among other things, the hideous 'entrance' and passageway to nothing represented the pervasive foreground meaninglessness of 'our time.' It conveyed a sense of the massive disintegration and emptiness of the state of deception."

Kate nodded in understanding. She commented: "If it was anything like the 'malls' I remember, I imagine that scene of horror presented an apparent contrast to the glittering lights and stacks of books in the megabookstore where you had met your friend. But your seeing the 'Mall Entrance' afterward was really an extension of the same experience. It was all about what you have called 'presence of absence' that you described in Pure Lust—*the expansion of emptiness that fills the mind and makes the victim absent to herself. Am I right?"*

"Yes, right you are, Kate," said Mary. "It was one more revelation of what that old misogynist Milton correctly called 'a kind of massacre' which 'strikes at that ethereal and fifth essence, the breath of reason itself, and slays an immortality rather than a life.' That complex experience happened only a short time after I had learned that three of my own books had been put out of print, as had many other Feminist books. While my friend was signing I found out more from a clerk at the information desk about specific targets of a current form of that massacre. During our extended conversation this woman informed me of scary details about the rapid disappearance of Feminist books and those of her own African American heritage." Turning to Anowa, Mary added: "So you see, this was one tactic used by snuffers and snudges in their attempt to snuff out the X-Factor." Mary took another deep breath of fresh air.

Kate commented: "I remember seeing an article in which you quoted a bore-ocrat who told you that the reason your books were not in the publisher's catalog was 'they just didn't sell.' When you asked how they could possibly sell if they were not advertised and were not in the catalog he responded in all seriousness: 'It's pure science, Mary.' I don't know how you kept your sanity in the face of such malignant idiocy, Mary!"

"Well, she wrote that Spirit refuses to die," I said.

"I've always believed that, Annie," Mary replied. "But I am trying to respond honestly to Anowa's question. It wasn't always easy. She's right that the atmosphere was lethal. Desperate Acts of Leaping were absolutely necessary. One reason I am Here with you is to tell you how it was."

"And we're Here to tell you that you Battle Axes won!" I said.

"I think it's time to open this jug of cider and celebrate our Victory,"

said Kate. With that comment she filled mugs for the four of us. As usual we toasted all Sister Survivors.

"Do you want me to bring specific messages back from you to Hags who refused to sell out in the moronizing 'millennial time'?" Mary asked.

"Please reassure them that they have our gratitude and respect," I said. "We wouldn't have arrived Here without them. And in fact we can't be Here without them, because their lives are interwined with ours. Wherever/whenever we are, they are also Here."

Anowa spoke next. "It's hard for those of us who were lucky enough to have been born on Found Continent to imagine living in a time of perpetual reversals and erasures of deep truths. But please let them know that in some way we are with them through it all."

"Please tell them that I remember the late 1990s only too well," added Kate. "So they have my deepest empathy. For me, one of the most frustrating manifestations of the state of deception during that period was the 'been there, done that' attitude that prevailed. When I was a student, if anyone tried to explain patriarchy and its horrors, she would frequently be interrupted not only by direct denial of this reality, but by statements to the effect that the subject was passé—that nothing more needed to be said or done about that 'old stuff.'"

"And this was in a time when Biggest Lies were as Big as Lies can get," said Mary. "Millions who followed 'The Trial of the Century' were stunned when they heard that the man who they were convinced stalked, battered, mutilated, and stabbed to death Nicole Brown Simpson was 'not guilty.' And he got custody of the children. The press found it titillating that one of the proposed potential means of income for this celebrity whom they believed to be the slasher/killer of his wife would be the invention and sale of 'O. J. Simpson cutlery.' And he could 'write a book.' Few mentioned that the acts attributed to Simpson were typical of batterers and woman-killers all over the United States and everywhere in the world. His 'victory,' of course, was in large measure made possible by the fact that he was rich and therefore could hire the most expensive, conniving lawyers and get away with anything. And the media somehow managed to make it acceptable."

"How disgusting!" said Anowa. "How did women escape from such massive physical and mental battering?"

"Some women sought safety wherever they thought they could find it," Kate replied softly. "Fundamentalism was one 'solution.'"

"And that brings us around to the principle that everything is connected with everything else," said Anowa. "Kate's observation about women seeking safety made me think about the section in Chapter Four on problems with patriarchal spirituality, which, of course, appeared to offer some security. It's been hard for me to understand how so many women at that time, including Feminists, were willing to hand over their autonomy—their minds, and in some cases their bodies—to gurus of various religions. This may seem naive, but I would have thought that their experience of christianity and escaping its grasp would have made women able to resist the influence of 'spiritual masters.' But learning that this was a time of grotesque flourishing and flaunting of Biggest Lies helps me to see it in context."

"It's true that in the context of the state of deception, every atrocity was connected with every other atrocity," Mary said. "But women whose minds were battered by deception often could not make the connections. In fact, they sometimes tended to particularize, to see all manifestations of the same syndrome as discrete and unrelated. For example, some might unquestioningly believe that an ashram could serve as a refuge where 'bliss' could be attained through subjection to a guru who was perceived by all to be holy. And even if the guru was raping a number of his female followers and amassing millions of dollars while supposedly living a 'simple' life—as happened in a few notorious cases—this would not be immediately visible in a closed community that was submerged in a state of mass hypnosis. Of course I'm not saying that no women benefited from studying some of the techniques, especially meditation and deep breathing methods, that were taught within the context of eastern religions, for example, in ashrams and in buddhist centers. But the context left something to be desired."

"Yeah, like autonomous Female power and action," said Kate. Turning to Anowa, she continued: "In spite of everything, Anowa, I can assure you that even during those bad times women's rage and grief were seething under *the surface. There was much ardent Searching for the Quintessential Goddess behind the possessed goddess symbols."*

"I have an urgent question," said Anowa. "Kate used the word 'ardent.' But my impression is that many, if not most, women during those times were quite subdued—sort of passionless. Were they ardently searching?"

"That's an important question," said Mary. "Although there were plenty of pseudopassions floating around, deep Passion was suppressed in many women. But I believe it was subliminally working in all. Those whom I often call Wild Women were overtly Passionate, and that was contagious and encouraging to others."

Anowa persisted. "But wasn't the prevailing dispassion discouraging?"

Kate answered the question. "To use an expression that was widespread at that time—'It sucked.' At times we were tempted to be very pessimistic, even cynical, about the pervasive conformity. I guess my own optimism—like Mary's—came partly from my history of being very lucky. For example, I had good parents. It also stemmed from deep memories of great Moments, and it was sustained by bonding with friends, even though we were often separated by enormous geographic distances. The spatial and temporal geography of the Background was very different from foreground geography. It was especially when we were engaged in our own creative work that we knew we were connecting with each other. Often after months or even years of apparent noncommunication, startling synchronicities happened." She paused and then announced earnestly: "And right Now I have a Passionate desire to get beyond the topic of dispassion and dullness!"

"I'll second that," said Mary. "I want to move on to the subject of the Fifth Element."

"I find it rather amusing that old misogynist Milton served as a springboard to get to the subject of the stifling of Radical Feminist Genius," Kate remarked.

"Well, sometimes I'm a kind of intellectual ragpicker, as you know," replied Mary. "Most of the men who did write books that remained in 'the canon' were misogynists. I saw no reason not to use the worst of them. Milton's Areopagitica was a tantalizing bit. Since he protested quite forcefully about

the murder of books (authored by men), he made a good springboard for Roaring about the massacre of Elemental Feminist books."

Anowa chimed in: "Mary, I'm interested to see how your analysis wove its way from the subject of the 'burning' of Feminist books to picking up threads of unfinished business from Beyond God the Father. You had been uncritical of Whitehead in that earlier book. But this time around you really wanted to nail him for his bland assumptions, didn't you? Especially for the assumption that 'people do not know what they are assuming because no other way of putting things has ever occurred to them.' Weren't you enraged when you wrote that section in Quintessence?"

"Right," said Mary. "I was in a fit of Wicked Rage, thinking about how many Other Ways of putting things have not only 'occurred' to many Feminists, but were Named, over and over, in our own writings and conversations."

"You were all proponents of an 'intellectual position' that Whitehead and his followers did not want to surface to such an extent that they would have to defend themselves against it," I said. "They had to erase the fact that you Shrews had unerased other ways of Naming reality."

"Mister White Head," giggled Anowa.

Despite her feelings of outrage, Mary had to laugh. "There were so many rich Mister White Heads running the patriarchal show, Anowa!" she exclaimed. "And they reestablished the 'canon' of literary and philosophical works they deemed 'worthy' of being taught in academia, dismissing works by women and so-called minorities as flawed."

"And this was done under the guise of protecting academic freedom against the 'tyranny' of 'political correctness,'" added Kate. "By means of this and other reversals the 'Great Books' fellows and their henchwomen got away with fixing the curriculum and shrinking students' minds. I know, because I was one of the students who refused to read a lot of the prescribed stuff. Mary managed to use some of these as 'springboards' for her writing, and I'm glad she did this. My problem as a student was that I was bored out of my mind. Can you guess which authors we were supposed to study—almost exclusively?"

"Only Mister White Heads!" Anowa and I recited in unison.

"Go to the head of the class, both of you!" Kate laughed.

We both goose-stepped up and down the garden path until Kate and Mary ordered us to halt.

After we had dropped back down on the grass, I said, "I'd like to talk about Ether. Where did the idea come from?"

"An early reference occurred in the work of Homer," said Mary. "There it meant 'fiery sky,' the upper atmosphere or celestial light. It comes from a Greek root, meaning 'to blaze.'"

"What an inspiring image for Fiery Hags!" I said.

"He probably got it from some ancient Greek Fiery Hag," said Anowa.

"No doubt," said Mary. "At any rate, some interpreters of Homer believed that his idea of aether *(ether) refers not only to the fiery upper atmosphere of the sun and stars, but also to celestial light which allows objects to be seen clearly.* Ether could be described as the 'ground' Element or field which allows the four elements of Air, Fire, Water, and Earth to interact."*

"I am interested in your comments concerning Ether as the unifying principle for the other elements," said Kate. "And I'm wondering how this relates to the idea that it is especially connected with the emotion of grief. This would seem to suggest that grief is a central and unifying emotion. But I hadn't thought that grief holds a central place in your writings."

"That's a thought-provoking comment, Kate," responded Mary. "It's true that whenever possible I have transformed grief/sadness into Rage, or some other Volcanic Passion. Sorrow by itself is often passive, whereas Rage can provoke us to action and creation. I have always tried to Name and overcome the oppressive conditions that are the occasions for unnecessary grief.

....

*A book I read in our Archives explains that Aristotle tried to identify Homer's aither *with his "quintessence," the fifth essence* (quinta essentia) *in the universe, postulating this quintessence as forming the heavenly bodies. He saw this as different from the elements out of which regular matter is made, but pervading these four elements. This has been described as a universal background of invisible ephemeral material. By his blending of ether and quintessence Aristotle was taking a position in an intellectual debate of his time. See Lawence M. Krauss,* The Fifth Essence: The Search for Dark Matter in the Universe *(New York: Basic Books, 1986).*

Grief/sorrow is the basis for Rage, which can be Metamorphic—but only if it is Righteous Rage. Obviously shallow ranting without Fierce Focus can't be transformative, any more than self-indulgent whining can. I think that Grief and Rage are profoundly interconnected with each other and with all of the Elemental Passions.

"For example?" asked Anowa.

"Hope, for instance," replied Mary. "Elemental Hope inspires Acts of Righteous Rage. If we were hopeless, we would not keep on fighting back. Hope inspired many women in their battles with the institutions of patriarchy."

"And Rage (which is rooted in Grief) inspires Acts of Hopping Hope," said Kate. "When members of the Anonyma Network made the great Leaps that brought us to Found Continent we were moved by Rage as well as by our Lust to reach Here. We had a great desire to overcome the state of patriarchal paralysis."

Anowa pursued her own train of thought. "Of course, we experience grief and Righteous Rage, especially over what has been done to women and nature in the patriarchal past. And there are residues of that past destruction that still linger in our environment and in our psyches. These sadden us. But there is a new configuration of our Passions, in which rage and grief play a less pivotal role than they did for women in the patriarchal era. New energy patterns are emerging. We have a yen to Spiral farther Out, and there's a temptation to forget the recent past, especially since so much of it was painful. But I think that such forgetting would be disastrous."

"And that's a major reason why I Conjured you, Mary," I said. "As you know, I wanted to strengthen our links to women of the patriarchal era. Otherwise our own Gynergy patterns will be skewed by 'skipping over' the atrocities of that time. We are coming to see how important such Re-membering is for re-establishing our Roots in a Time that preceded patriarchy, that is, in the Archaic Past. If we bypass the patriarchal past we won't reach the Archaic Past. As a result we won't be able to Spiral onward in the Archaic Future. This became more and more evident to me during our earlier conversations, and especially during and after our Time/Space trip to Fribourg."

"And don't forget that Found Continent is unique," said Kate. *"As you know, Mary, women elsewhere on Earth have been establishing Gynocentric societies, and at the same time some are relating to men as friends, lovers, co-workers, partners, and kin. There is still a lurking fear among these Sisters of a re-emergence of something like patriarchy. One of our functions Here on this continent, which is a Power center, is to generate Gynergy to our Sisters elsewhere. We need to remain mindful of history, so that the old order won't repeat itself."*

"Another point has emerged as very crucial during our discussions and experiences after your visits," I said. *"That's the fact that we have a responsibility to the women of your time. At first my motivation in Conjuring you was somewhat selfish. Mainly I wanted to learn from you, which is fine. But I have come to realize that this enterprise has to be a 'two-way street' (to use an antiquated expression from your time). This became clear especially after our conversations concerning Chapter Three. Since you and I have made this breakthrough in Transtemporal communication, we seem to have opened a path for transmission of Gynergy from us to you. I was deeply struck by your statement in that chapter that 'those who can pull us ahead may be our Fore-sisters of the Future.' As I understand this phenomenon, reciprocity is inherent in our connection."*

"Will you develop that thought further?" asked Mary.

"Sure," I said. *"This is a kind of recapitulation* and expansion *of what you wrote in the latter part of Chapter Four. Here goes: By creating Memories of the Future through your books and other recorded works, you and your Cronies affect us, and consequently we Re-Call you and your words and acts. And your knowledge of the effects of your work upon us pulls you on into the Future. But there is yet another dimension of our reciprocity that is coming into focus. This is Presence—our Transtemporal Presence not only to each other* but also to others."

"This brings us to the subject of the Fifth Direction, which is the Center," said Kate. *"The point at which we meet in these Transtemporal encounters—where/when we become Present to each other—is something like Mide, the expanding center of Ireland (as you implied). Through these encounters*

we're discovering the Fifth Direction together. As we move in this direction the flow of energy experienced by women who are in this New Time/Space radiates outward. It attracts others. So the Power of Presence of each of us enhances the ability of others to be Present to their Selves and to all other Biophilic beings."

"And when we meet in this way there is a shifting of the meanings of Past, Present, and Future," I said. "These words are in some sense relative to our own specific participation in Time." Turning to Mary I continued, "For example, as you have explained, in the course of such Momentous encounters you participate in the Present of 2048 BE, even though we members of Anonyma are not your 'contemporaries.' In these Moments, we all intensely experience the fluidity of Time, and we glimpse the complexity of the interrelationships between Past and Future. There are Shape-shiftings in our Sense of Time, and I think our Magnetic Powers evolve as we move into this surprising New Dance of Presence."

"And all of this is deeply related to the process of Centering and Focusing on our Final Cause," said Mary. "When we work alone and together to Realize our deep purpose we regain a sense of balance that we seem to have forgotten, but which 'feels right.' You might call this process a rediscovery and reclaiming of our cosmic place and perspective."

"It seems to me that we're not only in the process of overcoming the old habit of thinking of Time as a one-way series of events," said Kate. "We're experiencing a counterflow of Time. While Time moves from the Past to the Future, from another perspective it flows from the Future to the Past. We're Dancing (yes, I think 'Dancing' is the right word) in the middle, keeping the two streams of energy in balance. By our awareness of this we're learning to live in a Present which is alive, which is continually changing and expanding."

"And that observation makes me think again of the Fifth Cause, the Exemplar," said Mary. "We are in the process of Transtemporal creation of Nemesis. The Idea that each of us has in her mind of that which she is in the process of creating—but which is not yet—is what gives direction to her will. This Idea/Exemplar, no matter how inchoate, is an awareness of what she will create. *It is a window which allows the Future to stream into her mind. When Concreators actually work out our Ideas in the material world—when we actually engage in the work of creation—we move step by step (by writing words, painting on canvas, developing friendships, et cetera) in the direction of the Archaic Future."*

"So as we participate in Nemesis we're acquiring a Transtemporal sense of balance," I said. "And we're refinding and refining our Elemental connectedness across Time. The old sense of fragmentation seems to be dissipating. I'm astonished by our connections with women across Time! And I'm utterly amazed by our connections with all Elemental creatures, Past, Present, and Future!"

"I'm beginning to understand better why you wrote about the Sphinx just after discussing the Fifth Direction," said Anowa. "That image suggests the enormous achievement that is possible through our Transtemporal/Transspatial bonding and creation. It helps us to begin to imagine the vastness, depth, and intricacy of our interconnectedness with all of the animals, plants, seas, planets, and stars across Space and Time."

We all felt a shift in the energies among us . . . a kind of lightening of the atmosphere. Fenrir suddenly ran into the garden and began howling joyously. She bounded around in circles (perhaps they were spirals) greeting us all, and then began licking Anowa's face.

As soon as Anowa was able to extricate herself she casually remarked, "It seems that Fenrir agrees with us. Maybe she's telling us that we're beginning to move into a New/Archaic dimension of Interspecies awareness."

"And she's obviously sensitive to the fact that it's Time for us to 'wrap it up' for Now," said Mary, as she stood up and stretched. "See you in a Moment!" Then off she went. Fenrir accompanied her to the end of the garden path.

Chapter Five

Breaking into the Fifth Dimension:
Dis-covering the Light of Quintessence

I N O R D E R T O Break into the Fifth Dimension Journeyers can reflect upon our experience of the Fourth. The following description of
the Fourth Dimension can be useful for Spinsters to Spin off from:

> ... [I]magining the dimension might be likened crudely to recon-
> structing a moving picture film of a bud opening into a full-blown
> flower. If we cut apart each frame of such a film, stacked the whole
> film together frame by frame, and then looked at the unfolding flower
> simultaneously through all the frames, that might be the most we
> could do to appease our yen for imagining the fourth dimension.[1]

While any Wild Woman can "get the picture," this seems to be a con-
trived way of going about the task of "appeasing our yen for imagining
the fourth dimension." Any deeply aware woman has available to her an
array of vivid Momentous Memories over Time. If she Re-members
these, particularly in writing, she can see the Unfolding Moments along
the Spiraling Paths of her life simultaneously. That is, she can not only
imagine but also truly participate in the Fourth Dimension.

When a Seeker Sees, Names, and Acts in accordance with the Crone-
logical connections among her Moments/Movements across Time, her
knowing of the Fourth Dimension is enlivened, and she herSelf becomes more Alive. She is filled with Gynergy and is moved by a Lust to
Leap onward. She is impelled to Fly further into the Archaic Future
and Break into the Fifth Dimension, where/when she can ever more

consciously be Present, participating in the Be-Dazzling Dance of the Universe—the Cosmic Harmony which is Quintessence.

Of course, she is already Here—at least incipiently—in the Fifth Dimension. The feeling of New Time/Space is not foreign to her. But as she moves *further* into this dimension, there is a vaster sense of Newness as well as re-cognition in her encounters and Other magical Moments. In other words, the "plot" of her life continues to unfold . . . right Here.

Yet there is a problem for one who attempts to speak/write about the Fifth Dimension. This arises from the fact that although Canny Voyagers are arriving and Expanding Here we are not entirely Here. None of us possesses full consciousness of where/when we are, nor do we all have the same degree of such awareness. We sometimes seem to be silenced by the curse of fragmentation even as we strive to overcome it. And we still struggle to overcome silencing by the phallocratic taboo against Naming our Fifth Dimensional experiences. For Voyagers in this Dimension are Outlaws.[2]

Seers experience startling bursts of communication, which often take the form of synchronicities (Syn-Crone-icities). These seeming "coincidences," which are recognized as not really "coincidental," but rather very purposeful, are Known by Crones as Strangely significant.[3] Although it can be argued that these experiences are "nothing new" to Sinister Women, Seers are reporting that they are occurring in their lives with increasing frequency, and often in ways that shock. There is an interconnecting flow—with the Self, Other Women, Animals, all Elemental beings—that is revealed in these experiences to Spinning Women, such as the illustrator of this book.[4]

Such events are startling, but they "feel right." In fact, they *are* right. Syn-Crone-icities are common when we are in the flow of our creative work, following our deep purpose, our Final Cause, and Realizing our Ideas.

Why, then, are these occurrences so surprising? In part because they are not "supposed" to happen. Phallotechnocracy is working to make us unnaturally disconnected.[5] When we do break through and become psychically active/centered we move out from the patriarchal norm and become Eccentric Women who are able to bond in our uniqueness.

Patriarchy does not appreciate this. The reason for its disapproval of the Eccentricity of Wild Women is that we *are out* of its grasp, and *are moving ever further out,* in the direction of the Archaic Future, which we ourSelves are Concreating. The succession of creative acts by which Weird Women are Weaving the Future have as their Exemplar the Archaic Future itself, which is emerging in each of our minds. In our Creative Process/Journey, then, as the Future flows into our minds, drawing us onward, shaping our acts, we become more and more Present in the Fifth Dimension.

INTERFERENCE FROM DADDIES OF THE DEADZONE

There are enemies, of course, who attempt to block our way into this Dimension of Ultimate Adventure. These are the demonic daddies of the deadzone, the noncreators of the fake future, the drones who carry out the divine plan, perpetuating atrocious myths and insisting that we all con-form. They are ineffably unoriginal. The "future" they are noncreating is doodoo.

An important task for Wild Women is to See and Smell and Name this fact.

It is necessary for Journeying Women to get out from under the "sacred canopy"[6] of patriarchal myth Now. The pseudocreators who are working quickly and ruthlessly to impose their technologies of cloning and genetic engineering upon women, the indigenous peoples of the world, and all of nature are also extending their techno-colonization far into space. They are frenetically attempting to thrust upon us their pseudofuture.

A number of Mentally Alive persons have made this point with different emphases and in different contexts. As *Food & Water Journal* explains, in the 1950s the chemical and pesticide agriculture deceptively named "Green Revolution" marked the beginning of the Age of Cancer. Now there is a new "revolution":

> With bioengineering, transnational corporations are revoking the inherent knowledge of life cycles from the genes of seeds, dictating life and death, wiping out diversity, and interrupting evolution. Totally dependent upon their owners, bioengineered seeds and plants can no longer organize themselves internally and have no self-regeneration abilities—each seed is the end of its own line. . . . *Food & Water* believes that food bioengineering, the corporate manipulation and ownership of life and natural processes, is the most refined form of corporate violence yet.[7]

Vandana Shiva demonstrates connections between the encroachments of plant biotechnologies into the seed and the new reproductive technologies into the female body. As she explains:

> Women's bodies, the seed and the soil, the sites of creative regeneration, have been turned into "passive" objects which experts can manipulate for profit. The sources of renewal of life have thus been turned into dead, inert and fragmented matter, mere "raw material" waiting to be processed and manipulated into a finished product.[8]

Shiva also states:

> In modern childbirth, women's labor and knowledge are ignored; her only part in pregnancy and birth is to follow the instructions of the doctor. The direct organic bond with the foetus is substituted by machines and the knowledge of professionals.[9]

The same writer emphasizes that the advent of "the new reproductive technologies" has further accentuated the shift in power from mother to doctor, and from women patients to (mostly) male specialists. Indeed, mothers are reduced by medical experts to "environmental factors" for the fetus. Gena Corea predicts that by the year 2050 women will be divorced from their own procreative power.[10] That reproductive power, Shiva argues, "will have been destroyed by the colonizing forces of modern technology, professionalism, and commercialism."[11] In 1998 it is clear that such "progress" is happening faster than could have been foreseen in the mid-eighties and in the early nineties even by such far-seeing writers.

The necrofuture is already upon us. Its authors, who are Boundary-violators, plan to violate all life to achieve their "Grail"—their brave new world.[12] Their activities are legitimated by patriarchal myth. At this point I will examine some crucial manifestations/incarnations of christian patriarchal myths which have provided scenarios and models for the living hell on earth that is being "created" at the end of the twentieth century.

THE TRIUNE GOD AND NECROTECHNOLOGY

An androlatrous symbol that has affected western civilization for almost two thousand years is the christian trinity—the triune god, which is a reversal of the Original Triple Goddess.* The allegedly omnipotent, immutable trinity of "divine persons" functions/malfunctions to keep us trapped in a three-dimensional world. As dysfunctional symbol of transcendence, it would stop the Wild Journeying of Hags, Crones, and Spinsters which brings us into the Fourth and Fifth Dimensions.[13]

One manifestation of trinitarian conditioning and behavior in these

---

*In *Gyn/Ecology* I have shown that whereas the christian trinity is a model of totally stagnant self-absorption, the Triple Goddess represents an open Future. Unlike the christian closed triangle, the Goddess, one of whose names is *Trivia*—a name used equivalently with *Hecate, Artemis,* and *Diana*—represents diversity of possibilities. Hecate, Goddess of Witches, for example, was represented by statues set up at the crossing of three roads. The suggestion of open possibilities of movement in different directions is obvious. This possibility of diversity was reversed and stopped dead by the inversion of the crossroads (*tri-via*—three ways) in the closed triangular image of the christian trinity. See *Gyn/Ecology*, pp. 75–79.

times is the cloning of mammals. The christian trinity can be seen as a paradigm for cloning. According to traditional theology concerning "the processions of divine persons," the first person of the trinity (the father) brings forth the second person, the son, by thinking of himself. The first and second persons bring forth the third person, the holy spirit, by a mutual act of love. All three divine persons are said to be co-equal and co-eternal. They are "consubstantial." That is, they all are identical with the one divine essence. They are distinct persons only by reason of their relations to each other. They are said to be "subsistent relations."[14] The scenario is one of endless re-turning, that is, infinite immutability, ineffable sameness, and supreme narcissism.

The paradigm of the trinity is a product of christian culture, but it is expressive of all patriarchal patterning. Human males are eternally putting on the masks and playing the roles of "Divine Persons."[15] This scenario is grotesquely playing itself out in the field of biotechnology, most obviously in the phenomenon of cloning. And herein lies/lies a mythic connection between the nuclear weapons industry and the biotechnology business. Both are incarnations of the same necrophilic non-thought patterns. The Los Alamos scientists who were building the atomic bomb in 1945 referred to the first test under the code name "Trinity." In *Pure Lust* I analyzed this naming:

> Sadospiritual legitimation of this [necrophilic] lust and its technological ejaculations is illustrated not only by Oppenheimer's choice of the code name "Trinity" for the 1945 atomic test that took place at Alamogordo, New Mexico, but especially by his explanation of this choice. "Oppie," as he was known by his colleagues, recalled that he was influenced by a devotional poem by John Donne, which opened with the words: "Batter my heart, three person'd God." The battering of the Earth and of her creatures is the consequence of this disordered sentiment.[16]

While I would not say that the biotechnologists explicitly name or even consciously know this mythic connection, the paradigm and direction of both technologies are the same. In both instances the technodaddies indulge in narcissistic activities, remaining sublimely indifferent to the consequences.[17] Just as the nonpurpose of the bomb builders was the maintenance of world "peace," the nonreason for biotechnology is to cure illnesses and "improve" life by "creating" more and more destructive "cures."

Such self-serving nonreasoning is illustrated in the proposed use of genetically engineered "humanized" pig livers at a company called Nextran in Princeton, New Jersey, in 1997. The proposed trial required that blood from patients with liver failure be fed through a pig liver kept alive in a sterile container. Ten patients would be hooked up to a fresh pig liver for twenty-four hours at a time — a procedure which might need to be repeated twice a week over many weeks. The purpose of the procedure was supposedly to keep patients alive until a human donor could be found. John Logan, vice-president of research and development at the company, admitted that the pig livers used in such a trial are likely to contain dangerous viruses, but he affirmed his belief that the trial is justified. Logan is quoted as saying: "If we stopped and worried about everything that could go wrong in medical experiments we'd never achieve anything." Logan also described xenotransplantation (his desired goal) as "a tremendous medical opportunity."[18]

Leaving aside the ugly implications of "medical opportunity," there are hideous problems. It is quite possible that xenotransplantation will "create" new diseases. An animal organ affects the whole body of the recipient, especially because animal cells are dispersed throughout the body of the patient. Apparently researchers have uncontrollable desires to produce ever more complex chimeras, regardless of the enormous animal and human suffering involved. The chimera connection has not been missed by critics. In an article that skillfully detects false arguments and reveals the torture and violation of animals and humans involved in xenotransplantation Florianne Koechlin asks:

> What does it mean if "I" consist of many human and many baboon cells? Or what if my ears and hands are made up of human and pig cells? If I am a mixture of different creatures, how does this affect my sense of "self"?[19]

And we are not talking about science fiction here. This is real devastation by wannabe gods.

DEMONIC DISSOCIATION

Since they are not interested in the life-destroying consequences of their work, noncreators can sweep aside troublesome questions. Typically, Dr. Ian Wilmut, cloner of "Dolly," said in an interview that he wanted to clone animals for medical research but dismissed with predictable and deceptive clichés the idea of cloning humans. "There is no reason in principle why you couldn't do it . . . [but] all of us would find that offensive." Sure! Alas, there is blatant evidence that this is not the case.[20]

Although on the surface biotechnology/necrotechnology might appear less malevolent than the technology of nuclearism, both concur in promoting the destruction of nature. Both work on the assumption that there is no hope for halting the destruction and contamination of the environment (even if this were desired). Nectech feeds on this assumption, which makes its manipulations of genes appear to be the only exit from the plague of illnesses that supposedly can be "explained" solely or at least mainly by hereditary and "lifestyle" factors. This reasoning serves the dual purpose of legitimating nectech's own projects and letting contaminators off the hook.*

---

*This kind of reasoning is illustrated by the deceptive "research" that has been done on cancer. Ellen Leopold, who has been investigating the investigators, reports:

> In fact, of a total of 722 awards made to breast cancer research by the National Institutes of Health, only 33 (5%) involve a possible environmental connection.

Big Business does not want this information to have any impact. They want to prolong their cover-up of their own dirty business. The National Cancer Institute has been part of a concerted backlash against the environmentalist camp. The same author explains that the *Journal of the National Cancer Institute* attempted to "allay fears that unknown environmental hazards are responsible for the clustering of elevated mortality in the Northeast" by oversimplifying the problem under the banner of "lifestyle." In the infamous "Harvard Report on Cancer Prevention," as Leopold makes clear, "corporate and

The dissociation which the biotechnologists share with the nuclear weapons builders allows them to be indifferent to the suffering of the animals they "create," while denying the existence of this suffering.[21] Indifference characterizes also the ponderings of priests, politicians, and ethicists who pontificate on the subject of cloning. For example, John Cardinal O'Connor, roman catholic archbishop of New York, publicly stated that while he opposed the cloning of human beings, lawmakers need to be careful "not to cut off potentially valuable research."[22]

The demonic implications of such "potentially valuable research" are suggested in a statement by the writer Monette Vaquin:

> Today, astounding paradox, the generation following Nazism is giving the world the tools of eugenics beyond the wildest Hitlerian dreams. It is as if the preposterous ideas of the fathers' generation haunted the discoveries of the sons. Scientists of tomorrow will have a power that exceeds all the powers known to mankind: that of manipulating the genome. Who's to say for sure that it will be used only to avoid hereditary illnesses?[23]

Indeed, the fathers and the sons are processing still on their same funeral march. It does not occur to them that they themselves are not Alive.

Dissociated nonthought and atrocious mutilation constitute the nonfabric of necrotechnological society. In this society false distinctions are made to seem plausible. Women, who are classified as "humans," are

---

governmental responsibilities virtually disappear or are lost in vagueness." And this is not astonishing, since the list of donors who support such "research" consists of dozens of huge corporate contaminators such as Monsanto, Exxon, General Electric, and so on. Leopold sees an evil trend at work—shifting responsibility onto individuals in an attempt to privatize cancer causation. This extremely important article, entitled "Round Up the Usual Suspects," was published by Women's Community Cancer Project, c/o The Women's Center, 46 Pleasant Street, Cambridge, MA 02139, Spring 1997. It was originally published in *Sojourner: The Women's Forum.*

theoretically guaranteed better treatment than animals, who have no rights in the eyes of their new "creators." In reality the necrosociety reflects and perpetuates the oppression of both. This is illustrated in Ian Wilmut's naming of "Dolly," who he claimed had been "created" from DNA extracted from an adult sheep's mammary gland. "We couldn't think of anyone with a more impressive set of mammary glands than Dolly Parton," said Wilmut.[24]

This "joke" is a manifestation of the contempt for women which pervades the society in which scientists and others violate female human life and animal life. Janice Raymond gives abundant proof of the pervasiveness of misogyny among reproductive technologists.[25] It is important in this context to continue to listen to the warning of Andrée Collard that what is done to animals will next be done to us.[26]

THE NECTECH FUTURE I: THE END OF NATURE

The cloning of sheep is just the tip of the boringly proverbial iceberg. It is no coincidence that Dolly was cloned in Edinburgh where human genes had already been inserted into sheep embryos. Indeed, sheep are of particular significance. They (as well as some other animals) are being used as chemical factories:

> Researchers have successfully inserted human genes into sheep embryos that will cause the mature adult sheep to produce the human protein alpha-1-antitrypsin. . . . At Pharmaceutical Proteins Limited (PPL) in Edinburgh, Scotland, scientists have produced transgenic sheep that can churn out antitrypsin [normally extracted from human blood serum] at levels fifteen times what can be produced by blood plasma. The productivity gains are so spectacular that a flock of 1,000 ewes "could match the entire world production of the protein."[27]

The hidden iceberg, which includes increased profit margins for pharmaceutical companies, is indeed huge. In the new field called "pharming," transgenic animals are being manufactured in laboratories to serve as chemical factories. In the case of the sheep in Edinburgh proponents argue that this is being done "for a good cause"—producing antitrypsin to fight emphysema in humans. But it is important to look at the wide context of "pharming."

Biotechnology has invaded and continues to invade a great "wilderness area"—the genetic structure of living organisms. They are messing with "the blueprint of life." Activist attorney Andrew Kimbrell notes:

> With current technology, it is becoming possible to snip, insert, re- combine, edit, and program genetic material, the very blueprint of life. Using these techniques, the new life-engineers are rearranging the genetic structures of the living world, crossing and intermixing species at will to create thousands of novel microbes, plants, and animals.[28]

Kimbrell provides examples. There was "transgenic pig number 6707," for instance. Researchers for the U.S. Department of Agriculture wanted a super pig, so they implanted the human gene governing growth into the pig while it was still an embryo:

> To the surprise of the bioengineers, the human genetic material that they had injected into the animal altered its metabolism in an unpre- dictable and unfortunate way. Transgenic pig number 6707 was in fact a tragicomic creation, a "super cripple." Excessively hairy, riddled with arthritis, and cross-eyed, the pig rarely even stood up, the wretched product of a science without ethics.[29]

Technologists are committing the capital crime of Boundary viola- tion. While on the surface this may appear to be creation of "diversity," it is in fact pseudodiversity. It is idealized by some as "co-creation," or continuing creation. Theologian Ted Peters, for example, minimizes the problems inherent in biotechnology with a kind of do-gooder atti- tude about its potential for healing illnesses.[30] Ethicist Margaret Wer- theim writes: "In his enthusiasm to defend genetics from religious conservatives, Peters seems a little naive about the potential dangers in science itself."[31]

But the problem is not adequately Named as "potential dangers in science itself." *The problem is deeper than that.* From a Radical Elemental Feminist perspective such biotechnological meddling is simply and starkly evil. It is helpful to reflect upon Mary Shelley's exposé of the pseudocreativity of boundary violation. Doctor Frankenstein, the male supermother *par excellence,* pondered while making his monster from parts of corpses:

> A new species would bless me as its creator and source; many happy and excellent natures would owe their being to me. No father could claim the gratitude of his child so completely as I should deserve theirs.[32]

Indeed, no father could claim the gratitude which all phallotechnic mother-mimers appear to crave. But in the case of the biotechnologists, boundary violation goes to further hideous extremes. Not restricted to dismembering corpses and rearranging their parts to make monsters, contemporary nectechnologists *transgress biological boundaries and dismember living beings,* intermixing species "to create thousands of novel microbes, plants, and animals" (*and humans*), *attempting to replace the natural world.**

THE PATENTING OF LIFE FORMS

Life forms are now being patented. In June 1980, by a five to four margin, the U.S. Supreme Court decided to grant a patent to microbiologist

---

*This is consummate *assimilation,* which I have listed as one of the eight *deadly sins of the fathers. Assimilation* is "gynocidal/biocidal *gluttony* which expresses itself in vampirism/cannibalism, feeding upon the *living* flesh, blood, spirit of women and Others while tokenism disguises the devastation of the victims." See *Gyn/Ecology,* p. 31. See *Wickedary,* p. 71.

Anand Mohan Chakravarty, an employee of General Electric, for his genetically engineered oil-eating bacteria. Under a 1987 ruling, human beings were excluded from patentability. However the march of progress has continued. Women and indigenous peoples are especially targeted:

> The European Patent Office (EPO) has already received patent applications that would allow the patenting of women who have been genetically engineered to produce valuable human proteins in their mammary glands. The patent, jointly filed by the Baylor College of Medicine and Grenada Biosciences of Texas, was carefully crafted to include all female mammals—including humans—under its coverage.[33]

In 1990 a blood sample was obtained from a twenty-six-year-old Guaymi woman, who had contracted leukemia. Researchers cultivated a cell line from her blood. "Scientist Jonathan Kaplan of the Centers for Disease Control is listed on the patent application [November 1991] as an 'inventor' of the Guaymi woman's cell line."[34] Another significant case was the internationally denounced patent by the U.S. National Institutes of Health (NIH) on the human cell line of a Hagahai indigenous person from Papua New Guinea. After much pressure and charges of biocolonialism from around the globe, the NIH finally filed paperwork to disclaim the patent.[35]

Since that time there has been an escalation of fear that DNA research is becoming the latest tool of biological warfare against indigenous peoples. The U.S. military is engaged in genetic sampling of indigenous peoples internationally. Blood and tissue samples of indigenous peoples have been exchanged between medical researchers and U.S. military labs engaged in the production of biological warfare agents. Indigenous peoples were barred from the First International Conference on DNA Sampling, held in Montreal in September 1996, even though they had been the subjects of such research. An open letter endorsed by sixteen Indigenous Peoples' and public interest organizations proclaimed that the rights and safety of the peoples targeted by the collection, exchange, and commercialization of human genes is an exploitative and unscrupulous enterprise in the guise of disinterested science.[36] Because of such exploitation activists have called for cessation of the Human Diversity Genome Project and similar initiatives.

THE NECTECH FUTURE II: THE END OF WOMEN

In a book whose title, *The Code of Codes*, has mythic resonance ("King of Kings, Lord of Lords," et cetera, ad nauseam, Alleluia!), proponents of the human genome project oblige their readers with clues that can help us crack the symbolic code of their biological quest. Noting that the Nobel laureate Walter Gilbert has called the human genome "the grail of human genetics," they point out that the search for the biological grail has been going on since the turn of the twentieth century, but that it has reached its culminating phase with the creation of the human genome project.[37] One of the editors of *The Code of Codes*, Daniel J. Kevles, quite explicitly lets us know the nature of this "grail." He reports the situation in 1991:

> The human genome project was steadily gathering the technology, techniques, and experience to obtain the biological grail. The first complete human sequence was expected to be that of a composite person; it would have both an X and a Y sex chromosome, which would formally make it male, but this "he" would comprise autosomes taken from men and women of several nations—the United States, the European countries, and Japan. He would be a multinational and multiracial melange, a kind of Adam II, his encoded essence revealed for the twenty-first century and beyond.[38]

This "composite person," who is a "multiracial and multinational melange," presumably will not be white, black, red, or yellow. Perhaps, given the cultural bias of his makers, he will be just a bit "off white," or some neutral shade. It would seem that Adam II spells the end of ethnic and cultural diversity. However, the question of the sex of the "composite person" is handled differently. We are told that "he" will "formally" be male. Readers are left to wonder about the meaning of the word *formally*. We are told in no uncertain terms that his makers/mixers/assemblers will have taken autosomes (chromosomes not involved in sex determination) from women to make this new and perfected Adam. These will have been *assimilated* into Adam II.

In christian myth "the second Adam" is Christ, the god-man. It is not difficult to uncover this unmentioned thematic thread running subliminally through the discourse of biotechnologists. It should come as no surprise to find even more thorough erasure of Female Presence in the biotech version of the myth than in its christian paradigm: In the technological tale no attention is paid to Eve or to Mary, the "new Eve." Apparently they have been rendered obsolete, having been *assimilated* into Adam II. Perhaps Adam II—perfected to the point of having incorporated female procreative power—would be the source of a new Eve. After all, god—the original cloner—used a rib from the old Adam to fashion the old Eve. Perhaps the unoriginal cloners could use a cell from Adam II for the production of the new Eve, bringing the saga of male motherhood—the reversal of the millennia—to a heightened level of scientific sophistication.

Another noteworthy ingredient in the christian soup of symbols is the doctrine of "the mystical body of Christ," in which all members of the church, male and female, are said to participate. Since this model of the assimilation of women into a "formally" male body was established almost two thousand years ago, on a mythic level the deadly sin of assimilation[39] has already been committed on a grand scale. The biotechnological assembly of "the first complete human sequence" suggests an *incarnation* of the christological paradigm of the "mystical body." It represents supreme vampirism/cannibalism that feeds upon the living flesh, blood, and spirit of women.

We must ask: Why the messianic mad dash on the part of biotechnologists for this biological grail? The frenzied activity suggests that "time is running out."

On one level, this time urgency is suggested by the location of the human genome project at the sites of national weapons laboratories. The radioactive contamination that could kill most of the life on this planet needs an "antidote." But it is doubtful that nectech Draculas would be motivated to try to stop the contamination. Their funding—mythic as well as monetary—is from the same source. Their alleged motivation, to eliminate disease-causing genes, is unconvincing. Eco-psychologist Chellis Glendinning suggests their intention:

> The unabashed purpose of biotechnology is the control of biological evolution by manipulating the genes of living organisms.[40]

Radical Elemental Feminists naturally push the question of the purpose of biotechnology further. We begin by asking: Why the accelerated, frenzied activity of geneticists in recent years? In case the Haggard Searcher doesn't already have a clear idea of the probable motivation for this sense of urgency, she can find clues in an article that appeared on the front page of *The New York Times* on March 15, 1997. The article states that at some point in the distant past the Y chromosome's genes became obsolescent. As a result the Y shed them and consequently grew shorter and shorter:

> Its shrinkage seems likely to continue, to the vanishing point. But geneticists are not yet declaring men candidates for the endangered-species list. They believe a different mechanism of sex determination will eventually evolve, maybe with a single X causing maleness, or with the male-determining gene jumping to a new pair of chromosomes and the story of X and Y starting all over.[41]

The article goes on to describe the Y chromosome as "unstable and flighty" and to acknowledge the X chromosome's evolutionary stability.* This material may be anxiety-producing (de-stabilizing?) for flighty

---

*The material in this article was based in part on information from the obscure journal *Genome Research*. More explicit scientific and journalistic articles affirming the primacy of women were published in Germany in early 1997, specifically in *Bild der Wissenschaft*, 2/97, pp. 59–75.

male scientists, causing them to feel impelled to find "a different mechanism of sex determination," that is, to seize control of biological evolution by gene manipulation before the vanishing point arrives.

The news has been out for some time that males have a genetic deficiency. It simply has not been allowed to spread. Elizabeth Gould Davis and others before her stated that woman's reproductive organs are far older than man's and far more highly evolved and that parthenogenesis was the only means of reproduction in an all-female world.[42] Ashley Montagu wrote: "There appears to be a conspiracy of silence on the subject of the superiority of women."[43]

THE NECTECH FUTURE
AND THE PROGNOSTICATING POPE

Crones who are interested in the mythic context of the nectech future may find it useful to glance through the papal encyclical *Tertio Millennio Adveniente* (The Advent of the New Millennium), issued November 10, 1994, by pope John Paul Two. In this document the author describes a three-year preparatory period for the "Jubilee" year 2000, designed to take place from 1997 to 1999. The thematic structure of this three-year period was a partially reversed version of the trinitarian model. The first year of the period (1997) was to be dedicated to Christ, the second (1998) to the "Holy Spirit," and the third (1999) to "God the Father." The holy father repeatedly stated his wish to lead the church into the third millennium.

The place of Mary (Goddess dethroned) in this scenario is clearly defined, i.e., diminished. The encyclical states that she will be "indirectly" present in the whole preparatory phase but will be especially contemplated in the first year "in the mystery of her 'Divine Motherhood.'" We are reassured that her presence will not be overdone: "Veneration of her, when properly understood, can in no way take away from the dignity and efficacy of Christ the one Mediator. Mary in fact constantly points to her Divine Son."

Fascinated by the image of Mary's undoubtedly cramped pointing finger, Wild Women allow our minds to wander, i.e., focus upon the fact that the papally proclaimed paradigm is strangely coincidental with premillennial necrotechnological events. 1997, the year dedicated to the divine father's incarnate son/clone, who is known as the "Lamb of God," turned out to be the year of the famous cloned lamb.* The papal description of 1998, the year of the Holy Spirit, who impregnated Mary and guided her throughout her life by "his internal activity," is oddly suggestive of the advancing stages of nectech's obscene probing and meddling with genetic material and especially women's bodies. The papal vision of 1999, the year of the Father—is an appropriate trinitarian climax. There is no Mother. Instead, Mary is "the highly favored daughter of the Father." The superdoctor Frankensteins and their pontificating legitimators would seem to be winning in the foreground, as usual, of course.

MOVING BEYOND THE SAME OLD THING

Wild Women can "win the war" by Realizing what we have already won. Re-Calling our Archaic Past sets us on Course to reach the Archaic Future.

Deep Background consciousness empowers us to know that the only thing "new" about necrotechnology is that it dodders *further* along,

---

*Crone-ographers will not refrain from wondering whether these coincidences were staged/planned. Was the lamb possibly chosen for this public advent of cloning because of its symbolic significance? And was this event perhaps orchestrated as part of the media-made millennial program for the end of this century? It was difficult not to see in the bucolic AP photos of Dolly's cloner, Ian Wilmut, a sort of updated "Good Shepherd." In the foreground we could hear the sentimental but poignant question of the nineteenth-century poet William Blake: "Little lamb who made thee?" While Dolly chewed her clover, some of us ruminated the possibilities of semiconscious collaboration among cardinals, media men, and scientists disharmoniously plotting the grand finale of this century and the arrival of the third millennium. Crazy? Of course.

stumbling into more potholes of deadtime. On the foreground level the world has been dying in clonedom for a long time.

The pseudodiversity of "new" manmade species in a broad sense is a very dreary theme. Wild Women, drained by dummydom, flee shopping malls offering pseudovariety of unnecessary items, movie theaters where most of the films virtually have the same plot, bigbookstores which offer a glittering array of dumbed-down "best-selling" nonbooks, highways with the same paralyzing green signs, suburbs with the same green poisoned lawns, etc.

But the nectech nasties at the end of the twentieth century have crossed even their own proverbial line. Having taken up where the nazis left off, they have exposed the hell they are noncreating. Certain that they cannot be stopped, they are pursuing what Jerry Mander calls their "obvious, growing, and inherent bias against nature." Mander warns against "what is at stake in the last two big 'wilderness intervention' battlegrounds: space and the genetic structures of living creatures."[44] He adds:

> From there, it's on to the "postbiological age" of nanotechnology and robotics, whose advocates don't even pretend to care about the natural world. They think it's silly and out of date. . . . In the end, we can see that technological evolution is leading to something new: a worldwide, interlocked, monolithic, technical-political web of unprecedented negative implications.*[45]

---

*In the arena of nanotechnology "unprecedented negative implications" abound. Chellis Glendinning explains: "Molecular engineering, or nanotechnology, consists of machines so small that they cannot be seen with the naked eye, with moving parts no larger than a few atoms across. The idea is to direct these tiny machines *into* an organism (a tree, a dog) or a thing (a weapons silo, a nuclear containment building) to manipulate its molecular structure. One of the primary researchers of these minuscule machines, Eric Drexler of Stanford University, touts nanotechnology as the most effective way to deconstruct environmental disasters, transforming them from masses of toxic materials into harmless piles of nontoxic molecules. He speaks as well of nanoscopic electronic 'seeds' that will be planted on distant planets, moons, and asteroids and upon command,

Crafty Searchers note the unsurprising fact that nonfeminist sources offering useful information and critical analyses of the various tentacles of "biotechnology" do not Name the central unifying societal structure that generates these necrophilic activities. Hags/Wild Women have Constantly looked *patriarchy* in the eye (a glazed, empty, unfocused eye), Named it, Spat at it . . . Spat at that pit of evil, and Spiraled on. And Now, by Naming it and Spitting at it yet *again*, we arrive Here.

In Other Words: Because it takes Ultimate Stamina to Name and Act in this time of ultimate horror and braindead denial and paralysis, the powerful energy we Summon for this task is the Energy/Gynergy that can Spring us deep into the Fifth Dimension, toward conscious participation in Quintessence.

Spiraling on does not mean doing nothing. It means doing everything, vaporizing the pathetic mirror images of Fifth Dimensional reality—the "creations," the "telecommunications," the "information" of the nectech world.

Male critics have managed to summon up passion in the face of the horror. Jerry Mander writes of the possibility of a genetic holocaust resulting from reduction of genetic diversity.[46] Dr. Edwin Chargoff, envisioning mass production of human embryos, states that what he sees coming is "a gigantic slaughterhouse, a molecular Auschwitz in which valuable enzymes, hormones, and so on will be extracted instead of gold teeth."[47]

Can Radical Elemental Feminists be any less passionate? Our Re-Sounding denunciation of these unoriginal sins of the technofathers is rooted in our Original and Constant insight that it is *patriarchal* western civilization that invades and manipulates the Wild, proceeding full speed ahead on its superhighway of destruction, reiterating and surpassing Auschwitz.

The evil technocracy originates in the United States and Europe and

will use available elements to assemble space colonies." See *My Name Is Chellis and I'm in Recovery from Western Civilization* (Boston & London: Shambala, 1994), p. 114.

spreads throughout the Third World, vampirizing, dismembering, patenting, destroying all species that it can touch. It is not enlightening to overlook the fact that the U.S. and Europe are phallocratic/foolocratic, i.e., invasive, oppressive, destructive, life-hating, woman-hating. Nor is it helpful to erase the fact that nonwestern countries are also phallocratic. Andrew Kimbrell proposes "a new biodemocracy" in which "citizens" will express a "collective will to restrict biotechnology and to ban the patenting of life."[48] While applauding the optimism of this proposal, Crones insist upon an analysis that goes deeper, that acknowledges the effects of the miasma spewed by godfather, son, and company into the minds of millions. Wicked Women have learned to be wary of solutions that fail to take into account widespread naiveté, cynicism, and false hope.

Canny Women *know* in our core that the nectech empire, with its propensity for invading, poking, prodding, mutilating, destroying the core of living beings, is *rapist.* Nectech is ultimate *Rape of the Wild.*[49] Its visions are violently pornographic. Its enterprises are motivated by obscene and obsessive lust to invade and own.

TABOO-BREAKING INTO THE FIFTH DIMENSION

Untameable Women are Ablaze with Passionate Knowing of this violation. Our No to the spreading horror is Yes to the Call of Original Being, which is Inviolable and Wild. By breaking the manmade taboo against Naming the reality of such violation, we cast ourSelves further into the Fifth Dimension.

From the vantage point of this Dimension, Contrary-Wise Women see the ineffable contrast between Elemental Creativity, which is participation in Nemesis, and the carnage of the nectech nobodies who "create" biocidal blockages to the expression and expansion of Elemental Integrity.

Breaking taboos against Truth-telling, Terrible Women refuse to be silenced by rules of civilized discourse. We Name the fact that technological ghouls are vampirizing *living* flesh and blood. We Broadcast the fact that the ultimate cannibals and vampires *want to own patents on our cell lines.* We Announce to every grain of sand, every tree, every animal, every star that technofools are devoid of respect for the integrity of any and every Natural Being. We send out the message that they are producing hideous reversals of Elemental Connectedness, concocting boundary-violating variations of cellular and genetic mixtures in plants, animals, and humans. We prepare Intergalactic News Reports on idiot scientists who are sending probes to get under the "skins" of planets.[50] We contact all comets in the area, warning them that dirty big boys are planning to cut off and "study" their tails.*

Terrible Women send notes of profound apology to the Sphinx for the horrible perversion of her meaning that is happening at this time. We vow that we will not allow this desecration of her message of Elemental Integrity to go unavenged. We promise to partake ever more ardently in the work of Nemesis, shifting energy patterns and be-ing respectful of

---

*News of planned further rape of celestial bodies is reported in the media almost daily. On February 20, 1998, viewers were informed that scientists plan to do strip mining on the moon. It was suggested that in the not too distant future there will be "terra-forming" of other planets, making them more Earthlike. In December 1997 *Newsweek* reported: "As the millennium approaches, it is NASA chief Dan Goldin's goal to 'blacken the sky with spacecraft.'" Elemental Women were horrified to read the following:

> Champollion Deep Space 4 will launch in the summer of 2003, headed for comet Tempel 1, some 233 million miles from Earth. If all goes well, a harpoon will be shot from the spacecraft and anchor itself to the comet. Then a drill will dig in and retrieve something scientists have never seen—a sample of a comet's frozen core.

It is equally inspiring to read of other space-rape missions planned to head for Mars. We are informed that nine spacecraft are scheduled to drop in on the Red Planet over the next seven years. "Each consecutive mission will *bore deeper* [italics mine] into the planet's surface, looking for water and other organic material." See Tara Weingarten, "Harpooning a Comet—and Other New Space Probes," *Newsweek*, December 15, 1997, Vol. 30, No. 24, p. 16.

every Other's Originality. We solemnly swear that as Metamorphosing Women we will strive ever harder to Realize our Sphinxlike Selves and work to transform the world. We express our gratitude to her for inspiring our Quest for Elemental Cosmic connectedness. We thank her for inviting us to Dis-cover the Quintessential nature of Goddess under her many Names and for Calling us to participate in the Transtemporal and Trans-spatial Presence of all creation.

In response to us as Searchers the Sphinx opens our Eyes and Ears and Other windows of our souls to Quintessence.

We are not passive recipients of this gift, however. Journeying Women in the Fifth Dimension must work to overcome the patriarchal prohibition against Time/Space. Such Taboo-Breaking originates in Deep Desperation that accompanies seeing even further into the abyss of misogyny and nature-hating than was previously imaginable. And, Strangely, it helps us to understand more fully our potential for Ecstasy.

The makers of the patriarchal monoculture are working to block out the Background to such an extent that the Inhabitants of the Wilderness and Wild Women—including those who struggle to live on the Boundary—have become endangered species. The heavy miasma of the foreground now reveals itself more than ever as absolutely anti-Wild, anti-Nature, anti-Female. The Eye-opening that accompanies acknowledgment of this fact is an opportunity that we have sought, that we have longed for. It is our chance to move into a State of Natural Grace.

Following the Call of the Wild into a State of Natural Grace in this utterly unnatural time is less difficult than it might seem, especially when we recognize the impossibility of Living in the state of living death which is the encroaching techno-foreground.

This does *not* mean that Unsubdued Women leave the fight for others to carry on without us. It does mean affirming and Living our multidimensionality, so that we Spiral into the Fifth Dimension even as we are fighting "back there." Our participation in the Fifth Dimension strengthens us to overcome the destroyers of life. The further we Spiral on, the fiercer is our multiform expression of the power that flows from Biophilic Integrity.

And we have allies who are eager to help us Realize our Integrity! Among these are the animals, trees, stars, and Elemental Spirits (commonly known as angels) who are our traveling companions across Time/Space.

Encounters with all these beings are sources of natural grace. *Grace* in this context does not refer to the christian concept of a "supernatural" gift of god. The grace I am Naming here is Quintessentially natural. It is the innate source of our capacities to clearly intuit, think, will, sense, imagine, remember, feel, heal, teach ourselves and others, and act consistently with our knowledge and desires.* These natural powers are blunted but not killed in technocratic society by its physical destruction of the environment, especially by its continuing spread of toxins in the air, water, earth, and sunlight and in the electromagnetic field, and more recently by the biotechnologies purported to "solve" these problems.

The State of Natural Grace is qualitatively different from our condition under the state of possession which is phallocracy. Natural grace is a quality of the soul of one who is moving out of the unnatural state of captivity and contamination. It is often experienced as a gift, which may take the form of a flash of intuition, or a heightened sense of beauty — as of a sunset or glistening grass or the branches of a tree tossed by the wind. It may be found in acts of lovemaking, composition of music, interchange of energy that takes place in conversation with a friend.

Wild Women experiencing natural grace sense an impulse to thank the Universe. The further Wayward Women move into this state the less transitory it feels. We know that we have come home in some sense, even though we are still just arriving. We are more and more in commu-

---

*Charlene Spretnak expresses this concisely:

Experiencing grace involves the expansion of consciousness of self to all of one's surroundings as an unbroken whole, a consciousness of awe from which negative mind-states are absent, from which healing and groundedness result.

See Charlene Spretnak, *States of Grace: The Recovery of Meaning in the Postmodern Age* (San Francisco: HarperSanFrancisco, 1991), p. 26.

nication with our true be-ing. As we become more alive in the Fifth Dimension we find that we are changing in Elemental ways. This transformation could be described as participation in the powers of Elemental Spirits, that is, angels.

THE STATE OF NATURAL GRACE
AND OUR CONNECTION WITH ANGELS

Many Biophilic Women have experienced the Presence of angels. I am not referring here to popular caricatures but to the Wild, powerful, supremely intelligent Elemental Spirits about whom medieval philosophers and theologians wrote astonishing treatises.*

It is exciting to think and study about Elemental Spirits (angels), not only because we notice their Presence and are guided and guarded by them, but because this experience and reflection gives us vital clues about living in the Fifth Dimension. For in this Dimension we are invited to participate in powers that are beyond us. The powers of angels *are* beyond us, and yet they Touch us deeply, in myriad ways.

Despite their limitations, some medieval philosophers offered suggestive ideas about angels, which were known as "separate intelligences" and as "separate substances."[51] Angels were believed to be incorporeal, though they were thought to assume bodies at times in order to be seen and heard by humans. They are not "ghosts," i.e., souls of the dead. Indeed they cannot die. They are pure spirits. I will consider some

---

*I unabashedly cite these fellows because they had access to learning and writing at a time when women did not have such opportunities. In the Background of every phrase and sentence quoted here is a Howl of rage and grief for the brilliant women who were thus muted, and whose ideas and experiences were not honored or even recorded—and certainly not attributed to them. Yet they were in the air/aura of the medieval period, and Thomas Aquinas was, I think, unconsciously communicating those ideas/thought forms (which were reversed and in need of decoding, of course). These were transmitted to me during the years when I was studying his work in Fribourg, Switzerland. This realization was reinforced in a conversation with Jane Caputi, March 10, 1997.

of the qualities attributed to angels as these can afford insights to Wickedly Wise Women.

It is enlightening to consider the medieval view of the stunning diversity of angels. Reflecting the ancient Greek and medieval philosophical traditions, Thomas Aquinas contended that angels, "inasmuch as they are immaterial substances, exist in exceeding great number, far beyond all material multitude."[52] Citing Dionysius, he affirms that they surpass the weak and limited reckoning of our material numbers. He also wrote that it is impossible for two angels to be of one species.[53] This implies that each of these millions—billions—trillions of angels is a species distinct from every other individual/species. Numerically speaking, the vastness of such diversity is not comprehensible to us. But the implications can Spark the imaginations of Clairvoyant Crones.

Insofar as we have been trained to think of ourselves simply as members of the same species, our minds and imaginations have shriveled. Women are expected to categorize ourselves into divisions of class, race, nationality, age, et cetera, while failing to glimpse the astonishing potential for differentiation of individuals. Contemplating the diversity of angels can provide a leaping off point for creative imagining of Female Elemental potential for diversity. It also suggests the absolute diversity among all Elemental creatures.

Recognizing and honoring our deep differences is not a task for the faint-hearted. It involves overcoming the illusion of sameness, especially as this is used to stereotype women. It requires exploding out of the state of clonedom/boredom. When Eccentric Women open our minds/hearts to recognizing the diversity of our Genius, bursts of energy ensue. We become Unstuck. Unstuck Women Realize our capacity for deep communication, which is totally Other than the solipsistic, repetitious dis-course that fills the air under patriarchy.

Wayward Women will be intrigued to reflect on how angels are Present: They *are* where they *will* to be. They are where they choose to communicate:

So an angel can be in one place in one instant, and in another place in the next instant,without any time intervening.[54]

This idea sheds light upon our multiplying and intensifying experiences of synchronicity. Wild Women *are* Present to each other more often than we consciously realize. As we Realize the naturalness of this synchronicity it becomes a habit.

Many Life-Loving Women experience this kind of connection with animals and other Elemental creatures, such as trees, bodies of water, rocks, and comets, who are much more adept at such communication than we are. It is not unusual, in fact, to meet women who openly proclaim that animals, especially their Familiars, are their teachers. Others also acknowledge the speaking of stones, blossoms, and stars.[55] Moreover, there is no reason whatsoever to doubt that all Elemental beings experience synchronicities among themselves. It is we who have been backward. The rest of the Universe is already Here.

As Wandering Wanton Women become more rooted in the State of Natural Grace we recognize awareness of synchronicities/Syn-Crone-icities as a sign that we are coming into harmony with other Elemental creatures, that is, we are discovering Quintessence, which is the Ultimately Harmonious Integrity of the Universe and Source of Ecstasy.

QUINTESSENCE: THE MUSIC OF THE SPHERES

The multiple synchronicities experienced by beings in the Fifth Dimension constitute a symphony of the cosmos. The twelfth century Wise Woman and Mystic Hildegard of Bingen, Abbess of Rupertsberg, testified most eloquently to the reality of this cosmic harmony. Hildegard was a Genius of the first order. A gifted poet, composer, artist, doctor, preacher, and scientist, she wrote books on theology, medicine, science, and physiology, as well as seventy poems. She created a language of her own consisting of nine hundred words and an alphabet consisting of twenty-three letters, both of which have been lost to us.[56]

At the age of forty-two Hildegard began having visions, which were represented by her in thirty-six pictures or "illuminations." In one of these illuminations are painted seven rings. In the top ring she depicted Mary, Queen of Heaven, with the star-filled sky in the background. In the vision, which was also an auditory phenomenon, she heard "a sound resembling the voice of a multitude making harmony . . . a symphony of Holy Mary." She heard Mary praised as "the most brilliant gem and bright glory of the sun," and as "translucent matter."[57]

Since for many Nag-Gnostic Women the image of Mary suggests *Goddess* (albeit dethroned Goddess, tamed and possessed by the fathers), Hildegard's description of her vision, with its accompanying sounds, is of special interest. Discerning Women do not think of the word *Goddess* as Naming one individual deity with only one name. In fact, the words traditionally used to describe Mary are derived from descriptions of ancient Goddess images.* Moreover, Her-etical Hags do not think hierarchically, as if there were "one on top," especially if we think of *Goddess* not as a noun, but as a Verb.

---

*Barbara G. Walker writes:

Fathers of the Christian church strongly opposed the worship of Mary because they were well aware that she was only a composite of Mariamne, the Semitic God-Mother and Queen of Heaven, Aphrodite-Mari, the Syrian version of Ishtar; Juno the Blessed Virgin; Isis as Stella Maris, Star of the Sea; Maya the Oriental Virgin Mother of the Redeemer; the Moerae or trinity of Fates; and many other versions of the Great Goddess. Even Diana Lucifera the Morning-Star Goddess was assimilated to the Christian myth as Mary's "mother," Anna or Dinah. Churchmen knew the same titles were applied to Mary as to her pagan forerunners: "queen of heaven, empress of hell, lady of all the world."

The *Speculum beatae Mariae* said Mary was like the Juno-Artemis-Hecate trinity: "queen of heaven where she is enthroned in the midst of angels, queen of earth where she constantly manifests her power, and queen of hell where she has authority over the demons." According to the Office of the Virgin, she was the primordial being, "created from the beginning and before the centuries." Christian patriarchs therefore sought to humanize and belittle Mary, to prove her unworthy of adoration.

See Barbara G. Walker, *The Woman's Encyclopedia of Myths and Secrets* (San Francisco: Harper and Row, 1983), pp. 602–3.

The words used by Hildegard to convey her vision are suggestive of Quintessence, which in ancient Greek philosophy has been described as celestial clarity from heaven, as the fiery upper atmosphere of the sun and stars, and as scarcely material in form.[58] This is not to say that *Goddess* equals *Quintessence*, but that both words point to the same realm. *Goddess* is a Metaphor for the constantly unfolding Verb of Verbs — Be-ing. *Quintessence* also is a way of Naming Be-ing the Verb, with specific emphasis on its manifestations as source of integrity, harmony, and luminous splendor of form.

The joy of participation in Quintessence continually unfolds. This Sense of Be-Longing in the Universe sometimes feels like being part of a cosmic symphony. Our synchronistic communications are marked by rhythm, melody, harmony, and even counterpoint.

Journeying Women living ever more consciously in harmony with the Music of the Spheres cannot conveniently block out our knowledge of evil. Our intensified sensate and intellectual abilities enable us to understand atrocities and their interconnections on deep levels. Our sadness and rage are Alive and are assumed into the Quintessential Focus of Fierce Women.

Nothing that we do is small when it is seen in the Light of Quintessence. Size does not matter, nor does distance between separate beings participating in this Cosmic Concordance.[59] In Touch with Quintessence, Elemental Women become more than ever like trees and like angels. Extending our roots deeper, we are free to expand and participate in the creation of the universe.[60]

Cosmic Comments and Conversations
IN 2048 BE CONCERNING
CHAPTER FIVE

....

by Anonyma

A GROUP *of my Anonyma Network friends were sitting on the beach engaged in intense discussion. Many of us were in a state of nearly uncontrollable rage, especially as we talked about the genetic manipulation of species that preceded the Earth Changes and the great migration to Lost and Found Continent.*

"And to think how they claimed that animals don't suffer!" roared Anowa. "The stupidity and arrogance of those men!"

"And of the women who went along with it!" groaned Sung Hee. "It's hard to understand how the animals could ever forgive the 'human species' for its torture and destruction of the Earth's creatures."

"It was especially hideous that they 'created' monstrously deformed creatures—invading their genetic core," said Myoko.

Some of us were openly sobbing, not just for women but in some sense even more for the animals, who were not at all complicit in the horrible crimes against nature. I looked around at our Familiars who were clustered nearby, staring at us intently. Just a few minutes before our discussion they had all been going about their own business. Some had been playing happily. The seals had been barking and splashing; the parrots had been swooping among the trees; the snakes had been amusing themselves by hissing at invisible enemies; the rabbits had been hopping among the bushes.

This scene of peace and joy was transformed now into a solemn and silent ritual of listening and watching. The eyes of some of the animals were especially disconcerting, most tellingly the eyes of the pigs and the monkeys. It wasn't that they were angry. That would have been endurable. But instead they expressed an unfathomable sorrow. And beyond that they communicated . . . sympathy.

"They seem to be telling us that they forgive us," said Nassrin.

The scene was almost unbearable. None of us younger members of Anonyma had even been "there" before the Earth Changes, since we had either been born here on Found Continent or had come over as children. The older members, like Kate, had been deeply repelled by the atrocities and had tried to expose and resist them.

Instinctively I turned to Kate. "How are you feeling?" I asked softly.

"Terrible," she replied.

"But you fought and worked to oppose the evil," I began.

"Not hard enough" was all she could say. We knew that nothing would have been enough, so we waited for her to continue.

Kate looked around at the expectant group. After a while she smiled. The mood in the group subtly shifted. "Maybe we can do more Now," she said. "We are, after all, in the Fifth Dimension, which means that—upon occasion—we can communicate rapidly in Time and Space. And Annie has moved us further along by Invoking Mary, who can bring our messages back to her contemporaries. Then they can have an idea of how their times and their actions look from our perspective."

"So they can be influenced by us, if they choose to be," said Sophie. "Kate, are you saying that we can change the past?"

There was a surge of interest and energy emanating from the crowd of women. I glanced around at the animals and noticed that they were becoming excited. Some of the monkeys and parrots began chattering, and a few cats were frolicking in the tall beach grass. A kookaburra laughed. Nevertheless, they were all listening carefully to every word.

"We can't force anyone or anything," said Kate. "But we can attract attention to certain ideas and possibilities, and to the vast Transtemporal context. We can communicate our experiences, and we can beckon and warn."

"And you can give hope and energy and inspire us to bonding and action in Sisterhood," commented Mary, who came ambling into the group as an uninvited guest.

Everyone made some welcoming remarks, all at once. "Well, hello!" I shouted. "I was just thinking of Invoking you."

"'Just thinking' is sometimes enough," responded our guest. "I couldn't wait any longer for you to get around to issuing me a formal invitation." She then took a place on the sand next to Kate. "Please continue, Kate," she said.

"No, you continue," Kate laughed. "I like the part about inspiring you to bonding and action in Sisterhood."

"Well, yes. I think that is the core of what you are doing," said Mary. "Every time I return to 1998 after these visits my friends bombard me with questions. You know how it was at that time, Kate. You were there, then. So many women seemed to have amnesia about patriarchy, even though—or rather, especially because—we were drowning in it. 'Sisterhood' often seemed to have been demolished, and there was widespread exhaustion and discouragement. When I tell them about you they say: 'So there is hope! There is a Future Sisterhood. We were right all along. We won't be defeated after all!' And that reawakens Vision and Courage."

Kate was silent for a few minutes. Then she spoke calmly. "When I think of how it felt to be living then, I remember the sensation of being absolutely overwhelmed. For example, as word came out about the sickening effects of genetically engineered foods, some women were afraid to eat anything or to give their children food from a local supermarket. Almost everything was suspect as unsafe to eat or drink. And there was an unnatural proliferation of strange viruses and bacteria. Even when we decided not to 'fixate' on this, it was contributing to our overall anxiety. We all knew that it was important to act. But there were so many escalating crises toward the end of the century that it seemed there were hundreds of buttons we needed to push, all at the same time! We each had to figure out what our own priorities were . . . and Name the connections."

"What did you think was the most urgent crisis?" asked Anowa.

"On the deepest level, genetic manipulation was probably the worst assault against nature, and perhaps it was the most far-reaching in its destructive implications," replied Kate. "But this can't be understood if it is seen as disconnected from the widespread resurgence of fundamentalist misogyny

and terrorism against women. And there was the horror of sweatshop conditions around the world imposed by the United States government, the Third World governments, the Big Business elites, the International Monetary Fund, NAFTA, and so on. And that was connected with the worldwide escalation of female sexual slavery, since many poor women were forced to sell their bodies. At the core of all this was a fanatic phallic lust to own, control, and manipulate life. The fact is that all of the atrocities against women and nature were deeply interconnected."

Anowa pursued: "So how did you decide where to put your energies?"

"The important deciding factor was often personal inclination," Kate replied. "My point about the profound interconnectedness of the atrocities was to stress the importance of every well-focused Biophilic action, no matter how small it may have seemed. Each such act strengthened our capacity to Realize the flow of the Archaic Future into our minds at that time."

"And this enlarged our consciousness," added Mary. "To take one huge example, it enabled some of us to continue seeing through the nectech empire's self-justifying propaganda. This became increasingly difficult as the governments, allied with Big Business and Big Science, poured out more and more Lies."

"I'm interested in pursuing the subject of the connection between such giant Lies and the demonic dissociation you have written about, Mary," said Kate. "My own experience was that many of the women I knew back then seemed to become divided by such a maze of deception. For example, in the late nineties fewer and fewer women seemed to be able or willing to Name patriarchy as the fundamental and all-encompassing system of oppression. Some fixed their attention on 'Western civilization' as the main culprit. There was, of course, good reason to focus on western civilization, but the concomitant nonnaming of patriarchy narrowed vision, so that connections couldn't be seen."

"For example," said Mary, "it became difficult for many to Name the connections between the escalating oppression of women by fundamentalist movements and regimes around the world and the violation and destruction of women and nature by the nectech empire. The subsequent failure to con-

nect deep ecological concerns with Radical Feminist insight was debilitating."

"And that's why you issued your book as A Radical Elemental Feminist Manifesto!" said Sung Hee.

"Sure," Mary replied. "The French Feminist Françoise d'Eaubonne coined the term eco-féminisme (ecofeminism)in the early 1970s in her book Le Féminisme ou la mort (Feminism or Death). But I have always thought that term isn't strong enough. The word Gyn/Ecology says what I mean to say. The expression Radical Elemental Feminism spells out further the idea that Radical Feminism implies Elemental Feminism. That is, it is impossible fully to have one identity/commitment without the other."

"But you were not split off from the women who called themselves 'ecofeminists'?" asked Myoko.

"Definitely not," said Mary. "I respected the commitment and analyses of the women who used different terms. But I kept on trying to invent and retain words that I thought could enlarge the scope of vision and Name connections, so that we could continue to make our analysis deeper, and reach the roots of the problems."

"The inherent integrity of Radical Elemental Feminism became more and more obvious by the turn the century," said Kate. "Feminist scholars had been aware for some time that women were being cut off from our procreative powers by medical 'professionals.' The witchcraze of the fifteenth, sixteenth, and seventeenth centuries in western Europe, which targeted women healers and midwives for violent death, was followed in the eighteenth century by the takeover of midwifery by 'man-midwives' with their destructive forceps. In the nineteenth century 'gynecology' was invented in order to control women's powers, and toward the end of the twentieth century the 'new reproductive technologies' further diminished female self-knowledge and self-esteem. Connected with this was the fact that in the 1990s women's reproductive freedom was being taken away. By 1998, the twenty-fifth anniversary of Roe versus Wade, which had been a triumph for Free Choice, it had become increasingly difficult and dangerous for women to obtain an abortion. And in the 1990s the bioengineers were 'creating' seeds and plants with no self-regenerating *abilities. Animals, plants, and women were violated and castrated in the deepest sense by the nectech empire. It became ever more evident that the cause of women and the cause of nature were the same."*

"It is instructive to look back at reactions to the cloning of Dolly," added Mary. "In 1997 the most blatant patriarchs dispassionately stated that cloning of animals was acceptable but that humans should not be cloned. Their hypocrisy was obvious. Almost all the Feminists I knew were deeply repelled by such arrogant indifference to the fate of animals. And we all knew that if 'they' had not already cloned humans, they would soon attempt to do so. Our instinctive knowledge of our deep bond with all of nature was undeniable."

"I'd like to get back to our original discussion of how we, as your Future Foresisters, can help you and your 'Cronies' Now," I said. "I guess it would be helpful if we communicate the fact that you are not a cognitive minority, as you may have imagined yourselves to be. After all, we are Here, as are Foresisters of more ancient patriarchal times and from the Archaic Past. Seen in this wide Transtemporal context, you belong to the cognitive majority."

At this point in our conversation something wonderful began to happen. All of the carefully listening animals came closer and sat or stood among us. The women who were sitting next to each other shifted positions to make space between them for the animals. A beautiful turtle nudged her way between Kate and Mary, who greeted her warmly. A wombat crouched next to Suzanne, who addressed him as "Sweet Pea." A wild boar sat squarely between Anowa and Sung Hee, who both squealed in delight. While a small dog named Ricki nuzzled her friend Kay, a parrot whom I had seen flying around from time to time hopped on my shoulder and began gently nibbling my ear. Many others came and swelled our ranks.

We Time-traveling Cronies well understood that the animals were saying they belong to this majority. Or rather, to put it more accurately, they were inviting us to join their cognitive majority, which includes plants, rocks, planets, stars, angels—all Biophilic beings. They wanted to communicate their message not only to us but to their Foresisters. They were saying that our souls' work is their souls' work too, and that we have won. Telepathically we heard and joined in their chorus: "We have overcome!"

Then we all relaxed and listened together to the powerful symphony of the cosmos. The wind blew in cadence with the cosmic concert, swishing through the trees, whose branches moved in harmony with the celestial music. It danced through the grasses and sands and ruffled feathers, fur, and hair. It stirred the waves of the sea, which roared mightily.

As we listened to this concert and watched the dance of synchronicity we gazed at the glorious sunset. Soon the moon, planets, and stars became visible. Everything in the sky seemed to twinkle rhythmically with the whole symphony.

Everyone knew that this concordance is the vibrating light, sound, and breath of Quintessence, and that it is ultimately Unconquerable. And Now we send this joyful message and Memory of the Future to our Sisters of all kinds and all times so they too can always remember it.

Notes

AUTHOR'S INTRODUCTION
TO THE ORIGINAL 1998 EDITION

1. Jerry Mander, *In the Absence of the Sacred* (San Francisco: Sierra Club Books, 1991), p. 161.
2. Jane Caputi, *Gossips, Gorgons, & Crones: The Fates of the Earth* (Santa Fe, N. M.: Bear & Company, 1993), p. 12.
3. This expression came from Madeleine L'Engle, *A Wrinkle in Time* (New York: Dell Publishing Company, Yearling Books, 1962).
4. Elizabeth Cady Stanton, letter to Woman's Suffrage Convention, 1851, in *History of Woman Suffrage*, ed. by Elizabeth Cady Stanton, Susan B. Anthony, and Matilda Joslyn Gage (New York: Fowler and Wells, 1881), I, p. 816.
5. Susan B. Anthony, personal correspondence, cited in Ida Husted Harper, *The Life and Work of Susan B. Anthony* (Indianapolis: The Hollenbeck Press, 1898), p. 366.
6. This analogy for my succession of books was suggested by Jeanmarie Rindone, conversation, March 17, 1995.
7. The insight that *Wickedary* and *Outercourse* provided a Field of Force from which this book could Spring forth came from Jeanmarie Rindone, conversation, April 1, 1995.
8. Elizabeth Oakes Smith, speech delivered at Woman's Rights Convention, 1852, in *History of Woman Suffrage*, ed. by Stanton et al., op. cit., I, 522–23.

CHAPTER ONE
THE FIFTH SPIRAL GALAXY: EXPANDING HERE

1. I have developed the idea of *Quintessence* elsewhere in this book. See especially Introduction, Chapter Four, and Chapter Five.

2. See *Websters' First New Intergalactic Wickedary of the English Language*, Conjured in Cahoots with Jane Caputi (1987; 1993; London: The Women's Press, 1988. Cited as *Wickedary*. I first used this word in *Beyond God the Father: Toward a Philosophy of Women's Liberation* (1973; reissued with Original Reintroduction by the Author, Boston: Beacon Press, 1985), p. 194.

3. Susan Brownmiller, *Against Our Will: Men, Women, and Rape* (New York: Simon and Schuster, 1975), pp. 14–15.

4. See Toni Nelson, "Violence Stalks Women Worldwide," in *Vital Signs*, ed. by Linda Starke (New York: Norton/Worldwatch Books, 1996), pp. 134–35.

5. Naomi Neft and Ann D. Levine, *Where Women Stand: An International Report on the Status of Women in 140 Countries, 1997–1998* (New York: Random House, 1997), p. 158.

6. See Tom Post with Alexandra Stiglmayer, Charles Lane, Joel Brand, Margaret Garrard Warner, and Robin Sparkman, "A Pattern of Rape," *Newsweek*, January 4, 1993, pp. 32–36.

7. See Catharine A. MacKinnon, "Rape, Genocide, and Women's Human Rights," *Harvard Women's Law Journal*, Vol. 17, Spring 1994, pp. 5–16.

8. Ibid., p. 14.

9. Ibid.

10. Andrea Dworkin, "Free Expression in Serbian Rape/Death Camps," in *Life and Death* (New York: The Free Press, 1997), p. 75.

11. Ibid., p. 76.

12. Andrea Dworkin assured me that she knew some of this propaganda/pornography had spread to Germany. Conversation, June 1997.

13. MacKinnon, "Rape, Genocide and Women's Human Rights," op. cit., p. 13.

14. Ibid., p. 7.

15. See "Ihr Vater ist der Hass," *Stern*, 11 März 1993, p. 42.

16. Neft and Levine, *Where Women Stand*, op. cit., p. 158.

17. Gayle Kirshenbaum, "Jadranka Cigelj and Nusreta Sivac," *Ms.*, January/February 1997, p. 64.

18. Ibid., p. 68.

19. Ibid.

20. Susan Brownmiller, "Making Female Bodies the Battlefield," *Newsweek*, January 4, 1993, p. 37. Among other instances she cites the rapes by Pakistani soldiers in Bangladesh:

The mass rapes committed by Pakistani soldiers in newly independent Bangladesh were also called "unprecedented" in 1971, when
the government of Bangladesh appealed for international aid to help
with the aftermath. As in Bosnia now, Bengali women were ab-
ducted into military brothels and subjected to gang assaults. . . .

The plight of raped women as casualties of war is given credence
only at the emotional moment when the side in danger of annihilation cries out for world attention. When the military histories are
written, when the glorious battles for independence become legend,
the stories [of women] are glossed over, discounted as exaggerations,
deemed not serious enough for inclusion in scholarly works.

And the women are left with their shame.

21. Natalie Nenadic, "Femicide: A Framework for Understanding Genocide,"
in *Radically Speaking: Feminism Reclaimed*, ed. by Diane Bell and Renate
Klein (North Melbourne, Australia: Spinifex Press, 1996), p. 462.

22. See Andrea Dworkin, *Pornography: Men Possessing Women* (New York:
G. P. Putnam's Sons, A Perigee Book, 1981). See also Diana E. H. Russell,
ed., *Making Violence Sexy: Feminist Views on Pornography* (New York:
Teachers College Press, Athene Series, 1993).

23. See Andrea Dworkin and Catharine MacKinnon, "Questions and An-
swers," in Russell, *Making Violence Sexy*, pp. 78–96.

24. See Debra Michels, "Cyber-Rape: How Virtual Is It?" *Ms.*, March/April
1997, pp. 68–72. See also Carol J. Adams, " 'This Is Not Our Fathers' Pornography': Sex, Lies, and Computers," in *Philosophical Perspectives on
Computer-mediated Communication*, ed. by Charles Ess (Albany: State
University of New York, 1996), pp. 147–70.

25. I developed the idea of "Biggest Lies" in *Pure Lust: Elemental Feminist
Philosophy* (1984; 1992; London: The Women's Press, 1984. See also *Wickedary*, p. 66.

26. Rachel Carson, *The Sea Around Us* (New York: New American Library,
Mentor Books, 1961), p. 142.

27. Dale Spender, *Women of Ideas and What Men Have Done to Them* (Boston: Routledge and Kegan Paul, 1982), p. 18.

28. See Michael Dames, *Mythic Ireland* (London: Thames and Hudson,
1992), pp. 194–96.

29. Margaret J. Wheatley, *Leadership and the New Science: Learning About Organization from an Orderly Universe* (San Francisco: Berrett-Koehler Publishers, 1992, 1994), pp. 60–61.

30. Transatlantic telephone conversation with Io Ax, July 1994.

31. Conversation with Jeanmarie Rindone, Newton Centre, Mass., January 1995.

32. Cited in *The New York Times*, June 27, 1997, p. A11.

33. John H. Cushman Jr., *The New York Times*, January 29, 1997, p. A11.

34. Conversation with Jeanmarie Rindone, Spinning off from "Root," *Grolier Encyclopedia* (New York: The Grolier Society, 1957), Vol. XVII, p. 116, August 15, 1995.

35. Anjali Acharya, "Forest Loss Continues," in *Vital Signs*, ed. by Starke, op. cit., p. 122.

36. Kenton Miller and Lauren Tangley, *Trees of Life: Saving Tropical Forests and Their Biological Wealth* (Boston: Beacon Press, 1991), p. 2.

37. Acharya, "Forest Loss Continues," op. cit., p. 123.

38. Ibid., p. 122.

39. Ibid., p. 123. See also Odil Tunali, "Carbon Emissions Hit All-Time High," in *Vital Signs, 1996*, ed. by Stark, op. cit., p. 64.

40. See Paul Brown, *Global Warming: Can Civilization Survive?* (London: Cassell, A Blandford Book, 1996), pp. 13–14.

41. Cited by Barbara Leiterman, "Vandana Shiva Simply Wants to Change the World," *Ms.*, May/June 1997.

42. Vandana Shiva, *Staying Alive: Women, Ecology, and Development* (London: Zed Books, 1989), p. 67.

43. Ibid., pp. 76–77.

44. Virginia Woolf, *Three Guineas* (New York: Harcourt, Brace & World, Inc., 1938; Harbinger Books, 1966), p. 109.

45. Nelle Morton, *The Journey Is Home* (Boston: Beacon Press, 1985), p. xviii.

46. The refugee status of millions of women is a worldwide reality. The Human Rights Watch *Global Report on Women's Human Rights* (New York: Human Rights Watch, August, 1995) states on p. 100: "As of February 1995, twenty-three million people had fled across borders becoming refugees, and another twenty-six million had been internally displaced in their own countries. . . . Africa has nearly 7.5 million refugees and as many displaced; Asia has 5.7 million refugees and Europe six million, not including the internally displaced, especially in Bosnia. Women and children account for

roughly 80 percent of all refugees worldwide." Moreover: "While the conflicts that cause women to flee often make news headlines, the plight of women who become refugees and displaced persons frequently remains unpublicized. In many cases, refugee and displaced women flee conflict after being terrorized with rape and other sexual and physical abuse. Although they seek refuge to escape these dangers, many are subjected to similar abuse as refugees. United Nations High Commissioner for Refugees Sadako Ogata has called this widespread sexual abuse against refugee women a 'global outrage.'" And the situation worsens.

47. Morton, *The Journey Is Home*, p. xix.

48. See Mark Crispin Miller, "The Crushing Power of Big Publishing," *The Nation*, March 17, 1997, pp. 11–18. See also Tom Engelhardt, "Gutenberg Unbound," pp. 18ff in the same issue.

49. Conversation with Jeanmarie Rindone, Spinning Off from "Lightning," *Grolier Encyclopedia* (New York: The Grolier Society, 1957), Vol. XIII, pp. 14–15, October 31, 1995.

50. Conversation with Jeanmarie Rindone, October 31, 1995.

Cosmic Comments and Conversations in 2048 BE: *Concerning Chapter One*

BY ANONYMA

1. I read about these prophecies in one of Kate's books that she had brought over to Lost and Found Continent in 2018 BE. *This volume is* The Mayan Prophecies, *by Adrian C. Gilbert and Maurice M. Cotterell (Shaftesbury, Dorset, and Rockport, Mass.: Element Books, 1995). The authors interpreted the Mayan prophecies as forecasting the end of the world in 2012* AD.

2. Immanuel Velikovsky's Earth in Upheaval *(New York: Doubleday, 1955) was published in New York by Pocket Books in 1977. We have the Pocket Books edition in our Archives, and so the pages containing this information are numbered here as they occur in that later edition. The most pertinent pages are 124–25 and 239–40. Gilbert and Cotterell discuss the implications of these passages on pp. 191–93 of their book. From his studies of sunspot activities and the Mayan calendar Cotterell concluded that the Mayan prophecy for the end of "the fifth age" concerns a reversal of the Earth's magnetic field. He believed that this and its associated cataclysm would occur in 2012* AD. *See p. 192 of* The Mayan Prophecies.

3. *According to Norse mythology Fenrir was the cosmic doomsday wolf who was held by a chain and would be released by the Norns (triple Fate-goddess) to devour the heavenly father at the end of the world–an event which would be an omen of the destruction of all the gods.* See Barbara G. Walker, The Woman's Encyclopedia of Myths and Secrets *(San Francisco: Harper and Row, 1983), p. 243.* See also Wickedary, *p. 150. Fenrir is known in the mythology and Reality of Wild Women in the twenty-first century* BE *as the Great She-Wolf whom we released to devour the patriarchal god(s), thereby putting an end to their world, dooming the doomers, jumping off the doomsday clock, holding back "the end of the world." Fenrir has many daughters and granddaughters, all of whom bear her name. My Wondrous Fenrir is one of her Great-Granddaughters.*

4. *See Rupert Sheldrake,* A New Science of Life: The Hypothesis of Causative Formation *(Los Angeles: J. P. Tarcher, 1981), esp. chs. 4, 6, and 7. We have a copy in our Archives. The book was distributed by Houghton Mifflin Company in Boston and was widely available in the late twentieth century.*

5. *See Daly's book* Pure Lust *for a Radical Feminist explanation and critique of the traditional philosophy of virtues as well as her own philosophy of virtue. Among her sources are Aristotle's* Nicomachean Ethics *and Thomas Aquinas's* Summa theologiae I–II.

6. *Robert Graves gives abundant clues concerning the erasure of parthenogenesis by the mythmakers/myth reversers of Greece after the patriarchal takeover. See his book* The Greek Myths *(Baltimore: Penguin Books, 1955).*

7. *See Virginia Woolf,* Three Guineas *(New York: Harcourt, Brace & World, Inc., 1938; Harbinger Books, 1966), pp. 79–80.*

8. *Ibid., pp. 106–10.*

9. *See Daly,* Pure Lust, *pp. 4–7, and throughout. On p. 260 she cites Olive Schreiner, who wrote: "We are a race of women that of old knew no fear and feared no death, and lived great lives and hoped great hopes; and if today some of us have fallen on evil and degenerate times, there moves in us yet the throb of the old blood." This passage was published in "Rebel Thoughts," in* The Woman Rebel, *vol. 1, no. 3 (May 1914), p. 19.*

CHAPTER TWO

NEMESIS AND THE COURAGE TO CREATE

1. See Jan Goodwin, *Price of Honor: Muslim Women Lift the Veil of Silence on the Islamic World* (New York: Penguin Books, A Plume Book, 1994).

2. Ibid., p. 332.

3. Ibid., p. 331.

4. "Promise Keepers: A Real Challenge from the Right," *National NOW Times*, May 1997, pp. 1, 6.

5. Ibid., p. 6.

6. Ibid.

7. See Center for Democracy Studies, *Promise Keepers: The Third Wave of the American Right*, A Special Report. November 1996, p. 1.

8. Tony Evans, "Reclaiming Your Manhood," in *Seven Promises of a Promise Keeper*, ed. by Bill Bright et al (Colorado Springs: Focus on the Family, 1994), pp. 79–80. Cited in *Promise Keepers: The Third Wave*, op. cit., p. 15.

9. Tony Evans, *No More Excuses: Be the Man God Made You to Be* (Wheaton: Ill.: Crossway Books, 1996), p. 185. Cited in *Promise Keepers: The Third Wave*, op. cit., p. 15.

10. Wellington Boone, cited in Center for Democracy Studies, *Promise Keepers in Their Own Words*, 1997, pp. 5, 7.

11. At Los Angeles Coliseum PK Conference, April 19–20, 1996. Cited in *Promise Keepers: The Third Wave*, op. cit., p. 14.

12. *Promise Keepers: The Third Wave*, op. cit., p. 14.

13. Raleigh Washington, *Dallas Observer*, November 14, 1996.

14. This point has been made repeatedly by Radical Feminist writers, especially Andrea Dworkin and Catharine A. MacKinnon.

15. See my article "The Courage to See," in *The Christian Century* 88 (September 22, 1971), pp. 1108–11. See also *Wickedary*, p. 69.

16. See Daly, *Pure Lust*, pp. 274–80.

17. Ibid., pp. 276–77.

18. Ibid., p. 278.

19. Ibid., p. 280.

20. Millicent Garrett Fawcett, *The Women's Victory — and After: Personal Reminiscences, 1911–1918* (London: Sidgwick and Jackson, Ltd., 1920), 1966.

21. See Daly, *Wickedary*, pp. 62, 69.

22. See Daly, *Pure Lust*, pp. 216–18.

23. See Nevill Drury, *Dictionary of Mysticism and the Esoteric Traditions*, rev. ed. (Bridport, Dorset, England: Prism Press, 1992), p. 99.

24. Ibid.

25. For an ontology of anxiety, see Paul Tillich, *The Courage to Be* (New Haven: Yale University Press, 1952), pp. 32–63. This provided an early spring-

board for my analysis of the overcoming by Wild Women of the anxiety of nonbe-ing.

26. See *Wickedary*, p. 82.

27. Rollo May, *The Courage to Create* (New York: W. W. Norton & Company, 1975).

28. Ibid., p. 26.

29. Ibid., p. 27.

30. Ibid. It is true, of course, that *for women creators* overcoming patriarchal censorship an active battle with the gods is occurring.

31. Ibid., p. 28.

32. Conversation with Jeanmarie Rindone, Newton Centre, Mass., February 2, 1997.

33. In a conversation with Jeanmarie Rindone in Newton Centre, May 1, 1997, she suggested omitting *the* before Goddess(es). It became very clear to me in the process of writing this chapter that the insertion of the article *the*, especially before the singular *Goddess*, objectifies and diminishes that Name. *Goddesses* refers to the various manifestations and personae of "Goddess," such as Isis, Ishtar, and Hathor, who are not "entities" completely distinct from Goddess and should not be seen as comparable to "the gods" of patriarchy. All of this should be seen in the context of my Naming of *Goddess the Verb*, which is defined as "Metaphor for Ultimate/Intimate Reality, the constantly Unfolding Verb of Verbs in which all being participates; Metaphor for Metabeing." See *Beyond God the Father* and *Pure Lust*. See *Wickedary*, p. 76.

34. "The Young Physicists," *The New York Times*, January 31, 1984, pp. C1, C5.

35. *Wickedary*, p. 256.

36. See Andrew Kimbrell, "Biocolonization: The Patenting of Life and the Global Market in Body Parts," in *The Case Against the Global Economy and for a Turn Toward the Local*, ed. by Jerry Mander and Edward Goldsmith (San Francisco: Sierra Club Books, 1996), pp. 131–32.

37. Andy Coghlan, "One small step for a sheep . . . ," *New Scientist*, 1 March, 1997, p. 4.

38. Gina Kolata, "On Cloning Humans, 'Never' Turns Swiftly into 'Why Not?'" *The New York Times*, December 2, 1997, pp. A1, A24.

39. Ibid., p. A24.

40. Ibid.

41. Daly, *Beyond God the Father*, pp. 180–81.

42. Thomas Aquinas, *Summa theologiae* I, q.44, a.3c.

43. Elizabeth Oakes Smith, speech delivered at Woman's Rights Convention, 1852, in *History of Woman Suffrage*, ed. by Elizabeth Cady Stanton, Susan B. Anthony, and Matilda Joslyn Gage (New York: Fowler and Wells, 1881) I, pp. 522–23.

44. Daly, *Wickedary*, p. 182.

Cosmic Comments and Conversations in 2048 BE: Concerning Chapter Two

BY ANONYMA

1. See Robert O. Becker, M.D., Cross Currents: The Promise of Electro-medicine, The Perils of Electropollution *(New York: G. P. Putnam's Sons, A Jeremy P. Thatcher/Putnam Book, 1990), pp. 241–42. This volume, as well as the other books cited in these* Notes, *can be found in our Archives.*

2. Ibid., pp. 297–304. See also William Thomas, Scorched Earth: The Military's Assault on the Environment *(Philadelphia: New Society Publishers, 1995). See also Paul Brodeur,* The Zapping of America: Microwaves, Their Deadly Risk, and the Coverup *(New York: W. W. Norton, 1977).*

3. See Andrée Collard with Joyce Contrucci, Rape of the Wild: Man's Violence against Animals and the Earth *(Bloomington and Indianapolis: Indiana University Press, 1989; first published in London by The Women's Press Ltd., 1988).*

4. Robert O. Becker, M.D., Cross Currents, *op. cit., p. 184.*

5. Ibid., p. 187.

6. Ibid.

7. A "gigalapse" was explained as an Internet collapse in which a billion hours of access time are lost. See the article by Steven Levy entitled "The Internet Crash Scare," in Newsweek, *September 16, 1996, p. 96. Mary brought me a copy of this article, which is in our Archives.*

8. Ibid. An account of a prophecy of such a collapse appears in the same article.

9. See Virginia Woolf, "A Sketch of the Past," in Moments of Being: Unpublished Autobiographical Writings, *edited and with an Introduction and Notes by Jeanne Schulkind (New York: Harcourt Brace Jovanovich, 1976), p. 72.*

10. *See Peter R. Breggin, M.D.,* Toxic Psychiatry *(New York: St. Martin's Press, 1991), p. 32.*

11. *For sources, see Daly,* Beyond God the Father, *pp. 65–66.*

12. *See Lawrence Leamer,* The Kennedy Women: The Saga of an American Family *(New York: Villard Books, 1994), esp. pp. 318–23.*

13. *For example, the nineteenth-century "nerve specialist" S. Weir Mitchell tamed women with his infamous "rest cure," which he combined with ovariotomy. His most famous patient, i.e. victim, was the great Feminist activist, lecturer, and author Charlotte Perkins Gilman, whose story "The Yellow Wallpaper" is a chilling and exquisite exposé of Mitchell and his ilk. I found this information in chapter 7 of Daly's* Gyn/Ecology.

CHAPTER THREE
RE-AWAKENING THE X-FACTOR/FACULTY AND CREATING THE ARCHAIC FUTURE

1. Virginia Woolf, *Three Guineas* (New York: Harcourt, Brace & World, Inc., 1938; Harbinger Books, 1966), p. 64.

2. See Daly, *Pure Lust,* pp. 200–16.

3. Jeanmarie Rindone, personal communication, August 15, 1994.

4. As I have explained in *Pure Lust,* potted passions are stunted, artificially contained. "In a word, they are canned. Consequently, they are twisted and warped versions of genuine passions. Like the nine-inch-high potted bonsai tree that could have grown eighty feet tall, these passions are dwarfed; their roots are shallow. Moreover, since they are contorted, distorted, they bend in unnatural directions, stopping at the wrong objects." See pp. 206–11. Thus in the Cockocratic State women are tracked and trained to hope for the wrong things. For example, a woman might hope for equality within patriarchy, which is an inherently contradictory idea.

5. See Daly, *Gyn/Ecology: The Metaethics of Radical Feminism* (1978; reissued with New Intergalactic Introduction by the Author, Boston: Beacon Press, 1990), Chapter Ten: "Spinning: Cosmic Tapestries."

6. Colin Wilson, *The Occult: A History* (New York: Random House, 1971), p. 10.

7. Ibid., p. 59.

8. Ibid., p. 177.

9. Ibid., p. 582.
10. Elizabeth Gould Davis, *The First Sex* (New York: G. P. Putnam's Sons, 1971), p. 15.
11. Ibid.
12. Ibid., pp. 15–16.
13. Ibid., p. 18. For an extraordinary study of the erasure of women from history see Dale Spender, *Women of Ideas and What Men Have Done to Them* (Boston: Routledge & Kegan Paul, 1982).
14. Davis cites some of the evidence, especially in chs. 2, 4, and 5. Among her sources are J. J. Bachofen, Robert Briffault, Jane Harrison, and Robert Graves.
15. Monique Wittig, *Les Guérillères*, translated from the French by David LeVay (New York: Avon Books, 1969, 1971), p. 89.
16. Davis, *The First Sex*, op. cit., pp. 338–39.
17. See Julia Penelope, *Speaking Freely: Unlearning the Lies of the Fathers' Tongues* (New York: Pergamon Press, The Athene Series, 1990).
18. Renate Klein, "(Dead) Bodies Floating in Cyberspace: Post-Modernism and the Dismemberment of Women," in *Radically Speaking: Feminism Reclaimed*, ed. by Diane Bell and Renate Klein (North Melbourne, Australia: Spinifex Press Ltd., 1996), p. 350.
19. Woolf, *Three Guineas*, op. cit., p. 52.
20. An expert analysis of this situation can be found in Sheila Jeffreys' book, *The Lesbian Heresy: A Feminist Perspective on the Lesbian Sexual Revolution* (North Melbourne, Australia: Spinifex Press Ltd., 1994).
21. Woolf, *Three Guineas*, op. cit., p. 62.
22. Ibid., p. 74.
23. Ibid., p. 94. By *poverty* Woolf meant "enough money to live on." By *chastity* she meant "you must refuse to sell your brain for the sake of money." By *derision* she meant "that you must refuse all methods of advertising merit, and hold that ridicule, obscurity, and censure are preferable . . . to fame or praise." "By freedom from unreal loyalties is meant that you must rid yourself of pride of nationality in the first place; also of religious pride, college pride, school pride, family pride, sex pride and those unreal loyalties that spring from them."
24. Ibid., pp. 93–94.
25. Ibid., p. 36.

26. See Kathleen Barry, "Deconstructing Deconstructionism (or, Whatever Happened to Feminist Studies)," *Ms.*, January/February 1991, p. 83.

27. See Pauline Bart, "The Banned Professor or, How Radical Feminism Saved Me from Men Trapped in Men's Bodies and Female Impersonators, with a Little Help from my Friends," in *Radically Speaking*, ed. by Bell and Klein, op. cit., pp. 262–74.

28. See Elizabeth Grosz, *Space, Time, and Perversion* (New York: Routledge, 1995), pp. 45–46.

29. Klein, "(Dead) Bodies Floating in Cyberspace," op. cit., p. 350.

30. The word *academonic* was invented by Diana Beguine, personal communication, June 1984.

31. See Daly, *Gyn/Ecology*, pp. 130–33.

32. Denise Thompson, "The Self-Contradiction of 'Post-Modernist' Feminism," in *Radically Speaking*, ed. by Bell and Klein, op. cit., p. 325.

33. Ibid., p. 338.

34. John Rajchman, *Philosophical Events: Essays of the '80's* (New York: Columbia University Press, 1991), p. 119. Cited in Somer Brodribb, *Nothing Mat(t)ers: A Feminist Critique of Postmodernism* (North Melbourne, Australia: Spinifex Press Ltd., 1992), p. 10.

35. Christine Delphy, "French Feminism: An Imperialist Invention," in *Radically Speaking*, ed. by Bell and Klein, op cit., p. 384.

36. Ibid., pp. 384–85.

37. Ibid., pp. 389–90.

38. Ibid., p. 390. See Alice A. Jardine, *Gynesis: Configurations of Woman and Modernity* (Ithaca: Cornell University Press, 1985), esp. pp. 20–21. See also Toril Moi, *Sexual/Textual Politics* (London: Methuen, 1985). See also Toril Moi, ed., *French Feminist Thought: A Reader* (Cambridge, Mass.: Basil Blackwell, 1987). In Delphy's illuminating analyis, Moi is shown as employing the same tactics as Jardine. Delphy detects some of the same strategies in the writings of Rosemary Tong, who would not hesitate to classify Kristeva and Cixous as feminists, "despite their disclaimers." See Tong's work *Feminist Thought: A Comprehensive Introduction* (Boulder: Westview Press, 1989).

39. Kristin Waters, "(Re)Turning to the Modern: Radical Feminism and the Post-modern Turn," in *Radically Speaking*, ed. Bell and Klein, op. cit.,p. 289.

40. Ibid., p. 285.

41. Ibid., p. 281.

42. Judith Butler, *Bodies that Matter: On the Discursive Limits of "Sex"* (New York: Routledge, 1993), p. 91. Renate Klein makes the observation that, like the products of other postmodern body writers, Butler's writings on corporeality remain frozen within a hetero-relational framework. See Klein, "(Dead) Bodies Floating in Cyberspace," op. cit., p. 351.

43. Somer Brodribb, *Nothing Mat(t)ers*, op. cit., p. xxiii.

44. See Daly, *Wickedary*, p. 74, under the word *erasure*.

45. Ibid.

Cosmic Comments and Conversations in 2048 BE: Concerning Chapter Three

BY ANONYMA

1. Mary found this information for me in an article by Anton Foek, "Sweatshop Barbie: Exploitation of Third World Labor," The Humanist, January/February 1997, pp. 9–13.

2. Sarah Canner provided this information in "Health Notes," Ms., September/October 1996, p. 41.

3. This was explained in Foek's article, op. cit., pp. 10–11.

CHAPTER FOUR
THE FIFTH ELEMENT AND THE FIFTH DIRECTION

1. Erich Fromm, in his Afterword to George Orwell's *1984* (New York: New American Library, 1949), citing Orwell, wrote:

> "Doublethink means the power of holding two contradictory beliefs in one's mind simultaneously, and accepting both of them. . . . This process has to be conscious, or it would not be carried out with sufficient precision. But it also has to be unconscious, or it would bring with it a feeling of falsity and hence of guilt." It is precisely the unconscious aspect of doublethink that will seduce many a reader of *1984* into believing that the method of doublethink is employed by the Russians and the Chinese, while it is something quite foreign to himself. (p. 264)

2. See especially *Beyond God the Father*, pp. 95–97, and *Wickedary*, p. 93. See Valerie Solanas, *SCUM Manifesto* (Original edition, self-published, 1967; Olympia Press edition, 1968; Edinburgh and San Francisco: AK Press and Freddie Baer, 1996). Solanas' description of patriarchal behavior can be applied to the male product which is patriarchal religion. On pp. 3–4 she writes:

> Being an incomplete female, the male spends his life attempting to complete himself, to become female. He attempts to do this by constantly seeking out, fraternizing with, and trying to live through the female, and by claiming as his own all female characteristics—emotional strength and independence, forcefulness, dynamism, decisiveness, coolness, objectivity, assertiveness, courage, integrity, vitality, intensity, depth of character, grooviness, etc.—and projecting onto women all male traits—vanity, frivolity, triviality, weakness, etc. It should be said, though, that the male has one glaring area of superiority over the female—public relations. (He has done a brilliant job of convincing millions of women that men are women and women are men.) The male claim that females find fulfillment through motherhood and sexuality reflects what males think they'd find fulfilling if they were female.
>
> Women, in other words, don't have penis envy. Men have pussy envy.

3. June Campbell, *Traveller in Space: In Search of Female Identity in Tibetan Buddhism* (London: The Athlone Press, 1996; New York: George Braziller, 1996).

4. Ibid., p. 2.

5. Ibid., p. 102.

6. Ibid.

7. Ibid., pp. 101–3.

8. Ibid., p. 103.

9. See *Beyond God the Father*, *Gyn/Ecology*, *Pure Lust*. See Chapters Three and Five of this book.

10. Campbell, *Traveller in Space*, op cit., p. 70.

11. Cited in ibid.

12. Ibid., p. 71.

13. See my review article, "Women and Tibetan Buddhism," in *Women's*

Studies International Forum, Vol. 20, No. 1, January–February 1997, pp. 179–81.

14. Campbell, *Traveller in Space,* op. cit., p. ix.

15. Ibid., pp. 93–94.

16. Jane Ellen Harrison, *Mythology* (New York: Harcourt Brace, 1963), p. 97.

17. Robert Graves, *The Greek Myths* (Baltimore, Md.: Penguin Books, 1975), I, 14, c.

18. Daly, *Gyn/Ecology,* pp. 65–66.

19. Ibid., p. 64.

20. Ibid., p. 83.

21. Helen Diner, *Mothers and Amazons: The First Feminine History of Culture,* ed. and trans. by John Philip Lundin, introduction by Brigitte Berger (Garden City, N.Y.: Anchor Books, 1973), p. 4.

22. Norman O. Brown calls Dionysus "the [mad] god who breaks down the boundaries." See *Love's Body* (New York: Random House, 1966), p. 116.

23. See Janice G. Raymond, *The Transsexual Empire: The Making of the She-Male,* reissued with a New Introduction on Transgender (1979; New York: Teachers College Press, Athene Series, 1994).

24. Jeremy Rifkin, *The End of Work: The Decline of the Global Labor Force and the Dawn of the Post-Market Era* (New York: G. P. Putnam's Sons, A Jeremy P. Tarcher/Putnam Book, 1995), p. 119. Also see Jeremy Rifkin, *The Biotech Century,* (New York: G.P. Putnam's Sons, A Jeremy P. Tarcher/Putnam Book, 1998).

25. See Janice G. Raymond, *Women as Wombs: Reproductive Technologies and the Battle Over Women's Freedom* (San Francisco: HarperSanFrancisco, 1993; North Melbourne, Australia: Spinifex Press Ltd., 1997), pp. vii–xxxiii.

26. Patricia Monaghan, *The Book of Goddesses and Heroines* (New York: E. P. Dutton, 1981), p. 261.

27. Ibid.

28. John Milton, *Areopagitica* (1644), in *John Milton: Prose Selections,* ed. by Merritt Hughes (New York: Odyssey Press, 1947), pp. 206–7.

29. Mark Crispin Miller, "The Crushing Power of Big Publishing," *The Nation,* March 17, 1997, p. 17. See this entire issue of *The Nation* for important information on big publishing.

30. For a general analysis of the disappearing of books in the course of transfer-

ring information from card catalogs to online catalogs in libraries, see Nicholson Baker, "Discards," *The New Yorker*, Vol. 1xx, April 4, 1994, pp. 64–86. Also see Nicholson Baker, "The Author vs. the Library," *The New Yorker*, Vol. lxxii, October 14, 1996, pp. 50–53.

31. Alfred North Whitehead, *Science in the Modern World* (New York: Macmillan, The Free Press, 1925; paperback ed., 1961), p. 48. This passage served as an important springboard for the writing of *Beyond God the Father.*

32. See Dale Spender, *Women of Ideas and What Men Have Done to Them* (London and Boston: Routledge & Kegan Paul, 1982). Spender gives an excellent analysis and abundant evidence of this.

33. See Franklyn Sills, *The Polarity Process: Energy as a Healing Art* (1989; Rockport, Mass.: Element, Inc.,1991), pp. 50, 172–73.

34. Ibid., p. 173.

35. Ibid., pp. 53–55.

36. Michael Dames, *Mythic Ireland* (London: Thames and Hudson, 1992), p. 196

37. Ibid., p. 194.

38. Ibid.

39. Franklyn Sills, *The Polarity Process*, op. cit., p. 173. See also *A Source Book in Indian Philosophy*, ed. by Sarvepalli Radhakrishnan and Charles A. Moore (Princeton, N.J.: Princeton University Press, 1957), especially all references to *akasa*.

40. The idea of "OM as we Roam" was suggested by Melissa Fletcher, conversation, February 20, 1997.

41. See J. C. Cooper, "Directions of Space," in *An Illustrated Encyclopedia of Traditional Symbols* (London: Thames and Hudson, 1978), p. 51.

42. See Daly, *Pure Lust*, p. 26 and *passim*. See *Wickedary*, p. 88. Metaphors include the Fates, Changing Woman (Creatrix of the Navaho People), and Shekhina (Female Divine Presence in Hebrew lore).

43. See Barbara G. Walker, *The Woman's Dictionary of Symbols and Sacred Objects* (San Francisco: Harper and Row, 1988), p. 276.

44. Conversation with Jeanmarie Rindone, February 2, 1996.

45. See Barbara G. Walker, *The Woman's Dictionary*, op. cit., p. 276, illustration.

46. See Barbara G. Walker, *The Woman's Encyclopedia of Myths and Secrets* (San Francisco: Harper and Row, 1983), p. 957:

The riddle was: "What goes on four legs at dawn, two legs at midday, and three legs at sunset, and is weakest when it has the most support?" The answer was either man or god. The sun god, Ra, Hathor's offspring, grew old and feeble at the end of each day and walked with a third leg, a cane.

47. See J. E. Cirlot, *A Dictionary of Symbols*, translated from the Spanish by Jack Sage (New York: Philosophical Library, 1962), p. 289.

48. Barbara G. Walker's descriptions and analyses of Isis, both in her *Woman's Dictionary* and her *Woman's Encyclopedia*, are translucent with suggestions of Quintessence. As great Cow-Goddess she was the focus of the many-eyed gaze of the starry sky. In the *Dictionary* we read (p. 453): "Egyptian scriptures said, 'In the beginning there was Isis, Oldest of the Old. She was the Goddess from whom all becoming arose.'"

CHAPTER FIVE

BREAKING INTO THE FIFTH DIMENSION: DIS-COVERING THE LIGHT OF QUINTESSENCE

1. Huston Smith, "The Reach and the Grasp: Transcendence Today," in *Transcendence*, ed. by Herbert W. Richardson and Donald R. Cutler (Boston: Beacon Press, 1969), p. 14. Smith attributes this idea to William Witherspoon.

2. As are all Voyagers into further Dimensions. See Edwin A. Abbott (1838–1926), *Flatland: A Romance of Many Dimensions* (1880; New York: Harper Collins Publishers, 1983). In this entertaining work the author depicts a two-dimensional world in which the concept of three dimensions is unimaginable to all inhabitants but one, the narrator, who was visited by a Sphere who taught him the truth. Heresy concerning this matter was severely punished. Indeed the High Council passed the formal resolution "Death or imprisonment awaits the Apostle of the Gospel of Three Dimensions." The narrator is imprisoned for his declaration of his knowledge of the world of three Dimensions, and he fails to make a single convert to his vision.

3. *Syn-Crone-icities* are explained in *Pure Lust*, p. 416, where they are described as "meetings at crossroads of species, of souls," and in *Wickedary*, p. 170, where they are defined as "'coincidences' experienced and recognized by Crones as Strangely significant."

4. Sudie Rakusin, the illustrator of this book and of my two preceding books, *Wickedary* and *Outercourse: The Be-Dazzling Voyage* (1992; London: The Women's Press, 1993, has spoken with me about her many Syn-Crone-ici-ties with animals. One story she recounted to me (in February 1998) is the following:

> A while ago I was driving home on a country road and was really ex-cited because I had an appointment with an animal communicator [a psychic who transmits messages from animals]. I wanted to com-municate with my dog Willow—a beautiful black lab Irish setter mix—who had died in '93. Suddenly on the side of the road, on a chartreuse green hillock—just standing there looking at me—was a big beautiful black lab. I hit the brake pedal in order to slow down. "Oh, there she is!" I said to myself. Then she dashed down the hill-ock and ran across the road and disappeared into a field. I travel this road every day to and from my home. I had never seen this dog be-fore and have never seen her since then. I went home knowing that Willow had communicated with me.

5. Jane Caputi has Named this sort of blockage "jamming the wavelengths." Conversation, March 1997.
6. Sociologist Peter Berger developed this concept in *The Sacred Canopy: El-ements of a Sociological Theory of Religion* (New York: Doubleday, 1967). Professor Berger did not take kindly to my application of this analysis to pa-triarchy, which, of course, is an example *par excellence* of what he had writ-ten about. All the same, I continue to find his ideas on this subject useful.
7. Editorial in *Food & Water Journal*, Spring 1996, p. 6.
8. Vandana Shiva, "The Seed and the Earth: Women, Ecology, and Biotech-nology," *The Ecologist*, Vol. 22, No. 1, January/February 1992, p. 5.
9. Ibid. To illustrate the total takeover she cites a medical expert: "When a mother undergoes ultrasound scanning of the foetus, this seems a great op-portunity for her to meet her child socially and in this way, one hopes, to view him [*sic*] as a companion aboard rather than as a parasite. This should help mothers to behave concernedly toward the foetus." This astonishing piece, written by A. R. Dewsbury as a letter, was originally published under the title "What the Foetus Feels," in *British Medical Journal*, 16 Feb. 1980, p. 481, and was cited previously by A. Oakley in *The Captured Womb: A*

History of the Medical Care of Pregnant Women (Oxford: Basil Blackwell, 1984), p. 18.

10. Gena Corea, *The Mother Machine: Reproductive Technologies from Artificial Insemination to Artificial Wombs* (New York: Harper and Row, 1985).

11. Shiva, "The Seed and the Earth," op. cit., p. 5.

12. They speak for themselves. See *The Code of Codes: Scientific and Social Issues in the Human Genome Project*, ed. by Daniel J. Kevles and Leroy Hood (Cambridge and London: Harvard University Press, 1992).

13. On the subject of being trapped in a three-dimensional world, see Dionys Burger, *Sphereland: A Fantasy about Curved Spaces and the Expanding Universe*, translated from the Dutch by Cornelie J. Rheinbolt (1965; New York: Harper Collins, Harper Perennial, 1994). *Sphereland*, which was written as a sequel to *Flatland*, is coupled here with *Flatland* in one volume. As Isaac Asimov wrote in his introduction to *Sphereland*: "In between *Flatland* in 1880, and *Sphereland* in 1960, Einstein happened." In this book, those who saw "ahead of their time" (beyond three dimensions) also found that "the world" was not ready for their insights.

14. See Thomas Aquinas, *Summa theologiae*, I, q.29, a.4.

15. See Daly, *Gyn/Ecology*, p. 38:

> "The Processions of Divine Persons" is the most sensational one-act play of the centuries, the original *Love Story*, performed by the Supreme All Male Cast. Here we have the epitome of male bonding, beyond the "best," i. e., worst dreams of Lionel Tiger. It is "sublime" (and therefore disguised) erotic male homosexual *mythos*, the perfect all-male marriage, the ideal all-male family, the best boys' club, the model monastery, the supreme Men's Association, the mold for all varieties of male monogender mating.

16. See Daly, *Pure Lust*, p. 48.

17. Concerning the building of the first atomic bomb Oppenheimer wrote:

> It is my judgment in these things that when you see something that is technically sweet, you go ahead and do it, and you argue about what to do about it only after you have had your success. That is the way it was with the atomic bomb. I don't think anybody opposed making it; there was some doubt about what to do with it after it was made.

Cited in Robert J. Lifton, *The Broken Connection: On Death and the Continuity of Life* (New York: Simon and Schuster, Touchstone Books, 1979), p. 425.

18. Michael Day, "Tainted Transplants," *New Scientist*, 18 October 1997, p. 4. See also "Last chance to stop and think on risks of xenotransplants," *Nature*, Vol. 391, January 1998, pp. 320ff. This article warns strongly of the dangers of xenotransplants and declares that there is dire need for international regulation. It emphasizes the risk of xenozoonosis–the transmission of animal diseases via organ transplants or blood–and explains that trials could open a Pandora's box. The article was occasioned by the fact that U.S. regulations were soon to be released allowing trials of animal-to-human transplants.

19. Florianne Koechlin, "The Animal Heart of the Matter: Xenotransplantation and the Threat of New Diseases," *The Ecologist*, Vol. 26, No. 3, May/June 1996. In September 1995 two groups in Britain, Compassion in World Farming and the British Union for the Abolition of Vivisection, in the course of their campaign against genetic engineering and animal patenting which toured twenty-five towns throughout Britain, displayed a six-foot-high representation of a "chimera," which was a combination of a rat, beagle, pig, sheep, cow, and chicken–symbolizing the results of splicing together genes from different species. *The Ecologist* featured a photograph of this hideous representation on its cover plus information about the campaign. See Vol. 26, No. 5, Sept./Oct. 1996, p. 201.

20. See Gina Kolata, "On Cloning Humans, 'Never' Turns Swiftly into 'Why Not?'" *The New York Times*, December 2, 1997, pp, A1, A24.

21. An article which reports biologists' views on animal suffering but does not manage to criticize them is Gail Vines, "Who's suffering now?" *New Scientist*, 22 March 1997, pp. 30–33.

22. John Cardinal O'Connor, cited in *The New York Times*, March 24, 1997, p. A30.

23. Monette Vaquin, *La Vie en Kit: Éthique et Biologie* (Paris: L'Arche de la Defense, 1991), p. 25.

24. Ian Wilmut, cited in "Special Report: The Biotech Century," *Business Week*, March 10, 1997, pp. 79–80. A few researchers continued to express skepticism about the possibility of cloning from adults and maintained that it still remained possible that Dolly was not a true clone. See Gina Kolata, "Some Scientists Ask: How Do We Know Dolly Is a Clone?" *The New*

York Times, July 29, 1997, p. C3. In this article Kolata cites Dr. Norton Zinder, a professor of molecular genetics at Rockefeller University who stated: "They should have proved that Dolly was a clone by testing her mitochondria." The march of clones has continued, however. See Gina Kolata, "10 Cloned Cows Soon to Be Born, Company Reports, Duplicating a Lamb Experiment," *The New York Times,* August 8, 1997, p. A10. And the march of quibbles continues as well. On March 2, 1998, *Time* reported that, under pressure, Ian Wilmut conceded that Dolly could turn out to be the clone not of an adult ewe but of the fetus the ewe was carrying, but he put the odds at a million to one.

25. Janice Raymond, in *Women as Wombs: Reproductive Technologies and the Battle over Women's Freedom* (North Melbourne, Australia: Spinifex Press Ltd., 1994), cites women who "passed along the in vitro fertilization production line," describing their sense of utter degradation. Raymond discusses the violation and pain suffered by the women during procedures and the use of pornography in surrogate agencies to help men masturbate for sperm. She writes: "There is, in fact, a sense of pornography to the whole process of surrogacy and other new reproductive techniques." See p. xxx.

26. See Andrée Collard with Joyce Contrucci, *Rape of the Wild: Man's Violence Against Animals and the Earth* (Bloomington and Indianapolis: Indiana University Press, 1989; first published in London by The Women's Press, 1988).

27. Jeremy Rifkin, *The End of Work* (New York: G. P. Putnam's Sons, A Jeremy P. Tarcher/Putnam Book, 1995), p. 122.

28. Andrew Kimbrell, "Biocolonization: The Patenting of Life and the Global Market in Body Parts," in *The Case Against the Global Economy and for a Turn Toward the Local,* ed. by Jerry Mander and Edward Goldsmith (San Francisco: Sierra Club Books, 1996), pp. 131–32.

29. Ibid., p. 137.

30. See Ted Peters, *Playing God? Genetic Determinism and Human Freedom* (New York and London: Routledge, 1997).

31. Margaret Wertheim, "From Genesis to Genetics," Review of *Playing God?* by Ted Peters, *New Scientist,* 15 March 1997.

32. Mary Shelley, *Frankenstein: Or, the Modern Prometheus* (1818; New York: The New American Library, 1965), pp. 52–53.

33. Kimbrell, "Biocolonization," op. cit., pp. 136–37.

34. Ibid., p. 143. In response to international outrage, the patent claim was withdrawn by the U.S. Department of Commerce in November 1993. See *Gene Watch*, Vol. 9, Nos. 3–4, January 1994.

35. Reported in *Gene Watch*, Vol. 10, Nos. 4–5, February 1997, p. 6.

36. See Craig Benjamin, "Indigenous peoples barred from DNA sampling conference," *Gene Watch*, Vol. 10, Nos. 4–5, February 1997, pp. 5, 18, 19. Shrewd Women will not fail to note that this is analogous to the sort of unscrupulous exploitation that is practiced on women of all races all the time.

37. Kevles and Hood, *The Code of Codes*, p.19.

38. Ibid., p. 36.

39. See *Gyn/Ecology*, pp. 30–31.

40. Chellis Glendinning, "*My Name Is Chellis & I'm in Recovery from Western Civilization* (Boston and London: Shambala, 1994) p. 114.

41. *The New York Times*, March 15, 1997, pp. 1, 10.

42. Elizabeth Gould Davis, *The First Sex*, pp. 34–35.

43. Ashley Montagu, "The Natural Superiority of Women," in *The Saturday Review Treasury* (New York: Simon and Schuster,1957), p. 476.

44. See Jerry Mander, *In the Absence of the Sacred: The Failure of Technology and the Survival of the Indian Nations* (San Francisco: Sierra Club Books, 1991), p. 4.

45. Ibid.

46. Ibid., pp. 172–73.

47. Cited in ibid., p. 172. Dr. Chargoff is a professor of biochemistry at Columbia University Medical School.

48. Kimbrell, "Biocolonization," op. cit. pp. 144–45.

49. Again, Andrée Collard's expression is absolutely apt for the most extreme violation of all nature.

50. The words of Alice Walker in her article "Nuclear Exorcism" (*Mother Jones*, September/October 1982, p. 21) are a fitting response to this violation:

> And it would be good, perhaps, to put an end to the species in any case, rather than let white men continue to subjugate it and continue their lust to dominate, exploit, and despoil not just our planet but the rest of the universe, which is their clear and oft-stated intention, leaving their arrogance and litter not just on the moon but on everything else they can reach.

51. Thomas Aquinas, *Summa theologiae* I, q.51, a.1. What this means is that since angels are pure spirits they have no need for bodies to be attached to them. To put it another way, they can be considered as pure energy, that is, as pure integrity, not requiring a "union" (which implies a dichotomy) between matter and spirit.

52. Ibid., I, q.50, a.3.

53. Ibid., I, q.50, a.4.

54. Ibid., I, q.53, a.3 ad 3.

55. For example, Kay Cornish Mann, whose Native American name is Blue-stone and who identifies as an Intuitive and an Interspecies Communicator, communicates with extraordinary sensitivity especially with animals and with stones, which often Be-Speak to her.

56. See Hildegarde, St., *New Catholic Encyclopedia*, 1967, VI, 1117. Word-Witches continue to wonder and speculate about this "lost" language and "lost" alphabet. Destroyed by the church, perhaps?

57. See *Illuminations of Hildegard of Bingen*. text by Hildegard of Bingen, with commentary by Matthew Fox (Santa Fe, N. M.: Bear & Company, 1985), p. 117.

58. Lawrence M. Krauss, *The Fifth Essence: The Search for Dark Matter in the Universe* (New York: HarperCollins, Basic Books, 1989), pp. 11–13.

59. I have developed this idea in *Pure Lust*.

60. These realities are described vividly by Madeleine L'Engle in *A Wrinkle in Time* (New York: Dell Publishing Company, Yearling Books, 1962). Equally enlightening is another book by Madeleine L'Engle, *A Wind in the Door* (New York: Dell Publishing Company, Yearling Books, 1973).

Acknowledgments

A NUMBER of Musing friends have provided invaluable suggestions for Source materials—in some cases including Quintessential Sources. Several have offered encouraging and con-
structive comments on the manuscript at various stages. The following
"list" of names does not signify any hierarchical order of importance.
Rather, it is more like an interconnecting Web reflecting synchronistic/
Syn-Crone-istic events characteristic of this Time. So:

I thank Lori Getz, Krystyna Colburn, Kay Bluestone Mann, Betsy
Beaven, Suzanne Bellamy, Betty Farians, Jane Caputi, Carol Adams,
Cathleen Palumbo, Emily Culpepper, June Campbell, June Lampert,
Melissa Fletcher, Barbara Hope, Kamado, Pam McCarron, Annie Lally
Milhaven, Abbie Padgett, Mary Lou Shields, Diane Piedmont, Ti Anne
Reichwein, Ann Marie Palmisciano, Ger Moane, Ioma Ax, Mary Ellen
McCarthy, Karen O'Malley, Sandra Stanley, Robin Hough, Erika Wis-
selinck, Marisa Zavalloni, Pat Green, Gary MacEoin, Nancy Kelly,
Wendy Stein, Gail Bryan, Roseanne.

For their important work I am thankful to my thoughtful literary agent,
Jill Kneerim, and to my encouraging editor, Helene Atwan, Director of
Beacon Press. I am grateful to Natalie Maxwell of the administration department at Beacon for her generosity and attention to detail. Barbara
Flanagan was a helpful and efficient copy editor. Jeanmarie Rindone was
my ever Inspired and Inspiring Search assistant. Nilah MacDonald was
a skillful indexer.

I thank my Foresisters, Past, Present, and Future. In fairness, and as
usual, I thank my Self. And—Quintessentially Speaking—Thank Goddess!

Index

Words in boldface are New Words. Although many of these words are not new in the old sense, they are New in a New sense, because they are heard in a New way. Many can also be found in Mary Daly's Other works. Other New Words appear for the first time in this book.

Abbott, Edwin A., 255
ABC World News Tonight with Peter Jennings, 82
abortion, 32, 94, 235
academentia (Diana Beguine), 21, 134–44, 149; defined, 74n
academia, 195
academonic (Diana Beguine), 139, 144
ACLU, 35, 84
Acting, Powers of, 37
Acts: Biophilic, 24; **Courageous**, 62; **Desperate**, 190; **Original Creative**, 119
AD (obsolete), xiii
Adam, 68n
Adams, Carol J., 8, 241
Adwani (India), 48
Afghanistan, 79
Against Our Will: Men, Women, and Rape (Brownmiller), 28

agent deletion, 34n, 135
agribusiness, 109, 182
Áille Óg, 59n, 61
Air, 54, 105, 182, 196, 225; pollution of, 187–88
Akasha (Ether), 183, 254
Alamogordo (New Mexico), 207
Albright, Madeleine, 5
alchemy, creation as, 100
Althusser, 140
A-mazing, 76
A-mazing Amazons, xiii, 15
Amazon (rainforest), 47
Andrews, Lori, 93
Angelic Presences, 37
Angels, 56, 122, 225, 226–28, 230, 236; foreground images of, 151; individuals as distinct species, 227–28
animals, 39–40, 56, 62, 65, 66, 75, 105, 127, 182, 185, 203, 223, 225,

228, 231–32, 236; as chemical factories, 211–12; destruction and torture of, 109, 115, 123; migratory, 52; suffering of, 93, 123, 231–32, 258; transgenic, "pharming" of, 211–12

Anonyma (Annie), xi–xv, 9, 10, 56–77, 106–18, 148–63, 187–200, 231–37

Anonyma Book Club, 10n

Anonyma Netword, 10

Anonyma Network, xi(n), xiii, xiv, 9–11, 56–57, 110–14, 190, 197, 199, 230, 232

Anonymous, as a woman, xi

Anonymous Observer, The (Kate), 68n

anorexia, 152

Anowa, 187–200, 231, 233, 234, 236

Anthony, Susan B., 12, 89

anti-abortion, 81

antitrypsin, 211–12

Aquinas, Thomas, 98n, 99, 138, 226n, 227

Archaic Awakening, 129

Archaic Future, 2, 3, 11, 21, 87–88, 121, 124, 131, 143, 145, 149, 163, 175, 197, 200, 201, 204, 219; defined, xiv(n); Exemplar of, 204; **Realizing the**, xv, 6

Archaic Knowledge, 5

Archaic Memories, 162

Archaic Past, 21, 88, 174–75, 197; Memories of, 4; Memory Bearers of, 5; **Re-Calling the**, 219

Archaic Time: Deep Memory of, 133; defined, 127n; **Original**, 119, 127, 156

archetypal deadtime, 3, 87, 119

Archives, xi–xii, *passim* in *Cosmic Comments*

Areopagitica (Milton), 178, 194

Aristotle, 97–98, 98n, 138, 196n

Artemis, 206n

ashrams, 182, 193

Asia, developing countries in, 174

Associate, The, 91n

astronomy, Chinese and Toltec, 183

Athena, 178

Atlanta Clergy Conference, 81

Atlantis, 64

atomic bomb, 207–8

atrocities: against nature, 109; medical, 109, 173

Augurs, 88

Auschwitz, molecular, 221

Australia, 65

Ax, Io, 44

babblespheres, 123

Background (Denise D. Connors), xi, *and throughout book*; defined, 38n; geography of, 194

Background Dreams, 112

Background Self, 51

Background Time, 119, 121

backlash against Feminism, xiii, 51, 80, 82, 108, 134, 153, 154, 179, 181

bacteria, 214, 233

Baker, Nicholson, 253–54

Balaban, Evan, 123n

Bangkok (Thailand), 152–53

barbie dolls, 122, 152–53; manufacture of, 152; as role models, 152; subliminal influence of, 152; toxic substances in, 152

Barry, Kathleen, 137

Bauman, Batya, 8

BE. *See* **Biophilic Era**

"Beaver Hunt," 31

Becker, Robert O., 109–10

Be-Dazzling, 40, *and throughout book*

Be-Dazzling Dance of the Universe, 203

Be-Dazzling Journey, 101

Beguine, Diana, 74

Be-ing (the **Verb**), 39, 50, 183, *and throughout book*; active battle against, 91; defined, 183; Expanding Presence of, 54; Moments of participation in, 27, 89; Spring of, 125

Be-ing, Powers of, 183

Be-Laughing, 53; defined, 53n

Bell, Diane, 72n, 74n

Bellamy, Suzanne, 8, 236

Be-Longing, 3, 21, 50, 103, 125, 174; defined, 50n

Be-Speaking, 8, 12, 22, 49, 54, 88, 103, 182; defined, 54n

Beyond God the Father: Toward a Philosophy of Women's Liberation (Daly), 8, 13n, 15, 17, 39–40n, 97, 98n, 195

Big Brother, xii

biocolonialism, 214

biodiversity, 47

bioengineering of food, 205, 235; as corporate violence, 205

biological warfare, 214

Biophilia, defined, 7

Biophilic beings, 57, 104, 199, 236

Biophilic Bitches, 119

Biophilic Brotherhood (Jeanmarie Rindone), 67n–68n

Biophilic Communication, 76

Biophilic Creatures, 41, 104

Biophilic Era (**BE**), xi, *and throughout book*

Biophilic Integrity. *See* **Integrity: Biophilic**

Biophilic Intelligence, 55

Biophilic Reality, 20

Biophilic Will, 46

biorhythms, 72

biotechnology, 92–95, 207–24; 225; as cannibalism/vampirism, 24, 219; and control of evolution, 217; as evil, 213; and indifference to suffering, 210, 212; and nuclear weapons, 207; and patriarchy, 221; and plants, 205; and soil, 205; and women's bodies, 205

birds, 183, 185

Bishnoi community (India), 48

Bitches, 39, 49, 74, 188; **Be-Witching**, 39; **Bold**, 49

Blake, William, 219n

bodies, celestial: rape of, 223

Bonding, 74; **Interspecies**, 6, 11; **Transtemporal/Trans-spatial**, 6, 11, 200; **Underground/Background**, 74

bookstores, megalithic/monolithic, 179, 190–91, 200
Boone, Wellington, 82
Bosnia. *See* rape
Boundary, Living on the, 224
Boundary violation, 1, 206, 212
Brahma, 177
brain: adultery of the, 137, 169n; **prostitution of the**, 137, 169n; **selling of the**, 137, 169n (all listings attributed to Virginia Woolf)
brain transplants, 123
breast amputation, as torture, 30
Brodribb, Somer, 142, 144
Brownmiller, Susan, 28, 33, 240
buddhism, Tibetan, 167–70, 174; secret sexual practices in, 167–68, 174
buddhist centers, 193
bulimia, 152
Burger, Dionys, 257
Burruss, Robert, 123n
Butler, Judith, 143

Call of the Wild, 4, 8, 24, 224, *and throughout book*
Campbell, June, 167–69, 252, 253
cancer: age of, 205; research, 209n–10n
Caputi, Jane, 8, 226n, 256
carbon, 47
carbon dioxide, 47
Carson, Rachel, 39
caste, touchable: women as, 123

castration, female: genital, 143; mental, 135; of women's theories, 143
cataclysm, prophecies of, 59–60
cathedrals, medieval, 161–62
causality, Aristotelian theory of, 97–99
Cause, Final, 39, 101–2, 112, 128, 199, 203; Cause of causes, 99n, 102; defined, 39n–40n
Cayce, Edgar, 60, 64
Center for Democracy Studies, 83
Chakravarty, Anand Mohan, 214
Changing Woman, 254
channeler, 11
Chargoff, Dr. Edwin, 221
Chicago-Kent College of Law, 93
chickens, engineering of, 123, 123n
chimeras, creation of, 208, 258
Chipko, Movement (India), 47–49
Christ, 216; "mystical body of," 216
Christian Coalition, 81
chromosomes, X and Y, 217–18
Church and the Second Sex, The (Daly), xv(n), 13n, 14, 17, 88n
Cigelj, Jadranka, 33
Cirlot, J. E., 185–86
Cixous, Hélène, 141
Clinton, President, 45–46
cloning, 1, 23, 92–95, 204, 206, 209–12, 236; human, 93–94; mythic foreshadowings of, 22, 170–74; in rhesus monkeys, 94
Code of Codes, The (Kevles and Hood), 215
Cokorinos, Lee, 80–81

Collard, Andrée, 8, 109, 211
Color Purple, The (Walker), 44n
comets, 3, 223, 228; harpooning, 3, 223n
computer: crashes, 110; viruses, 110–11
"conception, virginal," 71
Concreation, 85, 88, 98–99, 101; defined, 85n; of Nemesis, 20, 85n, 85–87, 98–99, 102–3, 113
Connections: Crone-logical, 201; Magnetic, 59
Connors, Denise D., 38n
continents, seven, 65–67, 75
Contrucci, Joyce, 8
Corea, Gena, 71n, 206
Cosmic Concordance, 40, 230
Cosmic Conversations, 76
Cosmic Symphony, 228–30
Courage, 62, 105; Acts of, 27; Communication of, 57; Contagious, 62, 96, 129; Creative, 20, 95–97, 102, 112, 114, 117, 126; Elemental Courage to Create, 90; Existential, 15; Magnetic, 20, 55, 87–88, 110; morphogenetic field of, 62–63; Ontological, 87; Outrageous Contagious, 11, 86–87; pseudo-, 92–95; as virtue, 62–63, 88
Courage to Create, The (May), 90, 117
Courage to Name, 36, 127–28
Courage to See, 84, 88, 176
Crafty Searchers, 221
Creation of Feminist Consciousness, The (Lerner), 131n–32n

Creation of Patriarchy, The (Lerner), 131n
Creative Dis-order, 117
creativity: authentic, 91; and guilt, 91; as provoking jealousy of the gods, 90–91; pseudo-, 92–95
Creativity, Female, 73, 117, 131; blunted by fear and anxiety, 117; erasure of, 22
Crones, 15, 114, 203, 206, 218; Cackling, 90; Canny, 23, 111; Clairvoyant, 129; Contrary-Wise, 105; Encouraging, 42
Cronies, xii, 71, 73, 198, 236, and throughout book; Company of Caring, 61; Starlusting, 52
Culpepper, Emily, 27n, 126n, 143n
Cushman, John H., Jr., 46

Daly, Mary, xi–24, and throughout book
Dames, Michael, 181
Daring, Great Leaps of, 158
Das, Chandra, 169
Daughters, Divine, 71
Davis, Elizabeth Gould, 5, 129–35, 145, 157–58, 218
Davis, Karen, 123n
deadfellows, 180
Deadly Sins of the Fathers, 16, 165n–66n, 213; Aggression, 16; Assimilation, 16, 24, 213n, 216; Elimination, 16–17; Fragmentation, 16–17, 108, 203; Obsession, 16; Possession, 16; Processions, 16, 257; Professions, 16

deadzone, 204–6

d'Eaubonne, Françoise, 235

de Beauvoir, Simone, 135

deception, 165–66

Deep Background, 112, 219

Deep Breath of Con-Questing Voyagers, 54, 55

Deep Memories, 5, 37, 162, 178, 183; of Elemental Sounds, 54

deforestation, 46–49

Deleuze, Gilles, 135

Dellenbaugh, Anne, 173n

Delphy, Christine, 141–42

de Man, Paul, 135

demonic dissociation, 23, 209–11, 234

depression, 127

Derrida, Jacques, 135, 140, 141

de Sade, Marquis, 68n

Desperately Hopeful Knowledge, 146

Desperation, 3, 21, 190; **Acts of**, 158–59; **Deep**, 224; defined, 128; **Focused Acts of**, 21, 127–29, 156; **New**, 157–62

Devi, Amrita, 48

Devi, Bachni, 48

Diana, 206n

diaspora, 9, 19–20, 22, 44, 51–52, 57, 75–76, 123, 127–29, 147, 182; of African-Americans, 38n; defined, 49–52; as dismembering dis-ease, 86–87; of Elemental Women, 52; imposed, 49, 75; inflicted by patriarchal language, 57; internalized, 51; of Irish, 38n; isolation of, 57, 125; of late twenti-

eth century, 56, 76; negative, 49–52; omen of, 184; overcoming, 37–38, 49–53; of Radical Women, 53; spatial, 119; temporal, 56–57, 119, 151; of Wild Women, xiv

Diaspora, Positive, 20, 52–54, 76, 119; **Creative Movement of**, 128; **Metamorphic**, 165; **Transcendent**, 159; **Transtemporal**, 21, 147

dick-tionaries, 40

Diner, Helen, 172

Dionysius, 227

Dionysus, 22, 171–73

Direction, Sense of, 52, 64, 76, 86, 114, 183

Dis-cover, 3

diseases, sexual, 79

Dis-illusioning, 38, 111

Disney products, 152

dis-spiriting state, 123–27

DNA: reprogramming, 1, 95; research, 214

"Dolly" (sheep), 93, 209, 219n, 236, 258–59

dolphins, 3

Donne, John, 207

doomsday. *See* prophecies, doomsday

doomsday clock, 244

Doomsday Wolf. *See* Fenrir

doublethink, 165, 168; defined, 251

Drexler, Eric, 220n

Dworkin, Andrea, 31, 34, 100n–101n, 240

Dynamics (factory), 152

Early, Biddy, 59n

Earth, 3, 54, 61, 73, 105, 107, 109, 182, 196, 225; electromagnetic field of, 72, 107, 109; life on, 4; Self-cleansing of, 61, 106; Transformation of, 66

Earth Changes, 60, 62–66, 72, 75–77, 114, 118, 149, 231, 232

Earth in Upheaval (Velikovsky), 60

earthquakes, 60

ecofeminism, 7, 235

Edinburgh (Scotland), 211–12

"education," patriarchal, 137

Egypt, 78–80; Oxyrhyncus, 146

electromagnetic fields, man-made, 107–9

electromagnetic jungle, 109–10

electropollution, 108, 111

Elemental beings, 61, 105, 203, 228

Elemental Connectedness, 125, 223; Quantum Leap of, 58

Elemental Creatures, 43, 61, 75, 105, 109

Elemental Diversity, 37, 227

Elemental Emotion, 7, 16

Elemental energy, 77

Elemental Feminist Genius, 5, 20, 21, 41–45, 53, 55, 69–70, 73, 77, 97, 102, 104, 114, 117, 129, 133, 144, 169n, 180–81, 194; castration of, 135; and Creative Courage, 95–97; heritage of creative, 178; Quintessential, 40–43; Realizing, 55; Sparks of, 41, 70, 73; taming of, 134–44, 149; Wild Fire of, 41

Elemental Hope. *See* **Hope**: Elemental

Elemental Integrity. *See* **Integrity, Elemental**

Elemental Lust. *See* **Lust**: Elemental

Elemental Magnetism. *See* **Magnetism, Elemental**

Elemental Reality, 12, 20, 105, 121

Elemental Sensory Perception (ESP), 110, 112

Elemental Sisterhood. *See* Sisterhood, **Elemental**

Elements, 16, 16n–17n, 43, 54; five, 186; four, 185; unity with Quintessence, 186

El Niño, 3

El Saadawi, Nawal, 79–80

embryos, human: mass production of, 221

E-motion, 121; defined, 121n

endocrine system, 72

End of Manhood, The (Stoltenberg), 69n

energy: nuclear, 109; shifting patterns of, 61

erasure, 34, 115, 121, 132, 136, 138, 140, 188, 192, *and throughout book*

essentialist, 21, 134

Ether, 22, 23, 181–82, 186, 196; and "quintessence," 196n; roots of word, 196

ethnic cleansing (genocide), 30; rape as tactic for, 30–35

eugenics, nazi and nectech compared, 6, 210

European Patent Office, 214

Evans, Tony, 82

Eve, new, 216
evolution, control of, 217
Exemplar, 99–102, 117, 199, 204
Exile, 20, 75, 147
Exorcism, Acts of, 95
Expanding Here, xii, 19, 27–55, 77, 88–89, 99–100, 102, 104, 105, 112, 126–27, 183, *and throughout book*
Expanding Here and Now, 57
Expanding Now, 18–19, 112
Expanding Presence, xii
Exxon, 210n

Faculty X, 130–31
Fairy Time, 160
Faith, Fey, 96; defined, 96n
Falwell, Jerry, 35n, 81
Familiars, 40, 61, 64, 70, 228, 231; defined, 61n
Fates, 105, 254
Fawcett, Millicent Garrett, 87
Female Presence, 66; erasure of, 216
"feminine, persons gendered as," 135
Feminism, 74n, 155; backlash against, 51; pseudo-, 154
"feminism, French," 141–42
Feminism, Radical, 6–9, 154; characteristics of, 6n–7n; defined, 6n–7n
Feminism, Radical Elemental, 12, 74, 97, 119, 124, 235
Féminisme ou la mort, Le (d'Eaubonne), 235
"feminist," as insult ("the f-word"), 155

Feminist Books, xiii, 10n; **Be-Spelling**, 40; bookburning of contemporary, 179; destruction/killing of, 4, 179–81; dumping of, 179; massacre/bookburning of, 22, 191–95; remaindering of, 51; scattering of, 51
Feminist Bookstores, 52; massacre/killing of, 22
Feminist International Network of Resistance to Reproductive and Genetic Engineering (FINRRAGE), 72n
Feminist University/Diversity, 135
Feminists, Radical, xi, 8, 12, 21, 34, 50, 59, 72n, 96, 108, 111, 115, 130, 137
Feminists, Radical Elemental, 213, 215, 217, 221
feminist theory, pseudo-, 134–44
Fenrir, 61, 76, 77, 118, 200, 244; as cosmic doomsday wolf and her descendants, 244
fertility, 72
festival(s): Women's, 43; Michigan Women's Music, 43n
fetus, 94, 256
field: electromagnetic, 225; magnetic, 70, 72, 111, 114
Fierce Focus, 51, 197
Fifth Cause, 99–100, 101, 117, 199, 204. *See also* **Exemplar**
Fifth Dimension, 24, 28, 201–30, 232
Fifth Direction, 22–23, 28, 183–84, 198–200; as Center, 198
Fifth Element, 22, 28, 178–83, 180–82, 194

Fifth Essence, 179
Fifth Province (of Ireland). *See* Mide
Fifth Province (of women's minds), 180
Fifth Spiral Galaxy, The. *See* **Galaxy, The Fifth Spiral**
Fire, 40, 53, 54, 104–5, 137, 196
First Amendment, 35
First International Conference on DNA Sampling, 214
First Sex, The (Davis), 129–30, 135, 157–58
five (number), in numerology, 88–89
Five, Realm of, 101
Flatland, 255
Flynt, Larry, 35–36
Flynt, Tonia, 35n
food: genetically engineered, 233; irradiation of, 109
foolocrats, 55
footmaiming, Chinese, 115
Fore-Crone, 59
Fore-Familiars, 59; defined, 59n
foreground (flatland) (Denise D. Connors), 38, 89, 104; defined, 38n; geography of, 194; responsibilities, 89
Fore-Journeyers, 76
Foresisters, xii; of Archaic Times, 72. *See also* **Future Foresisters**
forests, 3, 47–49; destruction of, 109
Foretellers, 88
form, 101–2
Foucault, Michel, 135, 140
Found Continent, 189, 197, 198, 232. *See also* **Lost and Found Continent**
Fourth Dimension, 201, 206
Francoeur, Robert T., 71n
Frankenstein(s), Doctor, 213, 219
Freedom, Radical, 73
Freeman, Walter, 116
"free speech," pornography as, 35
Freud, Sigmund, 135, 141, 143
Fribourg (Switzerland), 157–62, 189–90, 197, 226n
fuels, fossil, 46–47
full-fillment, 122; defined, 122n
fundamentalism, religious: christian, 80–85, 94–95; islamic, 79–80; in Middle East and U.S., 20; movements, 234; state-created, 80
Furies, 15, 165, 184
Future, Memories of the. *See* **Memories of the Future**
Future, Real, 3, 87, 121; Foreknowledge of, 145; Magnetic Attraction of, 162
Future Foresisters, 11, 56, 58, 63, 69, 76, 113, 145–47, 163, 198, 236

Gage, Matilda Joslyn, 5, 63, 146
Galaxies, Four Spiral, 18
Galaxy, The Fifth Spiral, xii, 19, 27–55, 76, 85, 88–89, 128, 129, 182–83; Force Field of, 40, 54; Magnetizing Aura of, 40
Galaxy, The Fourth Spiral, 18–19
gasses, greenhouse, 45–47
"gender" jargon, 21, 134–35
gender studies, 155, 173

General Electric, 210n, 214

genes, 21, *and throughout book*

genetic engineering, 71, 93–95, 173, 204; of "humanized" pig livers, 208

genetic engineers, 93–95

genetic manipulation, xv, 109, 123, 173, 233

genetic wilderness, 1

Genius, Female: creative, 134–44; as Self-fulfilling prophecy, 73. *See also* **Elemental Feminist Genius**

Genius, Wild Elemental, 20, 104

genocide, 30–34, 31n

genome, 93, 210

genome, human, 24; as biological grail, 215–16; and christian myth, 216

gigalapses, global, 110–11; defined, 247

Gilbert, Walter, 215

Gimbutas, Marija, 132n, 158

Gingrich, Newt, 91

Glendinning, Chellis, 217, 220n

global warming, 45–47, 64

god: man becoming one with, 95; trinitarian, 219; triune, 23, 206–9

Goddess, 6, 122, 175, 184, 186, 194, 224; as "Blessed Lady," 162; death of, 94; as Metaphor for **Be-ing**, 95, 230; **Original**, 177; **Original Triple**, 206; and **Quintessence**, 230; **Quintessential**, 194; sacred grove of, 184; of a thousand names, 177n; unifying nature of, 186; as **Verb**, 229–30

goddess, "feminine," 121n

Goddess(es), 71, 91

Goddesses and Gods of Old Europe, The (Gimbutas), 132n

gods: and creativity, 90–91, 177; jealousy of patriarchal, 90–91; wannabe, 209

Goldberg, Whoopi, 91n

Good, Magnetizing Idea of the, 102

Goodwin, Jan, 29n–30n, 80

Gosden, Roger, 93

Gossips, Gorgons, and Crones (Caputi), 239

Graves, Robert, 244

"greenhouse effect, enhanced," 47. *See also* global warming

"Green Revolution," 205

Greer, Kelly Ali, 121n

Grief, Passion of, 182

Griffin, Susan, 8

gurus, religious, 167ff., 177, 193

gynecology, atrocities of, 115

Gyn/Ecology, 235

Gyn/Ecology: The Metaethics of Radical Feminism (Daly), 7, 13n, 15–17, 21, 31n, 38n, 71n, 115, 165n–66n, 206n, 213n, 235

Gynergy (Emily Culpepper), 61, 66–67, 73, 86, 160, 188, 197, 198, 201, 221; as Spinning, Spiraling, Whirling Movement, 160, 162

Gynocentric: society, 71, 132–33; tradition, 46; world, 66, 117, 161

gynocide, 30, 166n; defined, 30n–31n

Gynocratic world, 66

Hags, 15, 43, 76, 188, 192, 206, 221;
    Fiery, 196; Her-etical, 229; Outra-
    geous, 70; Radical, 46
Happiness, 50n; attainment of,
    98n; Re-Calling, 105
harassment, sexual, 122
Harmony: Cosmic, 186; New, 66
Harmony of the Spheres, 4
Harpies, 15
Harrison, Jane, 171
Hathor, 184, 186
healers, women, 235
Hearing, Deep (Nelle Morton),
    59
Hecate, 206n
Here, Expanding. *See* **Expanding
    Here**
Heritage, Archaic, 106, 185; hidden,
    53
Heritage Foundation, The, 81, 154
"Heritage Keepers," 85
Hildegard of Bingen, 228–30, 261
Himalayas, logging banned in, 48
hinduism, 177
holiness, illusion of, 168
holocaust, genetic, 221
Homer, 196
Hope: Elemental, 128, 156, 159,
    197; Leaps of, 160; unbounded,
    162
hope: foreground/false, 128; potted,
    128
Hopping Hope: Acts of, 197; de-
    fined, 56
hucksters, nutraceutical, 122
Human Diversity Genome Project,
    215

human genome project, 24
hurricanes, 60
Hurston, Zora Neale, 44n
Hwang, Hye Sook, 67n, 166n

incest, 79
India, 48–49
Indigenous Peoples (DNA sam-
    pling of), 260
Indonesia, 152
infertility, 94, 174
Inner Ear, 9, 59
Integrity, 11; **Biophilic**, 224; **Ele-
    mental**, 185, 223; **Female Ele-
    mental**, 134; **Leaps of**, 84;
    Original, 23, 40, 104, 129; viola-
    tion of, 168
Intergalactic Communication,
    52, 127
International Monetary Fund,
    234
Internet crashes, 110
Interspecies awareness, 200
In the Absence of the Sacred
    (Mander), 1
invalidation, Self-, 168
Iran, 79
Iraq, 79
Ireland, 198; Fifth Province of,
    50
Irigaray, Luce, 141
Isis, 186, 255

Jackson, Cindy, 152
Jardine, Alice, 141, 142
John Paul II, pope, 32–33, 218–19

Jordan (country), 79
Journeying, 50–51
justice, 86

Kalu, Rinpoche, 167
Kaplan, Jonathan, 214
Kennedy: Joseph P., 116; Rose, 116;
    Rosemary, 116
Kevles, Daniel J., 215
Kimbrell, Andrew, 212, 222
Kirshenbaum, Gayle, 33
Klein, Renate, 71n, 72n, 74n, 135,
    139
Koechlin, Florianne, 208
Krauss, Lawrence M., 196n
Kristeva, Julia, 141
Kuwait, 79

labor, cheap: women and children
    as, 152–53
Labrys, 19, 87
Lacan, Jacques, 135, 140, 141, 143
lama(s): "celibate," 167–68; de-
    fined, 169–70; guru(s), 167
"lamb of god," 219
Laughter: Lusty, 53; Roaring, 54
Lava, 5, 60
Lawrence Livermore Laboratory,
    92–93
lawyers, 192
Leaping: Desperate Acts of, 191;
    Metamorphic, 21
Leaps: Macroevolutionary, 105;
    Quantum, 43, 58, 70, 77
lechers, spiritual, 177
L'Engle, Madeleine, 239, 261
Leopold, Ellen, 209n–10n

Lerner, Gerda, 131n
Lesbians, 108, *and throughout book.*
    See also **Women: Brazen,**
    Contrary-Wise, Defiant, Des-
    perate, Disgusted, Eccentric,
    Outrageous, Terrible, Unstuck,
    Wayward, Wicked, Wild, *et*
    cetera
Levine, Ann D., 29, 32
Lie, Great, 92
Lies, Biggest, 192, 193
Life and Death (Dworkin), 100n–
    101n
Life, Elemental, 55; mutation of, 6
Light Bulbs, Radishes, and the Poli-
    tics of the 21st Century (Morgan),
    74n
Lightning, 53–55, 76, 112
"Lion King," 152
lobotomy: female victims of, 116;
    psychic, 116; surgical, 116
Logan, John, 208
Looking Glass Society, 169n–70n
Los Alamos, 207
Lost and Found Continent, 10,
    65–67, 69–75, 106, 107, 110, 114,
    118, 148, 158, 188, 190, 231; procre-
    ation on, 72. *See also* **Found**
    Continent
Lust: Elemental, 125; for risk and
    variety, 89
Lust to Leap, 201
Lusty Leapers, 53, 90, 105
Lyotard, Jean-François, 135, 140

McCartney, Bill, 81, 82, 83
McCaughey, Bobbi, 94

MacKinnon, Catherine A., 30–31, 32

Madonna, 122

Magnetic Course, 55

magnetic currents, 52, 76

magnetic field, Earth's: reversal in, 59

Magnetic fields, 88, 108

Magnetic Force Field, 55

Magnetic Magic, xiv, 19, 39–40, 58–59

Magnetic Presence, 39

Magnetic pulls, 161

Magnetic Storms, 88

magnetism, animal, 39

Magnetism, Elemental, 39–40; Acts of, 156

magnetize, 183; defined, 39, 58

Magnetizing, Momentous, 40

Magnetizing Aura, 40

Magnetizing Force, 102

Magnets, Women as, 39

Maio, Kathy, 35n

majority, cognitive, 236

male-functioning, 42, 111

male motherhood, 20, 94, 169–74, 216

Male Mothers, 94; wannabe, 71

management, business, 42

Mander, Jerry, 1, 220, 221

man-midwives, 235

Mann, Kay Cornish, 261

Mars, 223n

Mary: "Divine Motherhood," mystery of, 218–19; as Goddess, 229n, 229–30; as Goddess dethroned, 218; "mother of god,"

175; Queen of Heaven, 229; Virgin, 172

mass rape: in Bangladesh, 29; in Bosnia, 29–34; in Burundi, 29; in Cambodia, 29; in Croatia, 29–34; in Liberia, 29; in Peru, 29; in Rwanda, 29, 29n–30n; in Somalia, 29; in Uganda, 29. *See also* rape

masters, postmodern, 135–36

materialism, masculist, 133

Mattel Corporation, 152

May, Rollo, 90–91, 95, 117

media, 75, 192; mind muddiers of the, 184

meditation, techniques of, 193

Mejakic, Zeljko, 33

Memories, 3; Volcanic Eruptions of, 5

Memories of Desperation, 158

Memories of the Future, 126, 145, 146, 147, 149, 155, 156, 158, 159, 163, 198, 237

Memory, ancestral, 12

Memory, Archaic, 5, 113, 118

Memory, Deep, 125, 140

meta-, defined, 103

"Meta," Here and Now of, 118

Metabeing, 50n

Meta-dissolution, of patriarchal order, 20, 118, 119

meta-etymologies, 18

Metamystery, 99, 185; defined, 99n, 185n–86n

Metapatriarchal: defined, 70n; society, 70

Metapatriarchal Metaphor:

defined, 95n–96n; Goddess as, 95

Metapatriarchal Metamorphosis, 129

Metapatterning, 90, 102, 112

Meta-subversion, of patriarchal order, 20, 118, 119

Middle Ages, 161–62

Mide, 41, 50, 102, 181–82, 198

midwives, 235

migration, 20, 52–53, 76, 147, 183; of animals, 52–53; defined, 52

Migration: Massive, 53; Original, 76; Positive, 119

millennial dummydom, 113

millennial time, xiii, 1, 28, 49, 52, 59–60, 108, 192, *and throughout book*

millennium, 2, 64, 77, *and throughout book*; third, 218–19

Miller, Kenton, 46

Miller, Mark Crispin, 179

mindbindings, 57

minority, cognitive, 236

misogynism, 224; fundamentalist, 233

misogyny, patriarchal: in christianity, 22; in eastern religions, 22

Mitchel, S. Weir, 248

Moments: of Transtemporal Bonding, 56; **of Unforgetting,** 21, 125

Monsanto, 210n

monster, 213; defined, 185

Montagu, Ashley, 218

moon, 237; strip-mining of, 3

Moral Majority, 81

Morgan, Robin, 74n, 175n

"morphogenetic fields," 62

Morton, Nelle, 50–51, 59

mother-mimers, phallotechnic, 213

mothers, as "environmental factors" for fetus, 205–6

Movement: Leaping, 119; **Metamorphic,** 105

Ms., 33

murder, sexual, 32

Muses: Canny, 102; **Migrating,** 53

music, celestial, 237

Music of the Spheres, 186, 228–30

mutilation, emotional and spiritual, 168

mutilation: female genital, in African and Arab countries, 79, 115, 143

My Name is Chellis and I'm in Recovery from Western Civilization (Glendinning), 220n–21n

mysticism, Pythagorean, 11

myth, patriarchal, 204, 206; christian, 206–9

NAFTA, 234

Naming, 2, 19, 22, 23, 58, 65, 80, 101, 115, 121, 131n, 178, 182, 195, 203, 221, 225, 230; Act of, 42; phallocratic taboo against, 203; Powers of, 37

Nanadic, Natalie, 34

nanotechnology, 3, 220

National Cancer Institute, 209n–10n

National Citizen and Ballot Box (Gage), 63

National Institutes of Health (NIH), 214

National Organization for Women, 84

nature, 1, *and throughout book*; destruction of, 234; violation of, 234. *See also* **Biophilic Creatures; Elemental** beings; **Elemental Creatures**

nazis, 31n

Nazism, 210

necro/biotechnology, 23–24

necrofuture, 206

necrophiles, phallocentric, 139

necrophilia, 7

necrophiliac sir nothings, 55

necrophiliacs/nothing-lovers, 2, 74

necrophilic era, xiii

necrophilic state, 7

necrosociety, 211

necrotechnocracy, xv

necrotechnologists, 1, 6

necrotechnology, 209, 211, 213, 219; biotechnology as, 20, 92–95; indifference to suffering, 23

nectech, 4, 20, 21, 92, 209; as ultimate Rape of the Wild, 222. *See also* necrotechnology

nectech draculas, 217

nectech empire, 234

nectech future, 215–19; mythic context of, 218–19

nectech nasties, 220

Neft, Naomi, 29, 32

Nemesis, 20, 79–105, 111, 114, 122, 181, 186, 199–200, 223; **Concreation of**, 20, 85n, 85–87, 98–99, 102–3, 113; Metamorphic work of, 119; **Metapatterning** dance of, 90; and retribution, 85; Wrath of, 178

networking, underground, 45

"Network of the Imaginary Mother, The" (Morgan), 175n

Neuffer, Elizabeth, 33n

"new reproductive technologies," 205

New Space, 101

Newsweek, 30, 33

New Words, Tribes of, 17

New Word-Storms, 165

Nextran, 208

Nicholas, saint, 162

Nietzche, 135

1984 (Orwell), xiv, 119n

nirvana, defined, 166n

Nixon, President, 104

Nothing Mat(t)ers (Brodribb), 142

Notre Dame, Cathedral of, 162

Now, Expanding. *See* **Expanding Now**

Nowrojee, Binaifer, 29n–30n

nuclearism, 23, 209

ocean(s), 3, 39, 109

O'Connor, John, Cardinal, 210

Oedipus, 184–85

Omarska, 33

Oppenheimer, Robert, 207, 257
Oregon Primate Research Center, 94
Original Acts/Actions, xv(n), 87
Orwell, George, xiv, 119n
Other, 129; defined, 129n
Outercourse: The Be-Dazzling Voyage (Daly), 14n, 17–19, 28n, 162
Outsider's Society (Virginia Woolf), 22, 75, 119, 147, 163

Padgett, Abigail, 190
Pagan Past, 163
Paglia, Camille, 142
Pakistan, 79
Papua New Guinea, 214
parthenogenesis, 71–74, 172, 218
particularization, 193
Parton, Dolly, 211
Passion, Volcanic, 196–97
passions, potted: defined, 248
Past, Deep, 3, 5, 22
Past, New Presence of the, 58
patenting: of Guaymi woman's cell line, 214; of Hagahai person's cell line, 214; of human females, 214; of life forms, 23–24, 213–15, 223
patriarchal order, toxic residues of, 106
patriarchetype (Kelly Ali Greer), defined, 121n
patriarchy, xi(n), 41–43, 61, 65–67, 70, 72, 97–100, *and throughout book*; and takeover of Gynocentric cultures, 66; political powers

of, 32; scientists of, 71; "spirituality" of, 22
Paul, saint, 68n
Penelope, Julia, 34n, 135
peoples, indigenous, 204, 214, 260
People versus Larry Flynt, The, 35
pesticides, 109, 151
Peters, Ted, 212–13
phallocracy, 19, 41, 225
phallocratic/foolocratic, U.S. and Europe as, 222
phallocrats, 55
phallotechnocracy, 203
"pharming," 211–12
Phillips, Randy, 82
philosophers, medieval, 226–27
philosophy, 12–13; medieval scholastic, 100, 162; phallic, 22; western patriarchal, 97–99
pigs, transgenic, 212
planets, 223, 236, 237
plants, 235–36
poisoning: of mind, 151; of produce, 151
"political correctness," 195
pope, prognosticating, 218–19
pornography, 31–37, 222; in advertising, 36–37; causal connection with rape and torture, 34; in cyberspace, 36, 111; as depicting lynched blacks and beaten and mutilated Black and Asian women, 36; as "free speech," 35, 85; in the media, 36; as sexual/social subordination of women, 84; as stimulus for atrocities, 34; as vi-

olence of men against women, 36; in war, 30–34; as war propaganda, 31–32
Positively Revolting, 52, 193
Positively Scattered State, 75
Positively Scattering, 119, 147
"postbiological age," 220
Postchristian era, 14
postfeminism, 74
"postmodern feminist theory," 21–22, 134–44, 173
Power, Elemental, 73
Power of Presence, 199
Powers: Elemental Presentiating, 45; Elemental Sensory, 51; Magnetizing, 39, 109
Presence, 51; Be-Dazzling, 97; Expanding, 39; Female, 66; Magnetic, 58; New Dance of, 199; Ontological, 121; Real, 105; Transtemporal and Transspatial, 186, 198
presence of absence, 191
Present, Real, 119
prestige, phony, 167–68; 169n
"prick in the head, the," 143n
principalities and powers, 6
professionals, medical, 235
Promise Keepers, 20, 80–85; as anti-choice, 83; as anti-gay, 81, 83; cult-like nature of, 83; as political organization, 81, 83; and pornography, 83–85; racism of, 82–83; reversals in propaganda of, 83; "submission" of women in propaganda of, 80–85

Promise Reapers, 85
prophecies, doomsday, 59–61; of Edgar Cayce, 60; Mayan, 59, 243
prophecy, self-fulfilling, 42, 73, 172
prostitution, 32, 79
pseudocreativity, technological, 20
pseudodiversity, 212, 220
pseudofuture, 204
pseudopassions, 193
pseudovirtues, 75; patriotism as, 75
psychosurgery, 116
publishers, megalithic/monolithic, 179
Pure Lust: Elemental Feminist Philosophy (Daly), 7, 16–17, 50n, 86, 95n, 115, 122n, 125n, 191, 207, 248

Quintessence, 3, 6, 101, 103, 186, 221, 224, 228–30; as Cosmic Harmony, 203, 237; defined, 4, 11, 23; Elegant Wildness of, 88; Quest for, 2, 4, 96–97; as Source of Ecstasy, 228; as Verb, 4
"Quintessence" (garlic product), 122

racism, 8, 31n, 36, 82n–83n, 83, 106–7, 137, 191, 227. See also ethnic cleansing, genocide, pornography, Promise Keepers, rape
Radical Elemental Consciousness, 55
Radical Elemental Feminist Manifesto, 2, 6–9, 84, 119, 235
Radically Speaking: Feminism Re-

claimed (Bell and Klein, eds.), 72n, 74n

Rage, 22, 105, 111; Creative, 73; Female Elemental, 88; Righteous, 37, 53, 196–97

rainforests, 47

Rajasthan (India), 48

Rakusin, Sudie (illustrator), 203, 256

rape, 28–36, 79, 115, 173, 182; as conscious process of intimidation, 29; as genocide/gynocide, 30; mass, 29–34; of Muslim women by Serbs, 19; and pornography, 19; as strategy of war, 29–34; in U.S., 29; in war, 34–35; as war crime, 32. *See also* mass rape

rape/death camps, 19, 30–34

Rape of the Wild (Collard), 109

rapism, 222; defined, 8

rapists, space-, 3, 21

Raymond, Janice G., 71n–72n, 173, 211, 253, 259

"reality," phallocentric, 73

Realms, Subliminal, 99

Re-Calling, 58

Recklessness, Thoughtful Focused, 159

Refusing to Be a Man (Stoltenberg), 69n

religions, eastern, 193

remaindering of books, 51

Re-membering, 4, 87, 147

resonance, morphogenic, 66

reversal religion, 176

reversals, 83–87, 90–92, 94, 138, 155, 165, 166, 175, 252; Great, 92; by patriarchal "spirituality," 166–70; by redundancy and contradiction, 92

reversing reversals, 188

Ricki, 236

Rifkin, Jeremy, 173

Rindone, Jeanmarie, 67n–68n, 239, 242, 243, 246, 248, 254

river, Daly's work as, 13–14

rivers, 54

robotics, 220

rocks, 228, 236

Roe versus Wade, 94–97, 235

Roiphe, Katie, 142

Rootedness, 45–46; Intuition of, 74

Roots, 20, 44–49, 51, 75, 183; Discovering of, 88

Ross, Alfred, 80–81

Rwanda. *See* mass rape

"sacred canopy" (Peter Berger), 204

Sado-Ritual Syndrome, applied to "postmodern feminist theory," 139–44

sadosociety, 11, 68n, 73, 91, 103, 184

sado-sublimination, 124; defined, 124n-25n

Sappho, xi(n), 146

Sarasvati, 176–77, 178

satellites, military, 109–10

Saudi Arabia, 79

scatter, defined, 51

"scatter-brained," 51–52

Scattered State, 75

scattering, 20, 75; of feminist books, 51

Schreiner, Olive, 244

science, big, 234, 235

Scotland, 167

SCUM Manifesto (Solanas), 145n

Sea Around Us, The (Carson), 39

Searing Truth, 41

seas, 56, 60, 182, 237

"second Adam," Christ as, 216

Second Sex, The (de Beauvoir), 157

"second wave" (of Feminism), xiii

Seed, Dr. Richard, 1, 95

Seers, 185

Self-Realization, stoppage/inhibition of, 168

Semele, 171

sensory deprivation, world of, 187–88

sex determination, 218

Shakti, 177

Shape-shifting, 134, 199; defined, 75n

Shaw, George Bernard, 90

sheep, transgenic, 211–12

Shekhina, 254

Sheldrake, Rupert, 62, 244

Shelly, Mary, 213

Shiva, Vandana, 48, 205–6

shopping malls, 190–91, 220

Shrewd Shrews, 84, 103, 176

Shrewish Shrewdness, 52, 63

Simpson: Nicole Brown, 192; O. J., 192

Sinspiring/Firing, 86

Sisterhood, 52, 58, 232–33; as cosmic rainbow, 69; **Elemental**, 11; **Transtemporal**, 69

Sister Survivors, 192

Sisters: Animal, 75; Elemental, 52; Rock, 75; Star, 75; Tree, 75; Uncivilized, 71

Sivac, Nusreta, 33

skills: for adaptation, 76; migratory, 76

sky/skies, blackened with spacecraft, 3, 223n

slavery, female sexual, 79, 115, 153, 234

Smith, Elizabeth Oakes, 20, 102–3, 118

snookers, 111

snool, 68; defined, 68n

snudges, 111, 191

snuffers, 191

society, necrotechnological, 210

Sojourner, xi(n)

Sojourner: The Women's Forum, 35n, 210n

Solanas, Valerie, 145, 252

Sophie, 189, 232

"soul," 104

Sounding of Sirens, 165

Sounding, Elemental: Thunder as, 55

space, 220; probes, 223n; rape of, 223n

space-rape, 223n

Sparking, Intergalactic, 40

Speaking Freely: Unlearning the Lies of the Fathers' Tongues (Penelope), 34n species: of animals, 3, 95; endangered, 224; extinction of, 47; genetic manipulation of, 231; human, 6; mixing, 21; mutant, 93–95; "new," 6; patenting, 93; of plants, 3, 93, 95

Spender, Dale, 41

Sphereland, 257

Sphinx, 23, 184–86, 200, 223, 224; riddle of, 185, 255

Spinning, xii, 57, 128

Spinsters, 15, 73, 96, 128, 165, 201, 206

spiraling, 113

Spirits, Elemental (angels), 225, 226–28

spiritshed (Virginia Woolf), 121, 140

"spirituality": eastern traditions of, 166–69; institutionalized, 166; patriarchal, 193; reversals of, 166–74; "women's" new age, 121n

Spretnak, Charlene, 225n

stag-nation, 100

Stamina, 76; Ultimate, 221

Standing One's Ground, 52

Stanton, Elizabeth Cady, 11

stars, 56, 223, 225, 228, 236, 237

Statement from the Biophilic Brotherhood, 67–69, 156

state of: atrocity, 19, 28, 29, 37, 51, 85; **boredom/snoredom**, 85; **captivity and contamination**, 225; **clonedom/boredom**, 227; **confusion**, 21, 122, 151; **deception**, 13, 91, 187, 188, 190, 192, 193; **despair**, 128, 158, 159, 190; **diaspora**, 44, 75, 76, 105, 119, 128, 183; **dividedness**, 37, 52; **dividedness/diaspora**, 38, 49–53; **intellectual oppression**, 188; **isolation**, 55, 57; **living death**, 224; **mass hypnosis**, 193; **patriarchal paralysis**, 105, 197; **possession**, 225; **predatory prickery**, 113; **separation**, 119; **severance**, 127, 128, 156, 166; **staledom**, 127; **terror**, 19, 28–33, 36–39, 117; **torture**, 127

State of Natural Grace, 24, 224–28

States of Grace (Spretnak), 225n

Stockholm Environmental Conference, 48

Stoltenberg, John, 69

stones, 228

Storm, 76, 160; Great, 53

storms: electrical, 54

Subliminal Sea, 40; defined, 18

suffragists, xiv

sun, 182

sunlight, 225

surgery, cosmetic, 152

suttee, Indian, 115, 182

sweatshop conditions, 234

Sweet Pea, 236

synchronicity, dance of, 237

Syn-Crone-icities, 23, 105, 203, 228, 256; defined, 255

Taboo-Breaking, 224

Tangley, Laura, 46

technodaddies, 207

technodocs (H. Patricia Hynes), 71n, 94

technofathers, 221

technofools, 223

"technologies, new reproductive," 24, 71, 92–95, 115; and indifference to suffering, 93–94, 123, 210

technomadness, 5

tension, creative, 100

terraforming, 3, 223n

Terrible Taboo, 53n, 176

terror, subliminal, 36

terrorism, against women, 234. See also state of: terror

Tertio Millennio Adveniente (pope John Paul II), 218–19

Thailand, 152–53

Their Eyes Were Watching God (Hurston), 44n

theologians, medieval, 226

theology, medieval, 138, 162

theory, postmodern, 155

Third Eye, 9, 59

Third World, 222

Thompson, Denise, 140

Three Guineas (Woolf), 119n, 137, 169n

Thunder, 41, 53–55, 76, 112; as Be-Speaking, 54; defined, 54

Tibet, 167–71, 174–75

Tidal Time, 189

tide, 39

Tillich, Paul, 245

Time, 199–200, 201; counterflow of, 199; fluidity of, 199

Time, Background. See Background Time

timeshed (Virginia Woolf), 121, 140

token torturers, 143

tomfools, 74

Tomlin, Lily, 134n

toxins, 225

Transsexual Empire, The (Raymond), 173

transsexualism, spiritual, 170

Transtemporal Communication, 198

Transtemporal Conjuring, 148

Transtemporal Conversations, 10–11, 56–57, 106–8, 148–53, 187–200, 231–37

Transtemporal Desperadoes, 157

Transtemporal Encounters, 198

Transtemporal Sisterhood. See Sisterhood, Transtemporal

Transtemporal Synchronicities, 112

Transtemporal/Trans-spatial Travel, 9–10

travel: Time-Space, 3

trees, 19, 44–49, 51, 54, 56, 75, 182, 183, 223, 225, 228, 230; massacre of, 46–48

"Trial of the Century," 192

tricksters, 74

"Trinity" (code name for A-bomb test), 207

trinity, christian: as paradigm for cloning, 207; as patriarchal pattern, 207

Trivia (Triple Goddess), 206n

True Course, 55

tulku system, Tibetan, 22, 170, 174

Uncle Tom, as oppressive Black role model, 83

undoublethink, 188
Unforgetting, 22
United Arab Emirates, 79
United Nations Women's Decade, 48
Universe: Dance of the, 4; Harmonious Integrity of the, 228; Sense of **Be-Longing** in the, 230
Untamed Truthsayers, 57
U.S. Supreme Court, 35n, 213

Vach (Goddess of Speech), 176. *See also* Sarasvati
vampires, 223
vampirism, "divine," 166
vapor state: defined, 54
Vaquin, Monette, 210
Velikovsky, Immanuel, 60, 243
Verb of Verbs (Be-ing), 230
"Virgin Birth of Christ," 22, 172
Virtue: Metamorphosed/Metamorphosing, 99; **Volcanic**, 63
virtues, 62, 188
viruses, 233
Volcanic: Eruptions, 5; Flow, 6; Waves, 5
Volcanoes, 60
Voyagers: Canny, 203; **Daring**, 53; **Wild**, 87
Voyaging, Multidimensional, 89

Walker, Alice, 44n
Walker, Barbara G., 177n, 184, 229n
Washington, Raleigh, 83
water, 41, 54, 105, 196, 225, 228; Super Natural, 188

Waters, Kristin, 143
weapons: of death, 92; of life, 92; nuclear, 109
Websters, 180
Websters' First New Intergalactic Wickedary of the English Language (Daly in Cahoots with Caputi), 14n, *and throughout book*
Webster's Third New International Dictionary, 7, 39, 43, 50, 52, 54, 58, 103, 108, 185
Weingarten, Tara, 223n
Wertheim, Margaret, 212
West, Lawrence C., 92
whales, 3
Wheatley, Margaret, 42
Whitehead, Alfred North, 180–81, 195
White Heads, Mister, 195
Wicked Words, 40
Wild Cat, 59n, 61
wilderness: genetic, 1, 220; intervention, 220; space, 1, 220
Wildfire, 158, 159
"wild west," American, 89
Wilmut, Ian, 93, 209, 211, 258–59; as "Good Shepherd," 219. *See also* "Dolly"
Wilson, Colin, 129–32
wind, 40, 236
Wind, Great Raging, 49
Wisselink, Erika, 124
Witch-Crafty, 76
witchcraze, 58, 115, 235
Witches, 15, 52–53, 91, 105, 160
Wittig, Monique, 5, 133

Wolf, Donald, 94

Woman's Encyclopedia of Myths and Secrets, The (Walker), 177n, 229n

Woman's Rights Convention: of (1848), xiv, 10; of (1852), 103

women: atrocities against, 115; battering of, 173; boundary violation of, 173; destruction of, 234; end of, 215–18; patenting of, 214; patriarchal, 66; primacy of, 131–33; as refugees, 51, 242–43; reproductive freedom of, 235; sexual molestation of, 173; terrorism against, 234; tokenizing of, 169; veiling of 79–80; violation of, 234

Women, 211, 214; as Battle Axes, 191; Biophilic, 226; Bold, 57; Brazen, 41; Canny, 2, 42, 63, 70, 77, 103, 128, 166, 174, 177, 222; Catty, 8; Contrary-Wise, 127; Daring, 70, 128, 165; Defiant, 73; Desperate, 53, 129; Disgusted, 8, 85; Dis-illusioned, 38; Dragon-identified, 52, 54; Dreadful/Dreadless, 2, 39, 49, 53, 129; Eccentric, 72, 119, 204; Elemental, 44, 49, 53, 85–86, 177; Fantastic, 9; Fierce, 230; Fiercely Focused, 181; Glaring, Gorgonish, 2; as Haggard Searcher(s), 217; Journeying, 204, 224, 230; Life-Loving, 228; Lusty, 96; as Magnets, 39, 88; Memory-Bearing, 6; Metamorphosing, 97, 99, 126, 224; Musing, 91, 121; Nag-Gnostic, 229; Original, 121; Other-Wise, 3; as Outlaws, 203; Outrageous, 73; Phoenix-identified, 143; Pro-Choice, 94; Race of, 75; Radical, 44–45, 50, 86; Raging, 178; Revolting, 50; Rooted, 45; Shrewd, 23, 91, 129; Shrewish, 73; Sinister, 203; Sphinxlike, 186, 224; Spinning, 203; Stormy, 88; Terrible, 223; Tree-Like, 44–49; Truth-Saying, 3; Unstuck, 227; Unsubdued, 73, 224; Visionary/Volcanic, 88; Wandering Wanton, 228; Wanderlusting, 20, 45, 86; Wayward, 3, 225; Weird, 105, 176; as Whirling Dervishes, 129; Wicked, 91, 222; Wickedly Wise, 32; Wild, 2, 4, 6, 8, 9, 19, 22, 37, 47, 49, 50, 60, 61, 62, 63, 70, 71, 72, 74–77, 80, 96, 108, 110, 111, 114, 126, 134, 135, 137, 138, 165, 174, 177, 183, 189, 194, 201, 204, 219, 220, 221, 224, 225, 228; Wildly Hoping, 128; Wildly Witchy, 54; Wise, 52, 184, 227; Wolfish, 8; Wonderlusting, 20, 54

Women as Wombs (Raymond), 253

Women Philosophers (for our own kind), taboo against, 13

Women's Community Center Project, 210n

"Women's Month" (March), 154

Women's Movement, xiii, 82, 117, 153

Women's Resource Center: Andover Newton Theological School,
125–26, 156; Providence, RI, 156;
University of Redlands, 126n
Women's Space, 66, 68
Women's Studies, 21, 135–37; killing
of, 4
Wonderlust, 12–13
Woolf, Virginia, xi(n), 21, 22, 50, 75,
115, 119n, 120, 136–38, 140, 146,
158, 169n, 249
Words: as buried treasure, 40; erasure of, 51, 52; as Magical helpers, 40; Power of, 184; Weird/
Wise, 165
"world, end of the": prophecies,
59–61
World War II, 153
Worldwatch Institute, 29, 46
"wormism," 83

wristwatches, 76
Wylie, Philip, 142

xenotransplantation, 23–24, 208;
and "creation" of new diseases,
208, 258; and production of chimeras, 208; and sense of "self,"
208; and transfer of dangerous viruses, 208
X-Factor/Faculty, 21, 104–5, 118,
132, 149, 160, 162, 163, 180, 190–
91; defined, 104n; Re-awakening,
119–47. *See also* chromosomes,
X and Y
X-ing, 105

Yahweh, 91 *passim*

Zeus, 91, 171–72